The Student's Introduction to *Mathematica*

The use of *Mathematica* in university curricula has created a demand from undergraduate students for a compact introduction to this exciting software package. In writing *The Student's Introduction to Mathematica* Bruce and Eve Torrence have supplied such a text. The unique feature of their book is that they present concepts in an order that closely follows a standard mathematics curriculum, rather than structure the book along features of the software. As a result, the book provides a brief introduction to those aspects of the *Mathematica* program most useful to students. Furthermore, *Mathematica* commands are introduced as a means of solving problems and illuminating the underlying mathematical principles.

Following a brief introduction to Versions 3 and 4 of the *Mathematica* program, the authors discuss functions and graphs, algebra, calculus, and multivariate calculus, and finish with a chapter on linear algebra. No prerequisites other than high school level mathematics are assumed.

The *Student's Introduction to Mathematica* can be used in variety of courses, from precalculus, through single- and multivariable calculus, to linear algebra. Used as a supplementary text, it will aid in bridging the gap between the mathematics in the course and the *Mathematica* computer program. In addition to its course use, this book will serve as an excellent tutorial for those wishing to learn *Mathematica* and brush up on their mathematics at the same time.

Bruce F. Torrence received his Ph.D. in mathematics from the University of Virginia. He is currently serving as assistant chair in the Department of Mathematics and as codirector of the Honors Program at Randolph-Macon College.

Eve A. Torrence received her Ph.D. in mathematics from the University of Virginia. She is currently an assistant professor of mathematics at Randolph-Macon College.

The Student's Introduction to *Mathematica*®

A Handbook for Precalculus, Calculus, and Linear Algebra

Bruce F. Torrence   Eve A. Torrence

CAMBRIDGE
UNIVERSITY PRESS

PUBLISHED BY THE PRESS SYNDICATE OF THE UNIVERSITY OF CAMBRIDGE
The Pitt Building, Trumpington Street, Cambridge, United Kingdom

CAMBRIDGE UNIVERSITY PRESS
The Edinburgh Building, Cambridge CB2 2RU, UK   http://www.cup.cam.ac.uk
40 West 20th Street, New York, NY 10011-4211, USA   http://www.cup.org
10 Stamford Road, Oakleigh, Melbourne 3166, Australia
Ruiz de Alarcón 13, 28014 Madrid, Spain

First published 1999
Reprinted 1999

Printed in the United States of America

Typeset in Century Schoolbook 10.5/13 pt. and Avant Garde, in LaTeX 2_ε [TB]

*A catalog record for this book is available from
the British Library.*

Library of Congress Cataloging-in-Publication Data

Torrence, Bruce F. (Bruce Follett), 1963–
    The student's introduction to Mathematica : a handbook for
precalculus, calculus, and linear algebra / Bruce F. Torrence, Eve
A. Torrence.
        p.   cm.
    ISBN 0-521-59445-6 (hb). – ISBN 0-521-59461-8 (pb)
    1. Mathematica (Computer file)   2. Mathematics–Data processing.
I. Torrence, Eve A. (Eve Alexandra). 1963–   . II. Title.
QA76.95.T67   1999
510'.285'5369 – dc21   98-27788
                                                              CIP

ISBN 0 521 59445 6 hardback
ISBN 0 521 59461 8 paperback

For Robert and Alexandra

Contents

Preface

The mathematician and juggler Ronald L. Graham has likened the mastery of computer programming to the mastery of juggling. The problem with juggling is that the balls go exactly where you throw them. And the problem with computers is that they do exactly what you tell them.

This is a book about *Mathematica*, a software package often described as "a system for doing mathematics by computer." As software programs go, *Mathematica* is big – really big. If truth be told, it's a monster: the documentation alone consists of a book of 1400 pages, along with several separate publications dealing with such things as system-specific information, and the "standard" additions that ship with the software. Yes, *Mathematica* will do exactly what you ask it to do – but you have to know how to ask it, and that can be a formidable task.

That's where this book comes in. It is intended primarily as a supplementary text for high school and college students. As such, it introduces commands and procedures in an order that roughly coincides with the usual mathematics curriculum. The idea is to provide a coherent introduction to *Mathematica* that does not get ahead of itself mathematically. Most of the available reference materials make the assumption that the reader is thoroughly familiar with the mathematical concepts underlying each *Mathematica* command and procedure. This book does not. It presents *Mathematica* as a means not only of solving mathematical problems, but of exploring and clarifying the concepts themselves. It also provides examples of procedures that students will need to master, showing not just individual commands, but sequences of commands that together accomplish a larger goal.

Why *Mathematica*?

Mathematica is a comprehensive software package – it does many things extremely well. Among them: It can perform numerical calculations, it can operate on algebraic expressions (e.g., solve equations, factor polynomials), it can generate a wide variety of graphics, and it can produce publication-quality documents. In addition, it is a powerful high-level programming language, and as such it is possible to extend and enhance its native capabilities to suit a wide variety of specialized needs.

What exactly is desirable about having such a system? How does it differ from a good hand-held calculator? Do the benefits measure favorably against the time and energy spent learning its idiosyncrasies? The answers to these questions depend to some extent upon the type and amount of mathematics that you do. For most people a decent pocket calculator (together with a rudimentary understanding of arithmetic) provides an adequate system for "doing" the mathematics that daily life demands. But for students pursuing higher mathematics, or professionals dealing extensively with quantitative procedures, a time will come when the hand-held calculator meets its limitations: it cannot save and print files, it cannot provide accuracy beyond eight or perhaps sixteen digits, the screen resolution is abysmal, the programming language is awkward. *Mathematica* provides a long-term solution; it's not a program that you are likely to outgrow. The time invested in mastering its basic precepts will be amply rewarded as you continue to use the system. It is our experience that students who use *Mathematica* in one course will naturally and independently use it in subsequent math courses, as well as in other science courses.

A student edition of *Mathematica* is available for full-time students at a price roughly comparable to that of a top-end graphing calculator. To run it, make sure you have copious amounts of hard disk space and random access memory; in other words, it's not recommended if you just inherited your dad's eight-year-old PC. Files are portable across platforms, so it is not necessary to purchase hardware matching that of, say, your university's computer lab.

How to Use this Book

The first chapter provides a brief tutorial for those unfamiliar with the software. The second delves a bit deeper into the fundamental design principles, and can be used as a reference for the rest of the book. Chapters 3 and 4 provide information on those *Mathematica* commands and procedures relevant to the material in a precalculus course. Chapter 5 adds material relevant to single-variable calculus, and Chapter 6 deals with multivariable calculus. Finally, Chapter 7 introduces commands and procedures pertinent to the material in a linear algebra course.

⚠ Some sections of the text carry this warning sign. These sections provide slightly more comprehensive information for the advanced user. They can be skipped by less hardy souls.

Mathematica runs on many platforms, from Macs and PCs to Unix workstations. For the most part, it works exactly the same on each platform. There are, however, a few procedures that require platform-specific information. In such instances, we have provided explicit information for the Apple Macintosh and Microsoft Windows (including NT) platforms. If you find yourself running *Mathematica* on some other platform, you can be assured that the procedure you need is virtually identical to one of these. For those running the Solaris, X-Windows, or NeXT operating systems, the keyboard sequences closely mirror those of the Macintosh.

This text covers both versions 3 and 4 of *Mathematica*. For most of the applications and procedures discussed there will be little difference between the two. However, in a few instances separate instructions will be given for each version. For this reason, it's a good idea to know which version of the software you are using. This information will be prominently displayed on the welcome screen when you first launch *Mathematica*.

Acknowledgments

We extend thanks first and foremost to Robert and Alexandra (our children) for putting up with us throughout this endeavor, and for their frequent and pleasant interruptions. Special thanks to P. J. Hinton at Wolfram Research for help in converting the original *Mathematica* documents into LaTeX. We would like to thank Randolph-Macon College and the Walter William Craigie Endowment for the support we received throughout this project. We thank Alan Harvey at Cambridge for his thoughtful advice and encouragement. Last, but certainly not least, we would like to thank all the fine folks at Ashland Coffee and Tea for providing the perfect writing environment.

Chapter 1

Getting Started

1.1 Launching *Mathematica*

The first task you will face is finding where *Mathematica* resides in your computer's file system. If this is the first time you are using a computer in a classroom or lab, by all means ask your instructor for help. You are looking for an icon showing a *stellated icosahedron*. It looks like this:

It may have "*Mathematica*" written beneath it. When you have located the icon, double click it with your mouse. In a moment a welcome message will appear, followed by a blank window. This is your *Mathematica notebook*; it is the environment where you will carry out your work.

The remainder of this chapter is a quick tutorial that will enable you to get accustomed to the syntax and conventions of *Mathematica*, and demonstrate some of its many features.

1.2 The Basic Technique for Using *Mathematica*

A *Mathematica* notebook is an interactive environment. You type a command (such as **2 + 2**) and instruct *Mathematica* to execute it. *Mathematica* responds with the answer on the next line. You then type another command, and so on. Each command you type will appear on the screen in **boldface Courier** font. *Mathematica's* output will appear in plain Courier.

> After typing a command, you *enter* it as follows:
>
> - On a computer running the Mac OS: Hit the ENTER key (or the combination SHIFT–RETURN).
> - On a computer running Windows: Hit the combination SHIFT–ENTER.

1.3   The First Computation Is Slow

For your first computation, type **2 + 2**, then hit the ENTER key (Mac OS) or the SHIFT–ENTER combination (Windows). Then *wait*. Notice that the title bar for your notebook window now includes the text "Running...." It's a good idea not to type anything else until the task has been completed. Keep one eye on the window's title bar:

```
In[1]:= 2 + 2
Out[1]= 4
```

The reason that this simple task takes so long is that *Mathematica* doesn't start its engine, so to speak, until the first computation is entered. In fact, entering the first computation causes your computer to launch a second program called the MathKernel (or kernel for short). *Mathematica* really consists of these two programs, the Front End, where you type your commands and where output, graphics, and text are displayed, and the MathKernel, where calculations are executed. Every subsequent computation will be faster, for the kernel is now already up and running.

1.4   Commands for Basic Arithmetic

Mathematica works much like a calculator for basic arithmetic. Just use the **+**, **-**, *****, and **/** keys on the keyboard for addition, subtraction, multiplication, and division. As an alternative to typing *****, you can multiply two numbers by leaving a space between them. You can raise a number to a power using the **^** key. Use the dot (i.e., the period) for adding a decimal point. Here are a few examples:

```
In[2]:= 17 + 1
Out[2]= 18

In[3]:= 17 - 1
Out[3]= 16

In[4]:= 123456789*123456789
Out[4]= 15241578750190521
```

In[5]:= **123456789 123456789**
Out[5]= 15241578750190521

In[6]:= **17^19**
Out[6]= 2390724356851513248471S3

In[7]:= **9.1/256.127**
Out[7]= 0.0355292

In[8]:= **34/4**

$$Out[8]= \frac{17}{2}$$

This last line may seem strange at first. What you are witnessing is *Mathematica's* propensity for providing exact answers. *Mathematica* treats decimal numbers as approximations, and will avoid them in the output if they are not present in the input. When *Mathematica* returns an expression with no decimals, you are assured that the answer is exact. Fractions are displayed in lowest terms.

1.5 Input and Output

You've surely noticed that *Mathematica* is keeping close tabs on your work. Each time you enter an expression, *Mathematica* gives it a name such as *In[1]:=*, *In[2]:=*, *In[3]:=*. The corresponding output comes with the labels *Out[1]=*, *Out[2]=*, *Out[3]=*, and so on. At this point, it is enough to observe that these labels will appear all by themselves each time you enter a command, and it's okay:

In[9]:= **(1/2)^6**

$$Out[9]= \frac{1}{64}$$

You've surely noticed something else too, those brackets along the right margin of your notebook window. Each input and output gets its own *cell*, whose scope is determined by the leftmost bracket directly across from the respective input or output text. Cells containing input are called *input cells*. Cells containing output are called *output cells*. The brackets delimiting cells are called *cell brackets*. Each input–output pair is in turn grouped with a larger bracket immediately to the right of the cell brackets. These brackets may in turn be grouped together by still a larger bracket, and so on. These extra brackets are called *grouping brackets*.

At this point, it's really enough just to know these brackets are there and that they're okay, and to make the distinction between the innermost (or smallest, or leftmost) brackets, which contain cells, and the others, which are used for grouping. If you are curious about what good can possibly come of them, try positioning the tip of your cursor arrow anywhere on a grouping bracket and double click. You will *close the group* determined by that bracket. In the case of the bracket delimiting an input–output pair, this will have the effect of hiding the output completely (handy if the output runs over several pages). Double click again to open the group. This feature is useful when you have created a long, complex document and need a means of managing it.

Since brackets are really only useful in a live *Mathematica* session, they will not, by default, show when you print a notebook. And with the exception of the illustration above, we will not show them in this book. Further details about brackets and cells will be provided in Section 2.2 on page 22.

One last bit of terminology is in order. When you hit the ENTER key (Mac OS) or the SHIFT–ENTER combination (Windows) after typing an input cell, you are *entering the cell*. You'll be seeing this phrase quite a bit in the future.

1.6   The BasicInput Palette and Two-Dimensional Input

There may already be a narrow, light gray window full of mathematical symbols along the side of your screen. If so, you are looking at one of *Mathematica*'s palettes, and chances are that it is the **BasicInput** palette:

The BasicInput Palette

If you see no such window, go to the **File** menu and look for **Palettes**, and choose **BasicInput** from the pop-up menu. In a moment it will appear on your screen.

The **BasicInput** palette is indispensable. You will use it to help typeset your *Mathematica* input, creating expressions that cannot be produced in an ordinary one-dimensional typing environment. Palettes such as the **BasicInput** palette provide you with a means of producing what the designers of *Mathematica* call *two-dimensional* input, which often matches traditional mathematical notation.

For instance, use the ▣ button in the upper left corner of the palette to type an exponential expression such as 17^{19}. To do this, first type **17** into your *Mathematica* notebook, then highlight it with your mouse. Next, push the ▣ palette button with your mouse. The exponent structure shown on that button will be pasted into your notebook, with the 17 in the position of the black square on the palette button (the black square is called the *selection placeholder*). The text insertion point will move to the placeholder in the exponent position. Your input cell will look like this:

    17▪

You can now type the value of the exponent, in this case 19, into the placeholder, then enter the cell:

In[10]:= **17**^{19}

Out[10]= 2390724356851151324847153

⚠   Another way to accomplish the same thing is this: First hit the palette button, then type **17** into the first placeholder. Next hit the TAB key to move to the second placeholder. Now type **19** and enter the cell. This procedure is perhaps a bit more intuitive, but it can occasionally get you into trouble if you are not careful with grouping. For instance, if you want to enter $(1 + x)^8$, and the first thing you do is push the ▣ button on the palette, then you must type **(1 + x)** *with parentheses*, then TAB, then **8**. By contrast, you could type **1 + x** *with or without parentheses* and highlight the expression with your mouse, then hit the ▣ palette button, and then type **8**. The parentheses are added automatically when this procedure is followed.

> Speaking in general terms, the buttons on the top portion of the **BasicInput** palette (in fact all buttons containing a solid black placeholder on this and any other palette) are used this way:
>
> 1. Type an expression into a *Mathematica* notebook.
>
> 2. Highlight all or part of the expression with your mouse (by dragging across the expression).
>
> 3. Push a palette button. The structure on the face of the button is pasted into your notebook, with the highlighted text appearing in the position of the solid black square.
>
> 4. If there are more placeholders in the structure, use the TAB key (or move the cursor with your mouse) to move from one to the next.

If you don't understand what some of the palette buttons do, don't fret. Just stick with the ones that you know for now. For instance, you can take a cube root like this: Type a number and highlight it with the mouse, then push the $\sqrt[3]{\blacksquare}$ button on the **BasicInput** palette, then hit the TAB key, and finally type 3. Now enter the cell:

$$In[11]:= \sqrt[3]{50653}$$
$$Out[11]= 37$$

The buttons on the middle portion of the **BasicInput** palette have no placeholders. They are used simply to paste characters that are not usually found on keyboards into your notebook. To use them, simply position the cursor at the point in the notebook where you want the character to appear, then push a palette button.

For instance, the $\div$ symbol can be used for division:

$$In[12]:= 12^{23} \div 8^{16}$$
$$Out[12]= \frac{94143178827}{4}$$

Of course there is more than one way to skin a cat, and you could use only the two topmost buttons on the palette to accomplish the same task:

$$In[13]:= \frac{12^{23}}{8^{16}}$$
$$Out[13]= \frac{94143178827}{4}$$

1.7   Decimal In, Decimal Out

Sometimes you don't want exact answers. Sometimes you want decimals. For instance how big is this number? It's hard to get a grasp of its magnitude when it's expressed as a fraction:

$$In[14]:= \frac{17^{19}}{19^{17}}$$
$$Out[14]= \frac{239072435685151324847153}{548038685778480218593 9}$$

And what about this?

$$In[15]:= \sqrt[3]{59875}$$
$$Out[15]= 5\ 479^{1/3}$$

Mathematica tells us that the answer is 5 times the cube root of 479 (remember that a space indicates multiplication, and raising a number to the power $\frac{1}{3}$ is the same as taking its cube root). The output is exact, but again it is difficult to grasp the order of magnitude of this number. How can we get a nice decimal approximation?

If any one of the numbers you input is in decimal form, *Mathematica* regards it as approximate. It responds by providing an approximate answer, that is, a decimal answer. It is handy to remember this:

$In[16]:= \dfrac{17.0^{19}}{19^{17}}$

$Out[16]= 43.6232773140006969$

$In[17]:= \sqrt[3]{59875.0}$

$Out[17]= 39.1215$

A quicker way to accomplish this is to type a decimal point after a number with nothing after it. That is, *Mathematica* regards "17.0" and "17." as the same quantity. This is important for understanding *Mathematica*'s output on some occasions:

$In[18]:= \sqrt[3]{59875.}$

$Out[18]= 39.1215$

$In[19]:= \dfrac{30.}{2}$

$Out[19]= 15.$

Note the decimal point in the output. Since the input was only "approximate," so too is the output. Get in the habit of looking for decimal points in your output so that you can determine if the output is exact or approximate.

1.8 Use Parentheses to Group Terms

Use ordinary parentheses ( ) to group terms. This is *very* important, especially with division, multiplication, and exponentiation. Being a computer program, *Mathematica* takes what you say quite literally; tasks are performed in a definite order, and you need to make sure that it is the order you intend. Get in the habit of making a mental check for appropriate parentheses before entering each command. Here are some examples. Can you see what *Mathematica* does in the absence of parentheses?

$In[20] :=$ **3*(4+1)**
$Out[20] =$ 15

$In[21] :=$ **3*4+1**
$Out[21] =$ 13

$In[22] :=$ **(-3)^2**
$Out[22] =$ 9

$In[23] :=$ **-3^2**
$Out[23] =$ -9

$In[24] :=$ **(3+1)/2**
$Out[24] =$ 2

$In[25] :=$ **3+1/2**
$Out[25] =$ $\dfrac{7}{2}$

The last pair of examples above shows one benefit of using the **BasicInput** palette instead of typing from the keyboard. With the two-dimensional typesetting capability afforded by the palette there is no need for grouping parentheses, and no chance for ambiguity:

$In[26] :=$ $\dfrac{\mathbf{3+1}}{\mathbf{2}}$
$Out[26] =$ 2

$In[27] :=$ **3+**$\dfrac{\mathbf{1}}{\mathbf{2}}$
$Out[27] =$ $\dfrac{7}{2}$

The lesson here is that the order in which *Mathematica* performs operations in the absence of parentheses may not be what you intend. When in doubt, add parentheses. Also note: you do not need to leave a space to multiply by an expression enclosed in parentheses:

$In[28] :=$ **25(2+2)**
$Out[28] =$ 100

1.9   Three Well-Known Constants

Mathematica has several built-in constants. The three most commonly used are π, the ratio of the circumference to the diameter of a circle (approximately 3.14); e, the base of the natural logarithm (approximately 2.72); and i, the imaginary number whose square is –1. You can find each of these constants on the **BasicInput** palette.

```
In[29]:= π
Out[29]= π
```

Again, note *Mathematica's* propensity for exact answers. You will often use π to indicate the radian measure of an angle to be input into a trigonometric function. There are examples in the next section.

It is possible to enter each of these three constants directly from the keyboard, as well. You can type **Pi** for π, **E** for e, and **I** for i. The capitalizations are important. We mention this only because version 3 of *Mathematica* will typically use **E** and **I** in its output, rather than e and i:

```
In[30]:= e
Out[30]= E

In[31]:= (2 + i)²
Out[31]= 3 + 4 I
```

1.10   Typing Commands in *Mathematica*

In addition to the basic arithmetic features discussed earlier, *Mathematica* also contains hundreds of *commands*. Commands provide a means for instructing *Mathematica* to perform all sorts of tasks, from computing the logarithm of a number, to simplifying an algebraic expression, to solving an equation, to plotting a function. *Mathematica's* commands are more numerous, more flexible, and more powerful than those available in any hand-held calculator, and in many ways they are easier to use.

Commands are typically typed from the keyboard, and certain rules of syntax must be strictly obeyed. Commands take one or more *arguments*, and when entered transform their arguments into output. The typical syntax for a command is:

$$\texttt{Command}\,[argument] \quad \text{or} \quad \texttt{Command}\,[argument1\texttt{,}argument2]$$

> When typing commands into *Mathematica,* it is imperative that you remember a few rules. The three most important are:
>
> 1. Every built-in command begins with a *capital* letter. Furthermore, if a command name is composed from more than one word (such as **ArcSin** or **FactorInteger**) then each word begins with a capital letter, and there will be no space between the words.
> 2. The arguments of commands are enclosed in *square* brackets.
> 3. If there is more than one argument, they are separated by *commas.*

Here are some examples.

Numerical Approximation and Scientific Notation

The first command we will introduce is called **N**. You can get a numerical approximation to any quantity x by entering the command **N[x]**. By default, the approximation will have six significant digits:

In[32]:= **N [π]**
Out[32]= 3.14159

Very large or very small numbers will be given in scientific notation:

In[33]:= **N [17^{30}]**
Out[33]= 8.19347×10^{36}

In[34]:= **N [$\dfrac{1}{2^{50}}$]**
Out[34]= 8.88178×10^{-16}

If you were wondering, yes, typing **$17.^{30}$** has the same effect as typing **N[17^{30}]**. But the command **N** is more flexible. You can add an optional second argument that specifies the number of significant digits you require in your output. Type

N[x, m] to get a numerical approximation to x with m significant digits:

In[35]:= **N[$\frac{1}{2^{50}}$, 10]**

Out[35]= $8.881784197 \times 10^{-16}$

In[36]:= **N[π, 500]**

Out[37]= 3.14159265358979323846264338327950288419716900·.
3993751058209749445923081640628620899862803··.
4825342117067982148086513282306647093844609··.
5505822317253594081284811174502841027019385··.
2110555964462294895493038196442881097566593··.
3446128475648233786783165271201909145648566··.
9234603486104543266482133936072602491412737··.
2458700660631558817488152092096282925491715··.
3643678925903600113305305488204665213841469··.
5194151160943305727365759591953092186117381··.
9326117931051185480744623799627495673518857··.
52724891227938183011949

Trigonometric Functions

All trigonometric functions require that their argument be given in radian measure. The commands themselves and the square brackets are most easily typed, while the arguments (such as $\frac{\pi}{4}$) are best typeset with the **BasicInput** palette. Note carefully the placement of capital letters in these commands. You can choose from **Cos**, **Sin**, **Tan**, **Sec**, **Csc**, **Cot**, **ArcCos**, **ArcSin**, **ArcTan**, **ArcSec**, **ArcCsc**, and **ArcCot**:

In[37]:= **Cos[$\frac{\pi}{4}$]**

Out[37]= $\dfrac{1}{\sqrt{2}}$

In[38]:= **Sin[$\frac{\pi}{12}$]**

Out[38]= $\dfrac{-1+\sqrt{3}}{2\sqrt{2}}$

In[39]:= **ArcSin[$\dfrac{-1+\sqrt{3}}{2\sqrt{2}}$]**

Out[39]= $\dfrac{\pi}{12}$

$In[40]:=$ **Tan$\left[\frac{\pi}{12}\right]$**

$Out[40]=$ $2 - \sqrt{3}$

$In[41]:=$ **Sec$\left[\frac{\pi}{12}\right]$**

$Out[41]=$ $\sqrt{2}\ (-1 + \sqrt{3})$

$In[42]:=$ **Csc$\left[\frac{\pi}{12}\right]$**

$Out[42]=$ $\sqrt{2}\ (1 + \sqrt{3})$

If you must use degrees, enter the degree measure multiplied by the degrees-to-radians conversion factor of $\frac{\pi}{180}$. This will simply convert your degree measure to radian measure. For instance, the sine of 45 degrees is found as follows:

$In[43]:=$ **Sin$\left[45 * \frac{\pi}{180}\right]$**

$Out[43]=$ $\dfrac{1}{\sqrt{2}}$

Alternatively, you can use the built-in constant **Degree**, which is equal to $\frac{\pi}{180}$. Either type **Degree** or push the ⬚° button on the **BasicInput** palette. These have the effect of reading nicely, although in reality you are simply multiplying by $\frac{\pi}{180}$:

$In[44]:=$ **Sin[45°]**

$Out[44]=$ $\dfrac{1}{\sqrt{2}}$

Logarithms

Type **Log[x]** to find the natural logarithm of x:

$In[45]:=$ **Log[e]**

$Out[45]=$ 1

$In[46]:=$ **Log[e^{45}]**

$Out[46]=$ 45

Note that it is possible to build up input by nesting one command inside another. Before long you'll be doing this sort of thing without giving it a second thought:

$In[47]:=$ **N[Log[π],20]**

$Out[47]=$ 1.1447298858494001741

To find the logarithm of x in base b, type **Log[** b **,** x **]**. Here is a logarithm in base 10:

```
In[48]:= Log[10,100]
Out[48]= 2
```

And here is one in base 2:

```
In[49]:= Log[2,512]
Out[49]= 9
```

Of course you can always check an answer:

```
In[50]:= 2^9
Out[50]= 512
```

Factoring Integers

You can factor any integer as a product of prime numbers using the command **FactorInteger**. Type **FactorInteger[** n **]** to obtain a factorization of n:

```
In[51]:= FactorInteger[4832875]
Out[51]= {{5,3},{23,1},{41,2}}
```

The output here needs interpretation. It means that 4,832,875 can be factored as $5^3 \times 23 \times 41^2$. Try that with a pocket calculator! Again, it is easy to check the answer:

```
In[52]:= 5^3 23 41^2
Out[52]= 4832875
```

Factoring and Expanding Polynomials

Mathematica is very much at home performing all sorts of algebraic manipulations. For example, you can factor just about any imaginable polynomial. Type the command **Factor[** *polynomial* **]** (recall that a polynomial is an expression consisting of a sum of terms, each of which is the product of a constant and one or more variables each raised to a nonnegative whole number power). Typically, lowercase letters such as x or t are used to represent the variables in a polynomial. Here's an example that you could probably do by hand:

```
In[53]:= Factor[t^2-9]
Out[53]= (-3+t) (3+t)
```

But here's one that you probably couldn't do by hand:

In[54]:= **Factor[64 - 128 x + 48 x^2 + 144 x^3 - 292 x^4 + 288 x^5 - 171 x^6 + 61 x^7 - 12 x^8 + x^9]**

Out[54]= $(-2 + x)^6 (1 + x + x^3)$

Note that you do not need to leave a space between a number and a variable to indicate multiplication as long as the number is written first. For instance, **128x** and **128 x** both mean $128 \times x$.

You can also have *Mathematica* expand a factored polynomial by typing **Expand** [*polynomial*]. Below we confirm the output above:

In[55]:= **Expand[(-2 + x)^6 (1 + x + x^3)]**

Out[55]= $64 - 128 x + 48 x^2 + 144 x^3 - 292 x^4 + 288 x^5 - 171 x^6 + 61 x^7 - 12 x^8 + x^9$

The commands **Factor**, **Expand**, and a host of others that perform various algebraic feats are explored in Chapter 4, "Algebra."

Plotting Functions

Mathematica has a variety of commands that generate graphics. One of the most popular is the **Plot** command, which is used for plotting functions. **Plot** takes two arguments. The first is the function to be plotted, the second is something called an *iterator*, which specifies the span of values the independent variable is to assume. It is of the form

{*variable*, *min value*, *max value*}.

Here's an example. Note that we view the function on the domain where the variable *x* ranges from −3 to 3. *Mathematica* determines appropriate values for the *y* axis automatically:

In[56]:= **Plot[x^2 - 1, {x,-3,3}]**

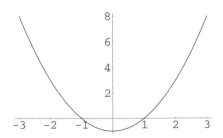

Here's a more interesting example:

$$In[57]:= \texttt{Plot}\left[\texttt{x}\,\texttt{Cos}\left[\frac{\texttt{10}}{\texttt{x}}\right], \{\texttt{x}, -\texttt{2}, \texttt{2}\}\right]$$

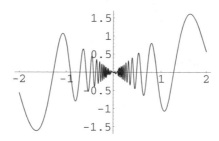

The **Plot** command is explored in greater depth in Chapter 3, "Functions and their Graphs."

Square Root Function

Here you have two choices. You can use the square root button on the **BasicInput** palette:

$$In[58]:= \sqrt{\textbf{144}}$$
$$Out[58]= 12$$

Or you can forgo the palette approach and type **Sqrt[x]** to get the square root of x:

$$In[59]:= \textbf{Sqrt[144]}$$
$$Out[59]= 12$$

⚠ It is a fact that every palette button with a placeholder (such as the square root button) has an equivalent square-bracket command that may be typed from the keyboard. In most cases you will find the palette version of the command easier to use. However, if you ever want to know the name of the square-bracket version of a palette command, follow this procedure: First use the palette version of the command to create an input cell. Then use a single click of your mouse to highlight the cell bracket for the cell. Go to the **Cell** menu and select **Convert to**, and choose **InputForm** from the pop-up menu. You should see the two-dimensional formatted command replaced by its square-bracket counterpart.

Real and Imaginary Parts of Complex Numbers

Every complex number is of the form $a + bi$. The real part of the number is a, and the imaginary part is b. You can extract the real and imaginary parts of complex numbers with the commands **Re** and **Im**:

In[60]:= **Re[2 + 3i]**

Out[60]= 2

In[61]:= **Im[2 + 3i]**

Out[61]= 3

In[62]:= **Re[(2 + 3i)^6]**

Out[62]= 2035

1.11 Naming Things

It is easy to assign names to quantities in *Mathematica*, and then use those names to refer to the quantities. This is useful in many situations. For instance, you may want to assign a name to a complicated expression to keep you from having to type it again and again. To make an assignment, type the name (perhaps a lowercase letter, or a Greek character, or even a whole word), followed by =, followed by the quantity to which the name should be attached. For example (look for θ in the **BasicInput** palette):

In[63]:= $\theta = \dfrac{\pi}{6}$

Out[63]= $\dfrac{\pi}{6}$

Now whenever you place θ in an input cell, *Mathematica* will replace it with $\frac{\pi}{6}$:

In[64]:= θ

Out[64]= $\dfrac{\pi}{6}$

In[65]:= **Sin[θ]**

Out[65]= $\dfrac{1}{2}$

In[66]:= **Sin[2θ]**

Out[66]= $\dfrac{\sqrt{3}}{2}$

In[67]:= **Tan[4θ]**

Out[67]= $-\sqrt{3}$

You can (and should) clear an assignment when you are done. This is accomplished with the **Clear** command:

In[68]:= **Clear[θ]**

No output will be produced when you enter the **Clear** command. You can check that no value is attached to the symbol θ by typing it into an input cell:

In[69]:= **θ**
Out[69]= θ

For a second example, we can assign to **p** the value of π rounded to 39 decimal places (the 3 followed by 39 decimal places makes a total of 40 significant digits):

In[70]:= **p = N[π, 40]**
Out[70]= 3.141592653589793238462643383279502884197

Using this approximation of π, we can compute the area of a circle of radius 3:

In[71]:= **p 3²**
Out[71]= 28.27433388230813914616379044951552595777

Note how *Mathematica*, in performing a calculation involving an approximate number (**p**) and an exact number (3^2), returns an approximate number with the same degree of accuracy as **p**.

For a final example, we'll assign values to words. Each word is treated as a separate entity. The terms **miles** and **hour** are not given values, but **distance** is assigned the value $540 \times$ **miles**, and **time** is assigned the value $6 \times$ **hour**:

In[72]:= **distance = 540 miles**
Out[72]= 540 miles

In[73]:= **time = 6 hour**
Out[73]= 6 hour

In[74]:= **rate = distance/time**
Out[74]= $\dfrac{90 \text{ miles}}{\text{hour}}$

We can clear all of these assignments in one shot with the **Clear** command — just put a comma between each successive pair of names:

In[75]:= **Clear[distance, time, rate]**

Since all built-in *Mathematica* objects begin with capital letters, it's a good practice to make all your names lowercase letters, or words that begin with lowercase letters. This practice assures that you will never accidentally assign a name that *Mathematica* has reserved for something else. The only Greek character that has a built-in value is π. All others make perfectly good names.

It is also alright to use numbers in your names, provided that a number is not the first character. For instance, you might use the names **x1** and **x2**. It is not alright to use the name **2x**, for that means $2 \times x$.

1.12 Saving Your Work and Quitting *Mathematica*

So you want to save a notebook that you created. Let's suppose that it is a freshly created notebook that has not been saved previously. Go to the **File** menu and select **Save**. You will be prompted by the computer and asked two things: What name do you want to give the notebook, and where would you like the computer to put it? Give it any name you like (it is good form to append the suffix ".nb" to notebooks created with *Mathematica* version 3.0 and later), and unless you are working on your own machine, save it to a floppy disk. The details of this procedure vary somewhat from one platform to the next (Mac OS, Windows, etc.), so ask a friendly soul for assistance if you are unfamiliar with the computer in front of you. Keep in mind that the saving and naming routine isn't a *Mathematica* thing; it's a process that will be similar for every program on the computer you are using. Anyone who is familiar with the platform will be able to help.

⚠ The file size of a *Mathematica* notebook tends to be quite small unless the notebook contains lots of graphics. Notebook files are also quite portable across computer platforms, as the files themselves are plain text files. The *Mathematica* front end interprets and displays notebook files in much the same way that a Web browser interprets and displays HTML files.

If you have created a large notebook file, and want to shrink its file size (so that it will fit on a nearly full floppy disk, for instance, or to make it easier to email to a friend) do this: Open the notebook and delete the graphics one by one. To do this, click once on a graphic's cell bracket to select it, then choose **Cut** in the **Edit** menu. Now save the notebook.

When you open the notebook next time, you can regenerate the graphics by entering the input cells that created them.

After a notebook has been saved once, the title bar will bear the name you have assigned. As you continue to work and modify the notebook, you can and should save it often. This is easy to do: choose **Save** from the **File** menu. This will write the latest version of the notebook to the location where the file was last saved. Should the power fail during a session, or should your computer crash for some reason, it is the last saved version of your notebook that will survive. Many hardened souls will save every minute or two.

To end a *Mathematica* session, select **Quit** from the **File** menu. If you have modified your notebook since it was last saved, you will be prompted and asked if you care to save the changes you have made since it was last saved. Answer **Save** or **Don't Save** as appropriate.

1.13 Some Frequently Asked Questions Regarding *Mathematica*'s Syntax

Why Do All Built-In *Mathematica* Objects Begin with Capital Letters?

Every one of the hundreds of built-in *Mathematica* commands begins with a capital letter. So do all built-in constants, built-in option settings, and so on. In fact, every built-in *Mathematica* object of any kind that has a name begins with a capital letter. Taken together, there are more than 1600 such objects.

Why capital letters? The main reason is that you will find yourself assigning names to quantities. Since you don't know the name of every built-in object, there is a danger that you may choose a name that coincides with the name of a built-in command or constant. Without getting into the technicalities, that would be bad. However, it can be avoided if you simply stick to lowercase letters when assigning names. By doing this you guarantee that you will never choose a name that conflicts with an existing *Mathematica* object.

Why Are Some Command Names So Long?

You will find that the majority of *Mathematica* commands are like **ArcSin** and **FactorInteger** in that cryptic or nonstandard acronyms are avoided. This makes it relatively easy to remember the names of commands. The only trade-off is that you sometimes have to type a little more; it's a small price to pay for consistency. The longer you use *Mathematica*, the easier it will be to make correct guesses regarding the names of new commands, or of old commands that you haven't used in a while.

Why Are the Arguments of Commands Enclosed in Square Brackets?

The numerical approximation command **N** is an example of what a mathematician calls a *function*; that is, it converts an argument x to an output **N[x]**. In *Mathematica*, all functions enclose their arguments in square brackets **[ ]**, always.

You may recall that in our usual mathematical notation, we often write $f(x)$ to denote the value of the function f with argument x. This won't do in *Mathematica*, for parentheses **( )** are reserved for grouping terms. When you write $f(12)$, for instance, it is not clear whether you intend for a function named f to be evaluated at 12, or whether you want the *product* of a variable named f with 12. Since parentheses are routinely used for these two very different purposes, the traditional notation is ambiguous. You and I can usually flush out the meaning of the notation $f(12)$ from its context, but a computer needs unambiguous instructions. Hence in *Mathematica*, square brackets are used to enclose function arguments, while parentheses are used to group terms.

When working with *Mathematica*, never use round parentheses for anything other than grouping terms, and never use square brackets for anything other than enclosing the arguments to functions.

What Happens If I Use Incorrect Syntax?

If you want to find the natural log of 7.3, you must type **Log[7.3]**, not **log(7.3)**, not **Log(7.3)**, not **log[7.3]**, not **ln[7.3]**, and not anything else.

What happens if you slip and muff the syntax? First of all, don't worry. This *will* happen to you. The computer won't explode. You will see error messages, big ugly blue error messages. And that's if you're lucky. The unlucky just get hopelessly wrong answers. Behold:

```
In[76]:= Log[7.3

        Syntax::bktmcp:Expression "Log[7.3" has no closing "]".
        Log[7.3
```

Here we are lucky, our input is close enough to the correct syntax that *Mathematica* suspects that we goofed, and tells us so. You will certainly generate messages like this at some point, so its good to acquaint yourself with one. Error messages are somewhat cryptic to the new user, and are rarely a welcome sight. But do read the text of the message, for you will often be able to make enough sense out of it to find the source of the problem. In this case we left off the closing square bracket. Note that in version 4 of *Mathematica* each opening bracket will appear brightly colored until the corresponding closing bracket is added, at which time both brackets will turn black. This makes mistakes of this type easy to spot. If an expression has one or more brightly colored brackets, it is incomplete and should not be entered.

Worse than getting an error message is getting no error message. Look at this:

```
In[77]:= ln(7.3)
Out[77]= 7.3 ln
```

No warning is given, but the output is not what we want. *Mathematica* has multiplied the meaningless symbol **ln** by the number 7.3 (remember round brackets are for grouping only). *Always* look carefully and critically at your output. There will certainly be times when you need to go back and edit and reenter your input before you get the answer you desire.

```
In[78]:= Log[7.3]
Out[78]= 1.98787
```

Chapter 2

Working with *Mathematica*

2.1 Opening Saved Notebooks

You can open any saved *Mathematica* notebook by double-clicking on its icon (or its name) with your mouse. It will appear on your screen exactly as it was when it was saved. You can open two or more notebooks at the same time if you wish. After the first notebook is open, go to the **File** menu and select **New** to get a new blank notebook. To open a saved notebook, go to the **File** menu and select **Open...**. A dialog box will appear. Use the mouse to navigate the directory tree to the desired file, then push the **Open** button. You can move between notebook windows with a mouse click, or by using the **Window** menu, which holds the names of all open notebooks and palettes.

2.2 Adding Text to Notebooks– An Introduction to *Mathematica's* Cell Structure

Mathematica has an integrated word processor that is simple to use once you are familiar with the cell structure of a *Mathematica* notebook (see Section 1.5, "Input and Output," on page 3 for a discussion of input and output cells). To add text to a notebook, you need to create a *text cell*. To do this, first go to the bottom of the **Format** menu and select **Show ToolBar**. A toolbar will appear across the top of your notebook window. Now position your mouse *between* any two cells in your notebook (or below the last cell in the notebook, or above the first cell) where you want to add text. The cursor will change from a vertical bar to a horizontal bar. Now click. You should notice a horizontal black line that runs completely across your notebook window. Next, use your mouse to select **Text** from the pull-down menu on the toolbar, and start typing. As soon as you do, a new text cell will be inserted in your notebook at the position of the horizontal black line, and it will contain the text you type.

A Notebook with the ToolBar Displayed

Mathematica's text environment is a joy to use. You don't need to hit the RETURN or ENTER key to get to the next line; it will wrap lines for you. You can use any palette to paste a mathematical symbol or expression into your text, just as you paste into an input cell. If you are using version 4 of *Mathematica*, there is a full-featured spell checker – just place the cursor where you want to start spell checking and choose **Check Spelling...** in the **Edit** menu. For these reasons, you may find yourself using *Mathematica* as your word processor of choice for technical papers. You can also highlight portions of text with your mouse and cut, copy, or paste (look in the **Edit** menu for these and other features). You can change the size, face, font, and color of highlighted text by choosing the appropriate item in the **Format** menu. There are buttons on the toolbar to control the centering and justification of your text. Use these features to make your notebook a masterpiece.

You can also cut, copy, paste, and format entire cells or groups of cells. You *select* a cell or group of cells by positioning the tip of the cursor arrow on a cell bracket or grouping bracket along the right side of the notebook window. The bracket becomes highlighted. Now choose **Cut** or **Copy** from the **Edit** menu, position the mouse where you wish to paste the selection (in the current notebook or in any other notebook that is open), click once, and select **Paste** from the **Edit** menu. Similarly, the commands in the **Format** menu will be applied to the text in any cell or group of cells whose bracket is selected.

You can also add a preformatted title or section headings to your notebook. Click between existing cells (or below the last cell in the notebook, or above the first cell), and then go to the pulldown menu in the toolbar and select **Title**, or **Section**, or **Subsection**, or the like, and start typing. Upon adding a title to a notebook, you will notice a gigantic grouping bracket on the far right of your notebook window that spans the entire notebook. Place the cursor anywhere along this bracket and double-click to *close the group*. You will see the title, but the rest of the notebook will disappear. Don't worry, it's still there; double-click again on the bracket to *open the group*. When you create sections or subsections, grouping brackets will appear to show their respective domains, and these too can be closed and opened with a double-click on the appropriate grouping bracket. These features allow you to keep your work organized, and minimize the amount of scrolling needed to navigate a large document.

If you click between cells in a notebook and then start typing, you will by default create a new input cell. This makes it easy to enter input during a *Mathematica* session; as soon as you get output from one computation, you can just start typing to generate a new input cell. You only have to specify cell type (**Text**, **Title**, **Section**, etc.) when you want create some type of cell other than input. By the way, you can forgo the toolbar if you want, and select your cell types from the pop-up menu that appears when you select **Style** in the **Format** menu.

If you accidently start typing text in an input cell, don't despair. The fix is simple: click once on the cell's bracket to select it, then use the toolbar (or go to the **Format** menu) to change the cell to a text cell.

There are a host of other features too numerous to mention, but here's one that's too much fun not to try: You can change the look of an entire notebook by changing the **Style Sheet** setting in the **Format** menu. After creating a notebook, give it a try. A style sheet contains different formatting parameters for each cell type. One style sheet might have input cells with purple backgrounds; another might have all titles, sections, and subsections in Helvetica font with a gray background, and 12-point Times Roman as the default text font. By choosing a new style sheet your notebook will take on a completely new look.

2.3 Printing

As long as your computer is properly hooked up to a printer, and the printer is turned on, you can print your current notebook by going to the **File** menu and choosing **Print...**. If your notebook contains graphics or two-dimensional input using special math fonts, it may take a minute or two to start printing, so be patient.

You can also select one or more cells to print, rather than printing an entire notebook. To print a single cell or a group of cells delimited by a grouping bracket, position the tip of the cursor arrow on the cell or grouping bracket and click once. This *selects* the cell or group. Now go to the **File** menu and choose **Print Selection...**.

To select several adjacent cells when there is no grouping bracket, hold down the SHIFT key and click on their cell brackets one by one. They will all become selected. To select several nonadjacent cells, hold down the ⌘ key (Mac OS), or the CONTROL key (Windows), while clicking on cell brackets. You can then print your selection as above: Go to the **File** menu and choose **Print Selection...**.

2.4   Creating Web Pages

If you would like to save a *Mathematica* notebook as an HTML (Hypertext Markup Language) document so that it can be posted as a web page, simply go to the **File** menu and select **Save As Special...**, then choose **HTML** in the pop-up menu. Your notebook will be converted, and any graphics will be saved as separate files (in the gif format).

We know of a student who was getting nowhere trying to explain a mathematics problem over the phone to a fellow student. He then typed the equations he was thinking of into *Mathematica*, saved the notebook as HTML, posted it to his website, and had the fellow student go to the freshly minted page. This seems a bit extreme, but if you are handy with creating and posting web pages, it's nice to know that it's a simple matter to compose in *Mathematica*.

2.5   *Mathematica's* Kernel

When you enter a command in *Mathematica*, it is processed by a separate program called the MathKernel, or kernel for short. This program is launched automatically when the first command is entered. It takes some time to launch this program, and that is why the first computation takes so long to be executed. The kernel is usually run on the same computer that you are using, but it need not be. It can be located on another, perhaps more powerful, computer. If you are running the kernel on your local computer, when you quit *Mathematica* the kernel quits as well. Each time you start *Mathematica* and enter your first command a new kernel is launched.

When you launch *Mathematica* by opening an existing notebook, the kernel is not needed. You can scroll through the notebook and view and even edit the contents. It is only when you place the cursor on an input cell and enter the cell, or type a new command line and enter it, that the kernel will be launched.

Numbering Input and Output

The command lines entered to the kernel and the outputs delivered by the kernel are numbered. They are numbered in the order that they are received by the kernel. After the *Mathematica* program is launched, the first command entered will be labeled *In[1]:=*, and its output will be labeled *Out[1]=*. The next input will be labeled *In[2]:=*, and so on.

Be mindful that the numbering is determined by the sequential order in which the commands are received by the kernel, and not necessarily by the order in which commands appear in the notebook. For instance, if you were to start a *Mathematica* session by opening an existing notebook, then scroll through to some input cell in the middle of that notebook, click on that cell and enter it, it would be labeled *In[1]:=*.

Reevaluating Previously Saved Notebooks

When you first open a previously saved notebook, you will notice that none of the inputs or outputs will be numbered any more. That's because the numbering refers to the order in which input cells were sent to the kernel and in which output cells were delivered from the kernel. When you save a notebook, this information is lost. You are now free to click on any input cell and enter it. That cell will acquire the label *In[1]:=*, and its output will be called *Out[1]=*.

It is important to realize that when you start a new *Mathematica* session by opening an old notebook, you should not enter any input cell that makes reference to another cell (or variable, or anything you created) that has not been entered in *this* session. For instance, suppose you opened a notebook that contained the following input and output cells (they are not numbered, since they have not been entered in this session):

> **a = 90**
> 90
>
> **a²**
> 8100

What would happen if you were to click on the *second* input cell (containing the text **a²**) and enter it? *Mathematica* would be unaware of the cell containing the assignment **a = 90** since that cell has not been entered in the current session. The resulting notebook would look like this:

> **a = 90**
> 90
>
> *In[1]:=* **a²**
> *Out[1]=* a²

In practice this means that when reopening an old notebook to continue work that you started in a previous session, you should reenter, one by one, all the cells to which you will refer later in the session.

You can automate this procedure if you like. After opening a previously saved notebook, go to the **Kernel** menu and choose **Evaluation**, then select **Evaluate Notebook** in the pop-up menu. This will instruct the kernel to evaluate every cell in the notebook, in order, from top to bottom. It's a handy way to pick up your work where you left off.

⚠ Many notebooks need certain input cells evaluated each time the notebook is used; this is often the case with notebooks created for students by teachers. Such notebooks can contain special types of input cells called *initialization cells*. When an input cell is an initialization cell, it can be automatically evaluated before any other input cells in the notebook. Typical initialization cells will define a special command to be used throughout the notebook, or load a *Mathematica* package (more on packages later in this chapter). When you send your first input to the kernel from a notebook containing initialization cells, you will be prompted and asked if you want to automatically evaluate all initialization cells in the notebook. If you ever see such a prompt, you should answer "Yes." Moreover, if you want to make an input cell in one of your own notebooks an initialization cell, select the cell by clicking once on its cell bracket (or SHIFT-click on several cell brackets), then go to the **Cell** menu and choose **Cell Properties**. In the pop-up menu, select **Initialization Cell**. You will notice that the cell bracket gets a little vertical tick mark at the top. Now when you reopen this notebook, the cell (or cells) that are initialization cells can be automatically processed by the kernel.

2.6 Tips for Working Effectively

Referring to Previous Output

In a typical *Mathematica* session you will enter a cell, examine the output, enter a cell, examine the output, enter a cell, examine the output, and so on. There are numerous little tricks that make it easier to deal efficiently with *Mathematica*'s input–output structure. Perhaps the most important is the percentage sign. When you need to use the output of the previous cell as part of your input to the current cell, just type %. *Mathematica* interprets % as the output of the last cell processed by the kernel (i.e., **%** represents the contents of the output cell with the highest label number):

$$In[2]:= \frac{21^{20}}{20^{21}}$$

$$Out[2]= \frac{2782184294469515486637196401}{209715200000000000000000000000}$$

$$In[3]:= \mathbf{N[\%]}$$
$$Out[3]= 0.132665$$

You can use **%%** to refer to the contents of the second-to-last output cell generated by the kernel:

$$In[4]:= \mathbf{N[\%\%, 30]}$$
$$Out[4]= 0.132664885257221006697271538258$$

You can also select **Copy Output from Above** in the **Input** menu. It will paste the contents of the output cell that resides *directly above* the position of the cursor into a new input cell, regardless of when that cell was processed by the kernel. You can then edit the new input cell and enter it.

Referring to Previous Input

You will often enter a cell and later want to enter something very similar. The simplest way to deal with this is to click on the former input cell and edit it, then reenter it. The cursor can be anywhere in the input cell when you enter it; it need not be at the far right. Once the cell is entered, its label number will be updated (for example from $In[5]:=$ to $In[6]:=$). The old output will be replaced with the output from the edited input cell.

If you want to keep the old input and output cells, click below the old output cell, go to the **Input** menu, and select **Copy Input from Above**. The old input cell will be copied into a new input cell, which you can then edit and enter.

Another option is to use your mouse to copy and paste text from one cell (input or output) to a new input cell. You can highlight text with your mouse to select it, then choose **Copy** from the **Edit** menu, click to position the cursor where you want the text to appear, and finally choose **Paste** from the **Edit** menu.

Postfix Command Structure

The typical structure for *Mathematica* commands is:

$$\mathbf{Command[}\textit{argument1}\mathbf{,}\ \textit{argument2}\mathbf{,}...\mathbf{]}$$

We've seen examples such as `Log[10,243]` and `Sin[`$\frac{\pi}{4}$`]`. When a command has only one argument, another way to apply it is in *postfix form*. The postfix form for a command is:

argument `//` `Command`

This form is useful when the command is applied to an existing expression as an afterthought. For instance, if you copy the contents of an earlier input or output cell into a new input cell, you can easily apply a command in postfix form to the entire copied expression. Here are some examples:

In[5]:= `Sin[`$\frac{\pi}{12}$`] // N`

Out[5]= `0.258819`

This is equivalent to entering `N[Sin[`$\frac{\pi}{12}$`]]`:

In[6]:= `(x - 1)(2 + 3x)(6 - x) // Expand`

Out[6]= $-12 - 4x + 19x^2 - 3x^3$

This is equivalent to entering `Expand[(x - 1)(2 + 3x)(6 - x)]`.

Undoing Mistakes

If you make a bad mistake in typing or editing, the kind that makes you say, "I wish I could undo that and return my notebook to its former state," chances are you can. Look for **Undo** in the **Edit** menu. It will reverse the previous action. The catch is that it will only undo the most recent action, so use it immediately after making your mistake.

Another option is to close your notebook (choose **Close** in the **File** menu), and answer **Don't Save** when you are prompted. You can then reopen your notebook (choose **Open** in the **File** menu). You will find your notebook in the state that it was in when it was last saved. Of course you should only do this if you have saved the notebook recently.

A more frightening scenario is entering an input cell and finding that *Mathematica* appears to be stuck. For a long time you see the text "Running..." in the notebook's title bar, but no output is being generated. You may have inadvertently asked *Mathematica* to perform a very difficult calculation, and after a few minutes you may get tired of waiting. How can you make it stop? Go to the **Kernel** menu and select **Abort Evaluation**. You may have to wait a minute or two before *Mathematica* stops. If this doesn't work, refer to Section 2.9, "Problems: Dealing with Them and Preventing Them" on page 39.

Keyboard Shortcuts

If you have quick fingers you may find it easier to type characters than make repeated trips to the menus with your mouse. Next to many menu items you will find keyboard shortcuts for accomplishing the same task. We summarize some of the most common in Table 2.1.

Table 2.1: **Keyboard Shortcuts.** When reading this table, COMMAND q means hitting the COMMAND key and the q key at the same time. Note that on a machine running the Mac OS, the COMMAND key is the one with the ⌘ symbol on it.

Task	Mac OS	Windows PC
Save your notebook	COMMAND s	CONTROL s
Cut	COMMAND x	CONTROL x
Copy	COMMAND c	CONTROL c
Paste	COMMAND v	CONTROL v
Undo an editing or typing mistake	COMMAND z	CONTROL z
Copy input from above	COMMAND l	CONTROL l
Copy output from above	SHIFT COMMAND l	SHIFT CONTROL l
Complete a command	COMMAND k	CONTROL k
Make command template	SHIFT COMMAND k	SHIFT CONTROL k
Abort an evaluation	COMMAND .	ALT .
Quit *Mathematica*	COMMAND q	ALT F 4

Typesetting Input–More Shortcuts

We have seen that a typical input cell contains symbols and structures both from the keyboard and from palettes (such as the **BasicInput** palette). As you get more familiar with *Mathematica*, you will want to find the easiest way to typeset your input. It is helpful to know that there are ways to get many symbols and structures directly from the keyboard without invoking the use of a palette at all. Table 2.2 shows some of the most often used. You can find others by opening the **BasicTypesetting** palette or the **CompleteCharacters** palette and positioning your mouse over a button. If that character has a keyboard entry sequence, it will be displayed at the bottom of the palette.

Table 2.2: **Keyboard Shortcuts for Typesetting.** Note that when reading this table [CONTROL]-[2] means hit the CONTROL key and the **2** key *at the same time*, while [CONTROL]**2** means hit the CONTROL key *followed by* the **2** key.

Type	To Get
[ESCAPE] **p** [ESCAPE]	the symbol π
[ESCAPE] **ee** [ESCAPE]	the symbol e
[ESCAPE] **ii** [ESCAPE]	the symbol i
[ESCAPE] **inf** [ESCAPE]	the symbol ∞
[ESCAPE] **deg** [ESCAPE]	the symbol $^\circ$ (for entering angles in degrees)
[ESCAPE] **th** [ESCAPE]	the symbol θ (no built-in meaning, but often used)
[ESCAPE] ***** [ESCAPE]	the symbol $\times$ (for multiplication)
[CONTROL]-[^] (or [CONTROL]-[6])	to the exponent position
[CONTROL]-[/]	into a fraction
[CONTROL]-[2] (or [CONTROL]-[@])	into a square root
[CONTROL]-[SPACE]	out of an exponent, denominator, or square root
[TAB]	from one placeholder to the next

For instance, you can produce the input

$$\pi^2 + \frac{x}{y}$$

by typing the following key sequence:

[ESCAPE] **p** [ESCAPE] [CONTROL]-[^] **2** [CONTROL]-[SPACE] **+ x** [CONTROL]-[/] **y**

And you can produce the input

$$\frac{\pi^2 + x}{y}$$

by typing the following key sequence:

[CONTROL]-[/] [ESCAPE] **p** [ESCAPE] [CONTROL]-[^] **2** [CONTROL]-[SPACE] **+ x** [TAB] **y**

Of course if you consider yourself a poor typist, you may want to use palettes more rather than less. Check out the **BasicCalculations** palette (under **Palettes** in the **File** menu). It contains buttons that will paste templates of the most often used commands into your notebook. This keeps your typing to a minimum, and helps you remember the correct syntax for commands. Whichever approach you take, you'll eventually find the way to typeset *Mathematica* input that works best for you.

Suppressing Output and Entering Sequences of Commands

There will be times when you don't want *Mathematica* to produce output. For instance when you make an assignment such as **x = 3** and enter it, *Mathematica* will output 3:

```
In[7]:= x = 3
Out[7]= 3
```

"Yeah," you might think, "tell me something I don't know."

If you would like to suppress the output of any input cell, simply type a semicolon **;** after typing the contents of the cell:

```
In[8]:= x = 3;
```

This will work provided the input does not generate graphics (as the **Plot** command does, for instance). A different means for suppressing graphical output is discussed in Section 3.8, "Superimposing Plots" on page 71.

You can enter a sequence of several commands in a single input cell by putting semicolons after all but the final command. Only the output of the final command will be displayed. When you are typing, you can use the RETURN key (Mac) or the ENTER key (Windows) to move to a new line in the same input cell, or you can keep it all on one line if it will fit:

```
In[9]:= x = 3;
         Expand[(x - y)^8]
```
$Out[9]= 6561 - 17496\ y + 20412\ y^2 - 13608\ y^3 + 5670\ y^4 - 1512\ y^5 +$
$\qquad 252\ y^6 - 24\ y^7 + y^8$

```
In[10]:= Clear[x]; Expand[(x - y)^8]
```
$Out[10]= x^8 - 8\ x^7\ y + 28\ x^6\ y^2 - 56\ x^5\ y^3 + 70\ x^4\ y^4 - 56\ x^3\ y^5 +$
$\qquad 28\ x^2\ y^6 - 8\ x\ y^7 + y^8$

A different means for suppressing output is found in the **Short** command. This command is useful if you generate output that is just plain too long. If you enter a cell and produce screen upon screen of output, append the text **// Short** to the input and reenter it. You will get the very beginning and end of the total output, with a marker indicating how much was chopped out of the middle. Here's an example that makes use of *factorials*. The factorial of a positive integer n is the product of n with every other positive integer less than n. So the factorial of 5 is equal to $5 \times 4 \times 3 \times 2 \times 1 = 120$. The common mathematical notation for the factorial of n and the *Mathematica* notation agree: type n!:

```
In[11]:= 1000!// Short
Out[11]= 4023872600770937735437024339230 ≪ 2506 ≫
            00000000000000000000000000000000
```

Here *Mathematica* tells us that there are 2506 digits missing from the output.

If you want to find out whose computer is faster, or if you want to know how long it takes *Mathematica* to arrive at an answer, use the **Timing** command. Wrap any input with this command, and the output will be a list containing two items (they will be separated by a comma). The first item in the list is the number of seconds that it took the kernel to process your answer (it doesn't include the time it takes to format and display the answer), and the second item is the answer itself. If the input to the **Timing** command is followed by a semicolon, the second item in the list will be the word "Null" rather than the answer. This is useful when the output is large:

```
In[12]:= 20!// Timing
Out[12]= {0. Second, 2432902008176640000}

In[13]:= 1000!;// Timing
Out[13]= {0.0333333 Second, Null}
```

2.7 Getting Help from *Mathematica*

Information on Known Commands

Type **?** followed by a *Mathematica* command name, and then enter the cell to get information on that command. This is useful for remembering the syntax for a command whose name you know, and for seeing the various ways in which a command can be used. For example:

```
In[14]:= ?N
         N[expr] gives the numerical value of expr. N[expr, n]
            attempts to give a result with n-digit precision.
```

Command Completion

Mathematica can finish typing a command for you if you provide the first few letters. This is useful if the command has a long name; it saves time and guarantees that you won't make a typing mistake. Here's how it works: After typing a few letters choose **Complete Selection** from the **Input** menu. If more than one completion is possible, you will be presented with a pop-up menu containing all of the options. Just click on the appropriate choice. Try it—type `Cos` in an input cell and attempt the completion. You will find that there are four *Mathematica* commands that start with these letters: `Cos`, `Cosh`, `CosIntegral`, and `CoshIntegral`.

Command Templates

If you know the name of a command, but have forgotten the syntax for its arguments, type the command name in an input cell, then choose **Make Template** from the **Input** menu. *Mathematica* will paste a template into the input cell showing the syntax for the simplest form of the command. For example, if you were to type `Plot`, and then choose **Make Template**, the input cell would look like this:

```
Plot[f, {x, xmin, xmax}]
```

You can now edit the cell (replacing `f` with the function *you* want to plot, `xmin` with the lower bound for *your* domain, etc.).

Command templates and command completions work well together. Type a few letters, complete the command, then make the template. It's an easy way to avoid syntax errors. See Table 2.1 for keyboard shortcuts.

The Help Browser

The Help Browser is the most useful feature imaginable; learn to use it and use it often. Go to the **Help** menu and choose **Help...** (version 3 of *Mathematica*), or **Help Browser...** (version 4 of *Mathematica*). In a moment you will see the Help Browser window.

There are six radio buttons beneath the text field near the top of the window. Push one (choose **Master Index** when in doubt). Now type some text in the text field and push the **Go To** button, or click on a topic in one of the columns below the radio buttons. When you have made a selection, the lower portion of the Help Browser will display text relating to the requested topic. The text displayed in the Help Browser is hyperlinked, so using it is much like surfing the Web. After you have found information on one topic, you can click once on any colored, underlined word or phrase to read about a related topic. It also contains live examples in the form of input cells, which can be edited and entered.

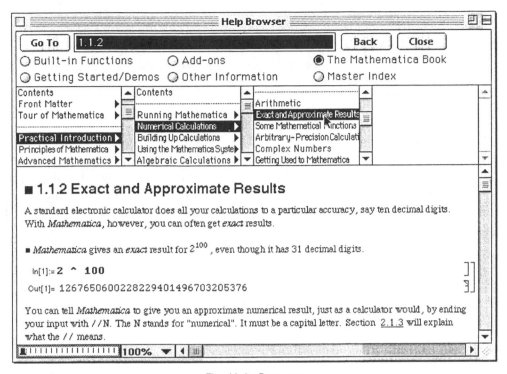

The Help Browser

The best way to get started is to push the **Getting Started/Demos** radio button, then click on **Using the Help Browser** in the first column. You will get a detailed account of how to use it.

Here are some of the ways you can use the Help Browser:

- To learn about a *Mathematica* command: Push the **Built-in Functions** radio button, then begin typing the command's name in the text field.
- To learn about a *Mathematica* topic: Push **The Mathematica Book** radio button. This is an online, hyperlinked version of the roughly 1400-page manual that comes with *Mathematica*. Search for a topic by typing a word in the text field and pushing the **Go To** button. If there are no matches, try clicking on **Contents** in the first column, then browse the table of contents.
- To learn about a menu command: Push the **Other Information** radio button, then click on **Menu Commands** in the first column.
- To learn about typesetting *Mathematica* input: Push the **Other Information** radio button, and select **2D Expression Input** in the first column.

- To learn about keyboard shortcuts: Push the **Other Information** radio button, and select **Keyboard Shortcuts** in the first column.
- To learn about standard *Mathematica Packages*, read the next section of this chapter; then push the **Add-ons** radio button, and browse the various topics.

2.8   Loading Packages

Mathematica comes with hundreds of built-in commands, but it is easy to add even more. It is possible to create or simply use a suite of custom-designed *Mathematica* commands for a particular application. A *Mathematica Package*, or *Add-on*, is a file that activates additional commands that are not ordinarily available. When you *load a package*, the commands in that package become available for you to use. *Mathematica* comes with a few dozen "standard" packages, and there are hundreds more in use around the world. Many are available to download (for free) from the following web sites:

```
http://www.wolfram.com
http://www.mathsource.com
```

You can find out about the standard packages in the Help Browser by clicking the **Add-ons** radio button and browsing the categories below.

It is highly likely that you will at some point need to load a package into *Mathematica*. For example, there is a useful package that allows you to easily convert units of measurement. To load it, enter a cell containing the text:

```
In[15]:= Needs["Miscellaneous`Units`"]
```

This must be typed with perfect precision. The argument to **Needs** is enclosed in double quote marks ", and the package name will invariably contain one or more *backquote* characters ` (try looking in the upper left portion of your keyboard for the backquote character. Do not use an apostrophe '). If the cell is entered properly, there will be no output. If you get an error message, chances are good that you didn't type the input exactly right; fix it, then reenter the cell. If you still get an error message, seek help from your instructor. Under no circumstances should you attempt to use the commands in the package until it has been properly loaded. You can check that the package loaded properly by typing and entering

```
In[16]:= $Packages
Out[16]= {Miscellaneous`SIUnits`, Miscellaneous`Units`,
          Global`, System`|
```

The output shows all currently loaded packages; your output may be slightly different. What you need to look for is the name of the package you tried to load. Since Miscellaneous`Units` appears in the output, all is well. If your package does not appear in the list, try using the **Needs** command again until it does.

Once the package has loaded you can use the commands it contains just as if they were ordinary *Mathematica* commands. The package **Miscellaneous 'Units'** contains the command **Convert**, which allows the conversion of just about any imaginable pair of measurement units. The syntax is:

Convert[*from, to* **]**

Remember to keep all units of measurement in the singular, and to capitalize as you would for any *Mathematica* command. For example, how many miles are there in a light year? How many teaspoons in a 16 gallon tank of gas? Bartenders take note: How many jiggers in a 1.75-liter bottle?

> *In[17]:=* **Convert[LightYear, Mile]**
> *Out[17]=* 5.87848×10^{12} Mile

> *In[18]:=* **Convert[16 Gallon, Teaspoon]**
> *Out[18]=* 12288. Teaspoon

> *In[19]:=* **Convert[1.75 Liter, Jigger]**
> *Out[19]=* 39.4497 Jigger

Note that all units of measurement are given in the singular, so you should type **Foot** rather than **Feet** and **Mile** rather than **Miles**. Note also that you may arithmetically combine basic units of measurement; for instance, you can convert miles per hour to feet per second like so:

> *In[20]:=* **Convert[90 Mile/Hour, Foot/Second]**
> *Out[20]=* $\dfrac{132 \text{ Foot}}{\text{Second}}$

You can deal in thousands with the prefix **Kilo**, which is simply equal to 1000. For instance there is no unit named Kilometer. Rather, you should use the product **Kilo Meter**.

This brings a natural question to mind: How do you find out what commands are available in a given package? For instance, what units of measurement are available in the **Units** package? To find out, use the **Names** command (do this *after* loading the package). The syntax for **Names** is just like that of the **Needs** command, except that you need to place an asterisk ***** between the last backquote and double quote (the asterisk is the "wild-card" symbol common in many computer applications and operating systems). You can save yourself some typing by clicking once under the input cell containing the **Needs** command, and choosing **Copy Input from Above** from the **Input** menu. Then edit the new cell, adding the asterisk and changing **Needs** to **Names**. (The output below has been abbreviated so as not to fill an entire page.)

```
In[21]:= Names["Miscellaneous`Units`*"]
```

```
Out[21]= {Abampere, Abcoulomb, Abfarad, Abhenry,
          Abmho, Abohm, Abvolt, Acre, AMU,
          Angstrom, Apostilb, ArcMinute, ArcSecond,
          ⋮
          Convert, ConvertTemperature, Cord, Cubit,
          ⋮
          Week, Wey, WineBottle, XUnit, Yard,
          Year, Yocto, Yotta, Zepto, Zetta|
```

Here we see that there are a host of objects defined in the package. Most of them are units of measurement, but two of them, **Convert** and **ConvertTemperature**, are commands. You can now find out about any of these names in the usual way:

```
In[22]:= ?ConvertTemperature
```

```
ConvertTemperature[temp, old, new] converts temp
   from the old scale to the new scale.
```

There is an important thing you need to know about packages. If you accidentally attempt to use a command defined in a package *before* the package has been loaded (you'll know you've done this when the command doesn't work; the output will simply match the input), you need to *remove* the command from *Mathematica*'s memory before loading the needed package. What happens is that upon entering an "undefined" command, *Mathematica* reserves the name of the command for you, and then will not allow the package to change the (empty) meaning of the command. For instance, if you had used the **Convert** command before loading the package, it wouldn't have worked, and if you then used the **Needs** command to load the package **Miscellaneous`Units`**, **Convert** still wouldn't work. To get out of this situation: As soon as you realize that you have prematurely used any commands or names that require the loading of a package, remove those objects from *Mathematica*'s memory by typing and entering an input cell of the form **Remove[***command***]**, then load the package and go happily on your way:

```
In[23]:= Convert[15 Gallon, WineBottle]
Out[23]= Convert[15 Gallon, WineBottle]

In[24]:= Remove[Convert, Gallon, WineBottle];
         Needs["Miscellaneous`Units`"]

In[25]:= Convert[15 Gallon, WineBottle]
Out[25]= 74.941 WineBottle
```

2.9 Problems: Dealing with Them and Preventing Them

The most common problem with learning *Mathematica* is adapting to a system in which spelling and syntax must be perfect. What happens if your syntax is wrong (say you typed a period instead of a comma, or forgot to capitalize a command name)? Usually you will get an error message. Getting an error message can be frightening; often the screen suddenly fills with a seemingly endless flow of cryptic messages in blue type. Don't panic. Most error messages can be traced to a simple typing mistake. Just go back to your last input cell, edit it, and reenter it. If you can't find your mistake, ask a friend or your instructor. You may also want to try the online help features discussed earlier. Also, the **BasicCalculations** palette (look in the **File** menu for palettes) has buttons available for pasting templates of the most frequently used commands. If you are not a very good typist, you may find it beneficial to paste, rather than type, commands.

In any event, if your input is either generating error messages, or not generating the output you want, look first for spelling or syntax problems. If you are reasonably certain that the command has been entered correctly, there are a few other things you might try. If *Mathematica* beeped when you attempted to enter your input cell, you can go to the **Help** menu and select **Why the Beep?...**. This will provide you with an explanation that may be quite helpful. Another tactic that cures a common source of problems is to clear the names of any variables appearing in your input, then try reentering the cell. For instance, if you have a variable called x, and somewhere long ago you typed **x = 3**, then *Mathematica* will substitute 3 for x every chance it gets for as long as the current kernel is running. You may have forgotten that you made such an assignment, and no longer want it. Type and enter **Clear[x]** to remove any previous assignment to x, then reenter your input cell (you will need to clear the values of all expressions that have been assigned values in *your* current session; such expressions may or may not be called x in *your* notebook). Get in the habit of clearing variable names as soon as you are done with them.

Another problem that arises from time to time is one in which an input cell suddenly contains lots of cryptic symbols, something like this:

```
In[26]:= \!\(\2\^5 - 2\^3\)\/\@2\)
```

There is a simple fix for this. Click once on the cell bracket of the afflicted cell (or shift-click on the brackets of several input cells if there is more than one) to select it. Next, go to the **Cell** menu and choose **Display As**, and select **StandardForm**. The gibberish will now look a little nicer. For instance, the mess above will look like this:

$$\frac{2^5 - 2^3}{\sqrt{2}}$$

While you're up in the **Cell** menu, make sure the **Default Input FormatType** and the **Default Output FormatType** are also set to **StandardForm**. That will keep this sort of thing from happening again.

⚠ *Mathematica* has four distinct *forms* for entering input and displaying output: InputForm, OutputForm, StandardForm, and TraditionalForm. Throughout this book we assume that you are using the most sensible of these, which is also the default: StandardForm. In StandardForm, you retain much of the standard mathematical notation developed over the past few centuries. At the same time, all the ambiguities of traditional mathematical notation are eliminated – for example square brackets are used to delimit the arguments of functions while round brackets are used for grouping. InputForm, by contrast, is highly untraditional. All InputForm commands require only standard keyboard characters, making elegant typesetting impossible. Its roots are in the command-line interface, prepalette versions of *Mathematica*. The gibberish we saw above can be had by pasting two-dimensional input into an InputForm cell. At the other extreme is TraditionalForm, which mimics traditional notation at the expense of internal consistency. In TraditionalForm you type **Sin(x)** instead of **Sin[x]**, for example, but there are instances in which the use of round brackets for both grouping and function arguments will get you into trouble. You could tell *Mathematica* to use TraditionalForm for output only, but then you could still run into trouble if you wanted to incorporate one output cell into a subsequent input cell. Our advice: avoid the temptation to use TraditionalForm as a default; use Standard-Form unless you have a compelling reason not to.

You can switch a cell into any form you like by selecting the cell, then going to the **Cell** menu and choosing the **Convert** submenu. More information about forms can be found in the Help Browser; push the **Master Index** radio button, and type `StandardForm` in the text field, then click on the link(s) referencing the *Mathematica* book.

Another reality that you may encounter at some point is that your computer can *crash*.

Recognizing a Crash

When you enter a command to *Mathematica*'s kernel, the title bar to the notebook window will display the text "Running. . . ." This label will vanish when the output appears. It is *Mathematica*'s way of telling you that it is working on a calculation. Some calculations are fast, but some are slow, and some are *very* slow (hours, days, even weeks). How much time a calculation will require depends on the complexity of the calculation and the type of computer being used. If you have entered a command and nothing seems to be happening, don't despair. It is likely that you have simply asked a difficult question (intentionally or not) and it will take *Mathematica* a bit of time to answer.

If you don't have time to wait and want *Mathematica* to stop, read on.

Or if (heaven forbid) the cursor does not respond when you move the mouse, and the keyboard does not seem to work, it is likely that a crash has occurred. Don't panic, and don't pull the plug just yet. Read on...

Aborting Calculations and/or Recovering from a Crash

The action that you should take depends to some extent on what type of computer you are using. Let's proceed by platform:

Mac OS Procedure

Under ordinary circumstances (the computer hasn't crashed), simply select **Abort Evaluation** from the **Kernel** menu. This will usually work, but not always. Wait a minute or two; take a deep breath. If all goes well you should eventually see the message `$Aborted` in your notebook window where the output would ordinarily appear. Mission accomplished.

If nothing happens when you attempt to abort, you will have to take slightly more decisive action: You will have to quit the kernel. To do this, go again to the **Kernel** menu, but this time select **Quit Kernel** (you then have to select the kernel that is running, usually the local kernel), then hit the **Quit** button when it asks if you *really* want to quit the kernel. The only consequence here is that if you wish to continue working, you will have to start a new kernel. This will happen automatically when you enter your next command. Remember that the new kernel will not be aware of any of your previous calculations, so you may have to reenter some old cells to bring the new kernel up to date (if your new commands make reference to your any of your previous work).

Now for those of you who have lost control of the mouse and keyboard due to a crash, none of the above is possible. Ideally, you would like to be able to quit *Mathematica* without losing any of your unsaved work. It's not always possible; this is why it's a good idea to save your work often.

First, try simultaneously hitting ⌘ and **.** (that's the period key). This is just the keyboard equivalent of selecting **Abort Evaluation** from the **Kernel** menu as described above. It probably won't work, but give it a try. We've seen instances in which the mouse failed in the middle of a long calculation. No crash, just a dirty mouse that died at an inopportune time.

If that doesn't work, try hitting ⌘-**q**. If this works you will be presented with a dialog box asking if you wish to save your work. Answer "Yes." In this case, the result will be quitting the entire *Mathematica* program (front end and kernel). You should restart your computer before resuming your work (look in the **Special** menu for **Restart**). This will decrease the likelihood of another crash.

If that doesn't work, simultaneously hit the ⌘-OPTION-ESCAPE keys. This is usually effective. The kernel will quit and you will then be able to save your notebook. Once you have saved your work, you should quit *Mathematica* and restart your computer.

As a last resort, you will have to turn off your computer manually. Any unsaved changes will be lost. If the computer has a reset button, use it. Otherwise find the "off" button (often on the back of your computer) and use it. Wait a few seconds and restart the computer in the usual way.

Windows Procedure

Under ordinary circumstances (the computer hasn't crashed), simply select **Abort Evaluation** from the **Kernel** menu. This will usually work, but not always. Wait a minute or two; take a deep breath. If all goes well you should eventually see the message $Aborted in your notebook window where the output would ordinarily appear. Mission accomplished.

If nothing happens when you try to abort, you will have to take slightly more decisive action: You will have to quit the kernel. To do this, go again to the **Kernel** menu and select **Quit Kernel** (you then have to select the kernel that is running, usually the local kernel), then hit the **Quit** button when it asks if you *really* want to quit the kernel. The only consequence here is that if you wish to continue working, you will have to start a new kernel. This will happen automatically when you enter your next command. Remember that the new kernel will not be aware of any of your previous calculations, so you may have to reenter some old cells to bring the new kernel up to date (if your new commands make reference to any of your previous work).

Now for those of you who have lost control of the mouse and keyboard due to a crash, none of the above is possible. Ideally, you would like to be able to quit *Mathematica* without losing any of your unsaved work. It's not always possible; this is why it's a good idea to save your work often.

First, try simultaneously hitting ALT and . (that's the period key). This is just the keyboard equivalent of selecting **Abort Evaluation** from the **Kernel** menu as described above. It probably won't work, but give it a try. We've seen instances in which the mouse failed in the middle of a long calculation. No crash, just a dirty mouse that died at an inopportune time.

If that doesn't work, simultaneously hit the CONTROL-ALT-DELETE keys. This is usually effective. You should be presented with a dialog box. Hit ENTER and you will quit *Mathematica* altogether. Any unsaved changes to your notebook will be lost. You should restart your computer before launching *Mathematica* again (use the reset button on the case). This will decrease the likelihood of another crash.

As a last resort, you will have to turn off your computer. Again, any unsaved changes will be lost. Use the reset button. If that doesn't work (very rare), turn the computer off, wait a few seconds, and then restart it.

Running Efficiently: Preventing Crashes

Mathematica makes heavy demands on your computer's resources. In particular, it benefits from large amounts of random access memory, or RAM. You should be aware of this so that you can help it along. Here are some tips:

First, quit any other programs (such as Netscape Navigator or Microsoft Works) before launching *Mathematica*. Other programs also require RAM, so running them at the same time steals valuable RAM from *Mathematica*. Also, even though it is possible to have multiple notebooks open at one time, avoid doing so unless it is necessary (as it is, for instance, if you are copying cells from one notebook to another). Each open notebook will consume memory. You should also save your notebook often. Doing so will allow *Mathematica* to put part of it on a floppy or hard drive, rather than storing all of it in RAM.

If you are a fiend for optimized performance, go to the Help Browser, click the **Getting Started/Demos** radio button, and begin typing **Memory** in the text field. You may need to go to the second column to choose your platform. Read up on memory management.

Memory Gauges for the Mac OS

If you are using a machine running the Mac OS, keep an eye on how much memory is available. There is a little black bar on the lower left corner of your notebook window. The black part indicates how much memory is being used by the front end; it's like a fuel gauge, except that full is bad. Big tick marks are megabytes. If it ever gets almost solid black, it's time to take action before you run out of memory. If you haven't saved your notebook recently, do so. If that doesn't help, consider quitting and restarting *Mathematica*, or perhaps closing the current notebook and creating a new one for your future computations. If you are running low on memory, be *sure* to save your notebook often.

The kernel has a gauge too, but it takes a little work to get to it. First, you need to make the kernel the current application. Use the application menu in the far upper-right corner of the screen; select **MathKernel**. Now go to the **File** menu and select **Show Memory Usage**. A little gauge will appear. You can grab it by the title bar and move it to a convenient location on your screen. If it gets close to being full, go to the **Kernel** menu and quit the kernel. Now continue working with a new kernel. Note that if you quit *Mathematica* with the kernel memory gauge showing, it will appear all by itself in future sessions.

These gauges are only available for Macs.

Chapter 3

Functions and Their Graphs

3.1   Defining a Function

A *function* is a rule that assigns to each input exactly one output. Many functions, such as the natural logarithm function **Log**, are built in to *Mathematica*. You provide an input, or argument, and *Mathematica* produces the output:

```
In[1]:= Log[1]
Out[1]= 0
```

You can define your own function in *Mathematica* like this (use the **BasicInput** palette to type x^2; see Section 1.6, page 4):

```
In[2]:= f[x_] := x^2 + 2 x - 4
```

This function will take an input x, and output $x^2 + 2x - 4$. For instance:

```
In[3]:= f[1]
Out[3]= -1
```

```
In[4]:= f[π]
Out[4]= -4 + 2 π + π^2
```

As a second example, here is a function that will return the multiplicative inverse of its argument (again, use the **BasicInput** palette to type the fraction):

```
In[5]:= inv[x_] := 1/x
```

Let's try it:

In[6]:= **inv[45]**

$Out[6]= \dfrac{1}{45}$

You can also create functions by combining existing functions:

In[7]:= **g[x_] :=N[inv[x]]**

In[8]:= **g[45]**

Out[8]= 0.0222222

Follow these rules when defining a function:

1. The name of the function (such as **f**, **g**, or **inv**) should be a *lowercase* letter, or a word that begins with a lowercase letter. This is because all built-in functions (such as **Log** and **N**) begin with capital letters. If your function begins with a lowercase letter, you will never accidentally give it a name that already belongs to some built-in function.

2. The function argument (in these examples **x**) must be followed by an underscore _ on the *left* side of the definition. This identifies the argument as a variable.

3. Use *square* brackets to enclose the argument.

4. Use the colon–equal combination **:=** to separate the left side of the definition from the right.

5. After typing the definition, enter the cell containing it. Your function is now ready for action.

⚠ The **:=** operator (called the *SetDelayed* operator) used in defining functions differs in a subtle way from the **=** operator (called the *Set* operator) used for making assignments (the **=** operator was discussed in Section 1.11, see page 16). Essentially, when you use **:=** the expression appearing to its right is processed anew by the kernel each time that the expression appearing to its left is called. The **=** operator, by contrast, evaluates the expression on its right at the time the assignment is made. In many settings, **=** and **:=** can be used interchangeably; however, there are cases when one is appropriate and the other is not. Using **:=** for function definitions will work in virtually every setting, and we will use it consistently for that purpose throughout this book.

For more information, go to the Help Browser and type **SetDelayed** in the text field, then follow the link to the appropriate section of the *Mathematica* Book.

3.2 Clearing a Function

A word to the wise: Once you are finished working with a function, get rid of it. Why? One reason is that you may forget about the function and later in the session try to use the name for something else. But *Mathematica* won't forget, and all sorts of confusion can result. Another is that in getting rid of a function you will clear out a little bit of memory, leaving more room for you to work. To see if a letter or word has been defined as a function, use the **?** command just as you would for a built-in *Mathematica* command:

```
In[9]:= ?f
        Global`f
        f[x_] := x^2 + 2*x - 4
```

This indicates that *f* is still retained in memory. You can use the **Clear** command to erase it, just as you would to erase the value of a constant:

```
In[10]:= Clear[f]
```

Now if you use the **?** command you will find no such definition:

```
In[11]:= ?f
         Global`f
```

⚠ The response Global`f indicates that the name *f* is retained in *Mathematica*'s memory, but that there is no meaning or definition attached to the name. Thus the **Clear** command has deleted the definition, but not the name itself. You can remove the name as well by typing and entering **Remove[f]**. After doing so, the **?f** querey will produce the response Information :: notfound : Symbol f not found.

You can clear several functions in one shot by entering all of them into the **Clear** command, separated by commas:

In[12]:= **Clear[g,inv]**

Many savvy users are in the habit of clearing a function's name just before it is defined. It's not a bad idea, as it guarantees that you will never attach two values to the same name. You can put it all in one cell: put a semicolon after the **Clear** command and hit RETURN (Mac) or ENTER (Windows) to get to the next line. Then write the definition for your function and enter the cell:

In[13]:= **Clear[f];**

$$\textbf{f[x\_] := } \frac{\textbf{Sin[x]}}{\textbf{x}}$$

3.3   Producing a Table of Values

It is often handy to produce a table of function values for various inputs. Here is a table of the squares of the first ten positive whole numbers:

In[14]:= **Clear[f];**

f[x_] := x^2

In[15]:= **Table[f[x],{x,1,10}]**
Out[15]= **{1,4,9,16,25,36,49,64,81,100}**

The **Table** command takes two arguments, separated by commas. The first (in this case **f[x]**) describes the contents of each table entry. The second (in this case **{x,1,10}**) is called an *iterator*, and it describes the span of values that the variable x takes. The curly brackets are essential in describing this span. In fact, *Mathematica* uses this iterator structure in numerous commands, so it warrants a bit of discussion. The first item (**x**) names the variable, and the next two items give the range of values that this variable will assume (1 through 10) in whole number increments. If you do not wish to have your variable increase in unit increments, you can add a fourth element to the iterator that will specify the amount by which the variable will skip from one value to the next. For example:

In[16]:= **Table[f[x],{x,0,50,5}]**
Out[16]= **{0,25,100,225,400,625,900,1225,1600,2025,2500}**

You can also shorten the iterator to contain only two items—the name of the variable and a stopping number. When you do this, *Mathematica* starts at 1 and increments the variable in steps of 1 until the stopping number is reached. So for instance, using the iterator **{x,10}** is the same as using the iterator **{x,1,10}**:

```
In[17]:= Table[f[x],{x,10}]
Out[17]= {1,4,9,16,25,36,49,64,81,100}
```

The iterator **{x,1,10}** is an example of a more general structure called a *list*. A list consists of items separated by commas and enclosed in curly brackets. The output of the **Table** command is also a list. Note also that the output in the last examples are a bit unruly – they don't look much like tables. The way to neaten up the output list is to put it in **TableForm**. When you input a list to this command, it will be nicely displayed as a column. For instance:

```
In[18]:= TableForm[{1,3,5}]
Out[18]//TableForm=
        1
        3
        5
```

One can produce the same effect like this, applying **TableForm** as a "postfix command" (discussed in Section 2.6, see page 28).

```
In[19]:= {1,3,5}//TableForm
Out[19]//TableForm=
        1
        3
        5
```

The point of all this is that you can use **TableForm** to smarten a table's appearance:

```
In[20]:= Table[f[x],{x,0,50,5}]//TableForm
Out[20]//TableForm=
        0
        25
        100
        225
        400
        625
        900
        1225
        1600
        2025
        2500
```

And wouldn't it be nice to display the inputs x that correspond to each of these outputs $f(x)$? This can be accomplished by giving the list **{x, f[x]}** as the first argument to the **Table** command, like this:

```
In[21]:= Table[{x,f[x]},{x,0,50,5}]//TableForm
Out[21]//TableForm=
        0    0
        5    25
        10   100
        15   225
        20   400
        25   625
        30   900
        35   1225
        40   1600
        45   2025
        50   2500
```

You can use powers of ten (or of any other number) as the values of the function variable:

```
In[22]:= Clear[f];
         f[x_] := Log[10,x]
```

```
In[23]:= Table[{10^n,f[10^n]},{n,1,6}]//TableForm
Out[23]//TableForm=
        10        1
        100       2
        1000      3
        10000     4
        100000    5
        1000000   6
```

As a last example, here is how you can make a table that displays two or more functions:

```
In[24]:= Clear[f,g];
         f[x_] := x^2;
         g[x_] := 2^x
```

In[25]:= **Table[{x, f[x],g[x]},{x,1,10}] // TableForm**

Out[25] // TableForm =

1	1	2
2	4	4
3	9	8
4	16	16
5	25	32
6	36	64
7	49	128
8	64	256
9	81	512
10	100	1024

Now is a good time to review the three most commonly used brackets in *Mathematica*. Parentheses **()** are used to group terms in algebraic expressions. Square brackets **[]** are used to enclose the arguments of functions. And curly brackets **{}** are used to enclose lists.

3.4 Plotting a Function

Plotting a function is very much like constructing a visual table of values for the function. The *Mathematica* command **Plot** works much like the command **Table** outlined in the previous section:

In[26]:= **Clear[f];**
f[x_] := x² - 2 x + 4

In[27]:= **Plot[f[x],{x, -1,3}]**

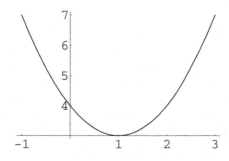

The **Plot** command has two arguments, separated by a comma. The first (in this case **f[x]**) is the function to be graphed, and the second (in this case **{x,-1,3}**) is an iterator specifying the name of the variable and the domain of values it is to assume. The variable always corresponds to the horizontal axis, while the values that the function assumes on the specified domain always correspond to the vertical axis.

Note that the axes in this plot do not intersect at the origin, but rather at the point $(0, 3)$. Every time you use the **Plot** command *Mathematica* decides where to place the axes, and they do not generally cross at the origin. There is a good reason for this. As often as not you will find yourself plotting functions over domains in which the graph is relatively far from the origin. Rather than omit one or both axes from the plot, *Mathematica* will move them into view, giving your plot a frame of reference. If you really want to produce a plot with the axes intersecting at the origin, you can. The details are provided in the next section of this chapter, "Using *Mathematica*'s Plot Options."

You can zoom in on a particular portion of a plot simply by editing the domain specified in the iterator, then reentering the cell. Let's take a close look, so to speak, at the function in the last example, this time with x values near 2. Notice how "flat" the graph becomes:

In[28]:= **Plot[f[x],{x,1.9,2.1}]**

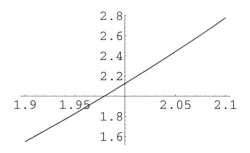

You can use the mouse to find the coordinates of any point in the graph. You really have to try this to appreciate it, so get yourself set in front of the computer and generate a plot. Now put the cursor anywhere on the graph and click once, then hold down the COMMAND key (on a Mac it's the key with the ⌘ on it). The coordinates of the point in the crosshairs will be displayed in the lower left corner of the notebook window. Move the cursor (keeping the COMMAND key depressed) and watch the coordinates change.

It appears from the graph that $f(2)$ is just a tad larger than 2.1. You could zoom in even more (say with a domain from 1.99 to 2.01) and get a more accurate estimate of $f(2)$. Of course, you could also do this:

$In[29]:=$ **f[2]**
$Out[29]=$ $\dfrac{17}{8}$

$In[30]:=$ **%//N**
$Out[30]=$ 2.125

Another little trick that's good to know about is how to make a graphic larger or smaller. This technique is best learned by trying it; so again, get yourself in front of the computer and produce a plot. Position the cursor anywhere on the graph and click once. A rectangular border with eight "handles" appears around the graph. Position the cursor on a handle and drag (hold down the mouse button and move the mouse) to shrink or enlarge the graphic. It's easy; try it.

When a function is defined by a complicated expression, its plot often demands careful investigation:

$In[31]:=$ **Clear[f];**
       f[x_] := $\dfrac{x^5 - 4 x^2 + 1}{x - \frac{1}{2}}$

$In[32]:=$ **Plot[f[x],{x, -3,3}]**

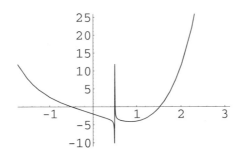

Something strange seems to be happening when $x = \frac{1}{2}$ (see that vertical blip?). What's happening is this: the function is not defined when $x = \frac{1}{2}$, since the denominator of f is equal to zero at this value of x. Think of there being an imaginary vertical line, an asymptote, at $x = \frac{1}{2}$ through which the graph of f cannot pass. In order to understand *Mathematica's* plot it is important to understand how the **Plot** command works. **Plot** samples several values of x in the specified domain and numerically evaluates $f(x)$ for each of them. It then plots these points and "connects the dots" with little line segments. There are so many that the graph appears in most places like a smooth curve. The important point here is that *Mathematica's* plots are not exact in a mathematical sense; they are only approximations. For instance, the vertical-looking segment that crosses the x axis near $\frac{1}{2}$ is not part of the true graph of f. As *Mathematica* plotted successively larger values of x just to the left of $x = \frac{1}{2}$, the function values got smaller and smaller. The last point that was plotted to the left of the true asymptote took a large negative value. The very next point plotted, just to the right of the true asymptote, took a large positive value. *Mathematica* then connected these two points with a line segment (so in fact that vertical-looking segment tilts ever so slightly from lower left to upper right). *Mathematica* had no way of knowing that in fact the true graph of f never crosses the vertical asymptote. Although technically inaccurate, this isn't a bad state of affairs. You can interpret the plot as the graph of f with the asymptote roughly drawn in. And an important lesson can be learned here: Never trust the output of the computer as gospel; it always demands scrutiny.

Beware also that vertical asymptotes (and other "narrow" features) in a plot will change in appearance as the specified domain changes. Asymptotes may disappear or become barely noticeable. For instance, here is another view of the function f, this time with the wider domain from −10 to 10. The asymptote appears to have vanished:

In[33]:= **Plot[f[x],{x, - 10,10}]**

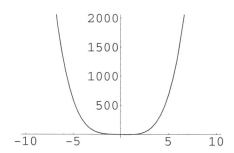

The asymptote is invisible because *Mathematica* (by chance) skipped over those values of x so close to the asymptote that $f(x)$ would take very large or very small values. The "true" graph of f still spikes up toward infinity just to the right of the asymptote and down to negative infinity just to the left of it. The point of all this is to make clear that the plots *Mathematica* produces are approximations. They may hide prominant features of a function if those features are sufficiently narrow relative to the domain over which the function is plotted. When it comes to finding asymptotes, for instance, looking for them on a plot is not necessarily the best way to find them. We'll discuss better methods for finding asymptotes (by finding explicit values of x for which the denominator is equal to zero) in the next chapter.

3.5 Using *Mathematica's* Plot Options

Many of *Mathematica's* commands have optional arguments; you can type additional arguments into a command to modify the behavior of that command. In this section we'll see how to tweak the **Plot** command so that you get the most out of your graphs. For example, here is the plot from the end of the last section:

```
In[34]:= Clear[f];
         f[x_] := (x^5 - 4 x^2 + 1) / (x - 1/2)
In[35]:= Plot[f[x],{x, -10,10}]
```

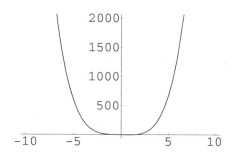

Notice how *Mathematica* only showed us a portion of what we asked for (the domain shown is only from -7 to 7 or so). This is because outside of this range *Mathematica* observed no interesting behavior; the graph kept going up on the left and up on the right. By only including this smaller domain we lost no information, and got a better view of the middle portion. *Mathematica* will do this by default.

But suppose you really want to see the function over the domain from -10 to 10. After typing the two arguments to the **Plot** command, type a comma followed by **PlotRange→All**. The arrow → is found on the **BasicInput** palette, or can be typed from the keyboard as [ESCAPE]->[ESCAPE]. You can also use a "minus" sign followed by a "greater than" sign, **->**, in place of the arrow:

```
In[36]:= Plot[f[x],{x, -10,10},PlotRange→All]
```

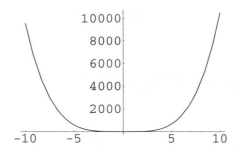

The optional argument **PlotRange** is set to the value **Automatic** by default, which will sometimes result in a graph whose ends are chopped off. You can specify a different value, such as **All** by adding **PlotRange→All** as an additional argument to the **Plot** command. It must be placed after the two requisite arguments. In general, you type the name of the option, followed by → (or **->**), followed by the desired setting of the option. You may add several options to the **Plot** command, and in any order you wish (provided each optional argument is listed *after* the two requisite arguments). Just use commas to separate them. Listed below are some common uses for plot options.

How to Get the Same Scaling on Both Axes

In order to get both sets of axes on the same scale use the option **AspectRatio→ Automatic**:

In[37]:= **Plot[2(x - 4)^2 +1,{x,3,5},AspectRatio→Automatic]**

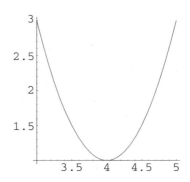

Be mindful that in many cases you definitely do *not* want your axes to have the same scale. You could very easily ask for a plot that was a few inches wide and a few miles high, and it is likely that you would crash *Mathematica* trying to render it. Imagine the plot at the beginning of this section if you are skeptical. That is why the default aspect ratio (the ratio of height to width) is set to scale the axes in such a way that the graph will fit into a rectangle of standard proportions. It's best to use the **AspectRatio → Automatic** option only after you have viewed the plot and determined that its use won't result in a plot that's too long and skinny.

Note that you can also set **AspectRatio** to any positive numerical value you like. The plot will have the height to width ratio that you specify. For instance, **AspectRatio → 3** will produce a plot that is three times as high as it is wide.

How to Get the Axes to Intersect at the Origin

Use the option **AxesOrigin → {0,0}**:

In[38]:= **Plot[2(x - 4)^2 + 1, {x, 3, 5}, AxesOrigin → {0, 0}]**

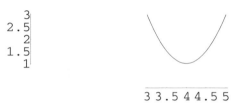

This may not be what you expected. *Mathematica* only includes those portions of the axes that are aligned horizontally and vertically with the graph. It's easier to determine where the darn thing is this way. If you really want those axes to be there, use the **PlotRange** option to specify both your *x* and *y* ranges, as follows:

In[39]:= **Plot[2(x - 4)^2 + 1, {x, 3, 5}, PlotRange → {{0, 5}, {0, 3}}]**

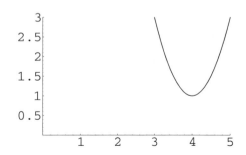

How to Add Color, and Other Style Changes

It's not hard to make a plot any color you like using the **PlotStyle** option. The abbreviation RGB stands for "red–green–blue." First, decide how much of each of these three colors should be used, on a scale of 0 (none) to 1 (all). For instance, the setting **RGBColor[1,0,0]** will produce a red graph, **RGBColor[0,1,0]** will produce a green graph, and **RGBColor[0,0,1]** will produce a blue graph. **RGBColor[.7,0,.7]** will produce a shade of purple, and so on. The output below is shown in grayscale. It will appear purple on your monitor:

$In[40]:=$ **Plot[2(x - 4)^2 +1,{x,3,5},
        PlotStyle → RGBColor[0.7,0,0.7]]**

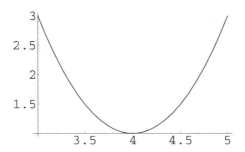

A simpler, but somewhat more cryptic way to add color is by specifying the value of the **PlotStyle** option in terms of **Hue**. **Hue** can take values from 0 to 1, and only experience will tell you which values correspond to which colors (green is near .3, blue is near .7, and red is near 1). You can use either **Hue** or **RGBColor** to add color to a plot. **Hue** is easier to type, **RGBColor** is easier to use to generate and blend specific colors:

$In[41]:=$ **Plot[2(x - 4)^2 +1,{x,3,5},PlotStyle → Hue[0.3]]**

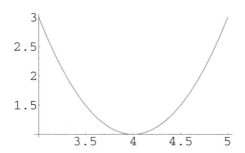

The **PlotStyle** option allows for all sorts of settings beyond changing color. Here's an example. When specifying several style options on a single plot, the option values appear in a list. **GrayLevel** can take any value from 0 (black) to 1 (white). **Thickness** is expressed as a fraction of the width of the entire plot.

Dashing takes a list as its argument. The list specifies the line segment lengths and space lengths (again, measured as a fraction of the width of the plot). For instance, **Dashing[{.05}]** produces a dashing line with dashes and spaces each 5% of the width of the plot, while **Dashing[{.05,.02}]** produces a dashing line with dashes that are 5% of the width of the plot, and spaces that are 2% of the width of the plot:

In[42]:= **Plot[2(x - 4)² + 1,{x,3,5},**
         PlotStyle → {GrayLevel[0.5],
         Thickness[0.01],Dashing[{0.05}]}]

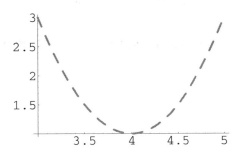

How to Remove the Axes or Add a Frame

To remove axes simply add the option **Axes → False**:

In[43]:= **Plot[2(x - 4)² + 1,{x,3,5},Axes →False]**

Without axes, you may at least want the scaling to be accurate:

In[44]:= **Plot[2(x - 4)² + 1,{x,3,5},**
         Axes →False, AspectRatio →Automatic]

To replace the axes with a frame around the entire graph, use the option **Frame →**
True:

$In[45]:=$ **Plot[2(x - 4)^2 + 1, {x, 3, 5}, Frame → True]**

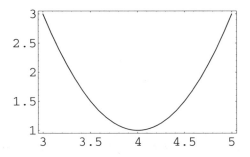

How to Add Grid Lines and Adjust Tick Marks

To add a grid to your plot, as if it were plotted on graph paper, add the option
GridLines → Automatic. With a color monitor, the grid lines will be blue by
default:

$In[46]:=$ **Plot[2(x - 4)^2 + 1, {x, 3, 5}, GridLines → Automatic]**

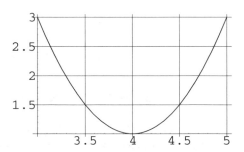

To change the spacing of grid lines, set **GridLines** as a list of two lists: the first consists of x values indicating the positions of the vertical lines, and the second consists of y values indicating the positions of the horizontal lines:

In[47]:= **Plot[2(x - 4)^2 +1,{x,3,5},**
           GridLines→{{3.25,3.75,4.25,4.75},{2,3}}]

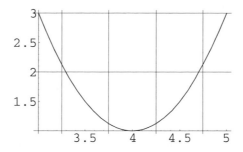

This gives you total control over the placement of grid lines, but it comes at the price of being somewhat cumbersome if you ask for too many of them. If you really want the graph-paper look, use the **Table** command to generate your lists of x and y values. For instance, replace the x list in the input above with **Table [x,{x,3,5,.1}]** to get vertical grid lines spaced in increments of $\frac{1}{10}$ of a unit.

You can follow a similar procedure to adjust the spacing of the tick marks and numeral placement on a plot without grid lines. Use the option **Ticks**, whose settings work exactly like those for **GridLines**:

In[48]:= **Plot$\left[$Sin[x]^2,{x,0,2π},**

           Ticks → $\left\{ \ \left\{ \dfrac{\pi}{2},\pi,\dfrac{3\pi}{2},2\pi \right\} ,$Automatic$\right\}\right]$

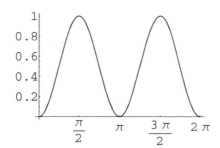

How to Label the Axes

If you want to add labels to the axes in a graph, use the option
AxesLabel→{"*xLabel*","*yLabel*"}

For example,

$In[49]:=$ **Plot[2(x - 4)^2 +1,{x,3,5},**
        AxesLabel→{"time","temperature"}]

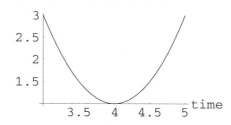

⚠ The double quotes surrounding the label names are not essential, but are recommended. For instance, if you do not use them, and if you had made the assignment **temperature = 72**, then the setting **AxesLabel→ {time,temperature}** would produce a plot whose y axis bears the label "72." Even if you had made no assignments, the setting **AxesLabel→{time of day, temperature}** would produce a plot whose x axis bears the label "day of time," since the label **time of day** is interpreted as a product of three items, and *Mathematica* sorts the factors in such a product alphabetically.

How to Give Your Plot a Title

To give your plot a name or title, add the option **PlotLabel→** *"name"*:

$In[50]:=$ **Plot[2(x - 4)^2 +1,{x,3,5},**
        PlotLabel→"My Favorite Parabola"]

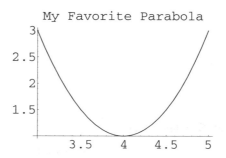

How to Change Fonts

Yes, of course you can change the fonts on your graphics. For instance, the Helvetica font in 12-point size (for both the labels and the numbers in a plot) is obtained as follows:

```
In[51]:= Plot[2(x - 4)^2 +1,{x,3,5},
            AxesLabel→{"time","temperature"},
            DefaultFont→{"Helvetica",12}]
```

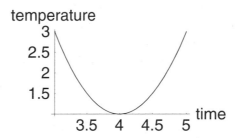

The **DefaultFont** option needs two arguments (expressed as a list). The first is the PostScript name of the font, and the second is the font size, in printer's points. The font size will be the specified size regardless of how you resize the graphic (by clicking and dragging on it, for instance). PostScript font names sometimes differ from font names used by other computer programs, especially for italicized or bold fonts. The best way to see which names correspond to which fonts is with an Adobe font catalog. Note also that there may be fonts that you are able to view on screen but not print on your printer. Sage advice: Stick to common fonts, and don't waste too much time trying to place a particular font on your graphic.

You'll get the most bang for your buck by adding the option **DefaultFont→ {"Times",10}**. This will replace the coarse Courier font on the plot with the always respectable Times font. If you want this to be the default font for all of your plots generated by the **Plot** command, type this once at the beginning of your session:

```
In[52]:= SetOptions[Plot,DefaultFont→{"Times",10}];
```

Now the option will be set as long as the current kernel is running, or until you use the **SetOptions** command to reset the default font to Courier:

```
In[53]:= Plot[x + Sin[x],{x,0,50},
            AxesLabel→{"Months","CO_2"}]
```

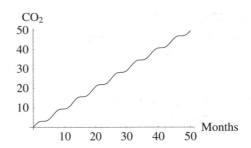

For the true control freaks: if you want to use one font for your plot label, and another for your axes labels, and a third for the numbers on the axes, you can do that too. Use the **DefaultFont** option to set the font for the numbers on the axes. Then use the command **StyleForm** to set any other fonts. To use **StyleForm**, replace

$$\textit{"text"} \qquad \text{with} \qquad \textbf{StyleForm[}\textit{"text"}\textbf{,}\textit{options}\textbf{]}$$

The *options* will specify the style of the text. Typical settings for **StyleForm** options include **FontFamily → "Times"** and **FontSize → 12**. Other possible settings can be found in the Help Browser by typing **StyleForm** in the text field. Here's an example:

```
In[54]:= Plot[2(x-4)^2+1,{x,3,5},AspectRatio→ 1/3,
        DefaultFont→{"Helvetica",10},
        PlotLabel→StyleForm["A Sinister Plot",
                FontFamily→"Times-Bold",
                FontSize→16],
        AxesLabel→{
          StyleForm["hell",
                FontFamily→"Helvetica-Oblique",
                FontSize→12],
          StyleForm["highwater",
                FontFamily→"Helvetica-Oblique",
                FontSize→12]
          }
        ]
```

How to Find Out About Other Options

The **Plot** command has more than twenty options. You can have it plot more points to get a more accurate graph, or change the background color to pink. To find out more type **??Plot**. The options for the **Plot** command (and their default settings) will be shown along with some other information:

```
In[55]:= ??Plot

        Plot[f, {x, xmin, xmax}] generates a plot of f as a
          function of x from xmin to xmax. Plot[{f1, f2, ... },
          {x, xmin, xmax}] plots several functions fi.
        Attributes[Plot] = {HoldAll, Protected}
        Options[Plot] = {AspectRatio -> GoldenRatio^(-1),
          Axes -> Automatic, AxesLabel -> None,
          AxesOrigin -> Automatic, AxesStyle -> Automatic,
          Background -> Automatic, ColorOutput -> Automatic,
          Compiled -> True, DefaultColor -> Automatic,
          Epilog -> {},
          Frame -> False, FrameLabel -> None, FrameStyle ->
            Automatic,
          FrameTicks -> Automatic, GridLines -> None,
          ImageSize -> Automatic, MaxBend -> 10.,
          PlotDivision -> 30.,
          PlotLabel -> None, PlotPoints -> 25,
          PlotRange -> Automatic,
          PlotRegion -> Automatic, PlotStyle -> Automatic,
          Prolog -> {}, RotateLabel -> True, Ticks -> Automatic,
          DefaultFont :> $DefaultFont,
          DisplayFunction :> $DisplayFunction,
          FormatType :> $FormatType, TextStyle :> $TextStyle}
```

To find out more about a particular option, say **Background**, type **?Background**:

```
In[56]:= ?Background

        Background is an option which specifies the background
          color to use.
```

Unfortunately this doesn't tell you what the legal settings are for this option. For this information, complete with examples, type and highlight the option name, go to the **Help** menu, and select **Find in Help...** (version 3 of *Mathematica*), or **Find Selected Function...** (version 4 of *Mathematica*).

3.6 Working with Piecewise Defined Functions

Sometimes functions are defined by different rules over different regions, so-called *piecewise defined functions*. For instance, a function may be defined by the rule $f(x) = 1 + x$ when x is zero or negative, and by the rule $f(x) = 1 - x$ when x is positive. How can this be conveyed to *Mathematica*? Append to the function definition the symbol **/;** followed by a *condition* (such as $x > 0$). This will restrict the function definition so that it will only be applied if the condition is true. This enables you to give a function different definitions over different intervals:

```
In[57]:= Clear[f];
         f[x_] := 1 + x /;  x ≤ 0
         f[x_] := 1 - x /;  x > 0

In[58]:= Plot[f[x], {x, -1, 1}]
```

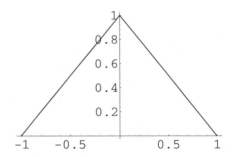

The **/;** operator can be read as "provided that." Note that $x \le 0$ means "x is less than or equal to zero," while $x > 0$ means "x is strictly greater than zero"; so the two domains butt up against each other but do not overlap. Note also the similarity to the traditional mathematical notation:

$$f(x) = \begin{cases} 1 + x, & x \le 0, \\ 1 - x, & x > 0. \end{cases}$$

Here's a second example:

```
In[59]:= Clear[g];
         g[x_] := 1          /;  x ≤ -1
         g[x_] := 2 - x²      /;  -1 ≤ x < 1
         g[x_] := 2          /;  1 ≤ x
```

In[60]:= **Plot[g[x],{x, -2,2},PlotRange→{{ -2,2},{0,2}}]**

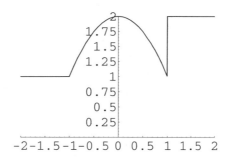

Here is another instance in which the plot is not accurate: the vertical-looking segment is not part of the actual graph of *g* (in fact no *function* has a vertical segment anywhere in its graph). Keep in mind how the **Plot** command works: it plots a bunch of points using the formula for *g*, then connects the dots. In this case it joined points which in fact should not be joined, for if *x* is just a little less than 1, the point $(x, g(x))$ lies on the parabola, while if *x* is 1 or greater, the point $(x, g(x))$ lies on the horizontal line $y = 2$. There are no points that lie on the vertical segment. We say the function *g* is *discontinuous*; its true graph cannot be traced without lifting the pencil from the page. Beware that *Mathematica* will have trouble rendering discontinuities.

Here is an example of three parabolas "pasted" together to form a bell-shaped curve. This function is not only continuous, but also smooth in the sense that its graph has no sharp corners. Piecewise defined functions can look very much like functions defined by a single equation:

In[61]:= **Clear[h];**
h[x_] := 0   **/; x < 0**
$$h[x\_] := \frac{x^2}{2} \qquad /; \ 0 \le x < 1$$
$$h[x\_] := -x^2 + 3x - \frac{3}{2} \quad /; \ 1 \le x < 2$$
$$h[x\_] := \frac{1}{2}(3-x)^2 \qquad /; \ 2 \le x < 3$$
h[x_] := 0   **/; 3 ≤ x**

Here's a plot of *h* with vertical grid lines added to show where the breaks occur:

```
In[62]:= Plot[h[x],{x, -0.5,3.5},
          Frame→True,GridLines→{{0,1,2,3},None}]
```

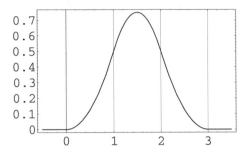

3.7 Plotting Implicitly Defined Functions

An *implicitly defined function* is given as an equation relating two variables, such as $x^2 + y^2 = 1$, which describes a circle of radius one. Here the y variable is not given *explicitly* as a function of the x variable, but rather the x and y terms are wrapped up in an equation; hence the term "implicitly" defined function. In order to plot implicitly defined functions, you will need to load the standard package **Graphics`ImplicitPlot`** into *Mathematica*. The following command will perform this action:

```
In[63]:= Needs["Graphics`ImplicitPlot`"]
```

Type carefully! Note the use of the backquote, and of the double quotation marks. There will be no output if the cell is entered properly. Do not even try to use the commands described below until the cell above has been entered successfully. The reason is that the command **ImplicitPlot** (used below) will not be available until the package has been loaded. See the Section 2.8, "Loading Packages," on page 36 for more information on using *Mathematica*'s packages.

Now to plot an implicitly defined function, use the command **Implicit Plot**:

```
In[64]:= Clear[x,y];
         ImplicitPlot[x² + y² == 1, {x, -3,3}]
```

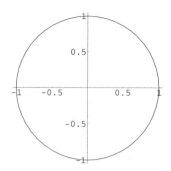

The first argument is an equation involving two variables. You *must* type == (or use the == button on the **BasicInput** palette) to enter an equation. The reason is that the single equal sign is used to assign names to quantities, an essentially different operation. The second argument to **ImplicitPlot** is the standard iterator specifying the span of values to be assumed by the variable on the horizontal axis. When in doubt about an appropriate span of values, be generous. **ImplicitPlot** is smart enough to crop off those regions where the graph doesn't exist (the iterator in the example above specifies that x ranges from -3 to 3, yet the plot only shows the relevant region from -1 to 1).

Note that unlike the **Plot** command, **ImplicitPlot** will by default produce a plot in which the x and y axes have the same scale. This will occasionally result in an awkwardly scaled graphic. You can use the **AspectRatio** option (described in the first subsection of Section 3.5 on page 56) to set the ratio of height to width to any value you like:

$In[65]:=$ **ImplicitPlot$\left[\dfrac{x^2}{144} + y^2 == 1, \{x, -12, 12\}\right]$**

Here is the same plot scaled so that it is half as tall as it is wide:

$In[66]:=$ **ImplicitPlot$\left[\dfrac{x^2}{144} + y^2 == 1, \{x, -12, 12\}, \right.$**
        $\left. \text{AspectRatio} \rightarrow 0.5\right]$

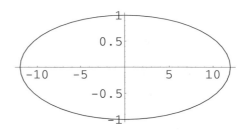

It is worth noting that **ImplicitPlot** will accept most of the options accepted by the **Plot** command, so you can leave off the axes, make the plot appear in color, and so on, using the techniques described in the previous section.

In certain cases, **ImplicitPlot** will not be able to solve the equation for the dependent variable, and hence will not be able to produce a plot. This typically happens when the equation contains "transcendental" functions, such as trigonometric functions:

In[67]:= **ImplicitPlot[Cos[x²] == Sin[y²], {x, - 2π, 2π}]**

Solve::incnst : Inconsistent or redundant
    transcendental equation. After reduction, the bad
    equation is ArcSin[Sin[y²]] == 0.

ImplicitPlot::epfail : Equation Cos[x²] == Sin[y²] could
    not be solved for points to plot.

Out[67]= ImplicitPlot[Cos[x²] == Sin[y²], {x, -2 π, 2 π}]

No need to get frustrated. In such cases just add a third argument to **ImplicitPlot**, an iterator specifying the range of values the second variable is to assume. A different algorithm is then implemented that *will* produce a plot, although it's often a bit jagged:

In[68]:= **ImplicitPlot[Cos[x²] == Sin[y²], {x, -2π, 2π},
        {y, -2π, 2π}]**

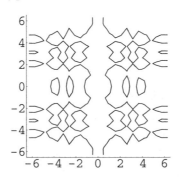

You can improve the quality of any **ImplicitPlot** by using the **PlotPoints** option. The higher the value, the more points will be sampled, and the greater the quality of the resulting image. Of course, you may end up waiting a while (or depleting the available memory) if **PlotPoints** is set too high:

```
In[69]:= ImplicitPlot[Cos[x^2] == Sin[y^2], {x, -2π, 2π},
            {y, -2π, 2π}, PlotPoints → 300]
```

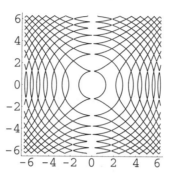

Now is a good time to review the three types of equal signs that are used in *Mathematica*. A single equal sign = is used to assign names to quantities, such as **a = 3**, or **mygraph = Plot[2x+1, {x, 0, 3}]**. A double equal sign **==** is used to present equations, such as those used in the **ImplicitPlot** command. Finally, a colon–equal sign **:=** is used for defining functions. Mercifully, that's all of them (at least in this book). Unless you get into some fancy programming, you won't be encountering any new equal signs in your later dealings with *Mathematica*.

3.8   Superimposing Plots

It is often desirable to view two or more plots together. If you simply want to plot several functions on the same set of axes, enter a *list* containing these functions as the first argument to the **Plot** command, and you'll have it:

```
In[70]:= Clear[f, g, h];
         f[x_] := 1 + x;
         g[x_] := x^2;
         h[x_] := f[x] + g[x]
```

In[71]:= **Plot[{f[x],g[x],h[x]},{x, -1,1}]**

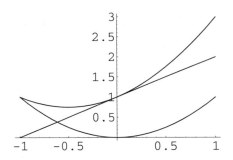

In such situations it is handy to make each of the three graphs distinctive by giving them three different styles. This is accomplished with the **PlotStyle** option (described earlier in this chapter, see page 57 for details). Here's how to enter the settings to make *f* red, *g* green, and *h* blue (they are shown here in grayscale; on a color monitor they will have the proper color):

In[72]:= **Plot[{f[x],g[x],h[x]},{x, - 1,1},**
        PlotStyle → {RGBColor[1,0,0],RGBColor[0,1,0],
        RGBColor[0,0,1]}]

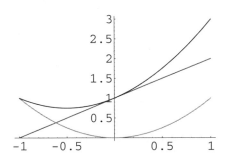

If you need a hard copy of your plot and do not have access to a color printer, you might replace the **RGBColor[...]** settings with **Dashing[...]** settings:

In[73]:= **Plot[{f[x],g[x],h[x]},{x, -1,1},**
        PlotStyle → {{},Dashing[{0.05}],
        Dashing[{0.01}]}]

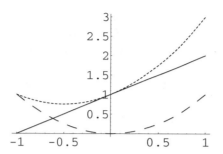

If you are willing to work just a little, you can add a legend to a plot that will explain which plot style goes with which function. To do this, first load the package **Graphics`Legend`**:

In[74]:= **Needs["Graphics`Legend`"]**

In[75]:= **Plot[{Tan[x],Sec[x]},{x,0,2π},**
            Ticks→{{π,2π},Automatic},
            PlotRange→{-3,3},
            PlotStyle→{GrayLevel[0.6],Dashing[{0.03}]},
            PlotLegend→{"Tangent","Secant"},
            LegendPosition→{1,-0.5}]

The option **PlotLegend→{"Tangent","Secant"}** will place the legend on the plot. The position of the legend will be in the lower left corner by default. If you care to move it, the position is set with the option **LegendPosition**. The setting for this option is a coordinate pair, in a coordinate system where the origin is in the center of the plot, and the longest edge of the plot runs from −1 to 1. Specify the coordinate position of the lower left corner of the legend box in this coordinate system as the setting for **LegendPosition**.

Since *Mathematica*'s **Table** command generates lists, it is possible to use it to generate a list of functions to plot. However, there is a special consideration that comes into play when the expression that you plot is one generated by another *Mathematica* command, such as **Table**. In such instances it is necessary to *wrap* the expression with the **Evaluate** command:

In[76]:= **functionList = Table[n x^2, {n, -40,40}];**

In[77]:= **Plot[Evaluate[functionList], {x, -2,2}]**

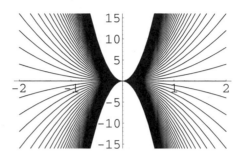

The necessity of the **Evaluate** command is a subtle business. What would happen without it? A string of error messages would result. The **Plot** command works by numerically evaluating its first argument for each of several values of x. If that argument consists of a *Mathematica* command such as **Table**, *Mathematica* will evaluate a new table for each of several numerical values of x (resulting in a list of numbers for each value of x, something the **Plot** command has no idea how to deal with). Instead, you need to tell *Mathematica* to evaluate a single table of functions, and *then* plot the functions in that table. The **Evaluate** command tells *Mathematica* to do just that. In general, you will usually need to use **Evaluate** whenever you plot an expression generated by some other *Mathematica* command.

A different way to superimpose plots is needed if you wish to combine the output of a **Plot** command with the output of some other plotting command, such as **ImplicitPlot**. The easiest way to do this is to first generate the two (or more) plots and give them names, then put them together with the **Show** command. Here is an example. Note that you only need to load the **ImplicitPlot** package if you have not already done so in your current *Mathematica* session:

In[78]:= **Needs["Graphics`ImplicitPlot`"];**
            Clear[x, y]
In[79]:= **circ = ImplicitPlot[x^2 + (y - 0.5)^2 == 0.25, {x, -1,1}]**

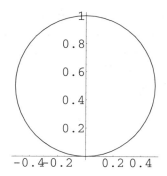

In[80]:= **parab = Plot[x², {x, -1, 1}]**

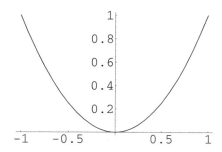

The **Show** command allows you to display any number of graphics objects at once:

In[81]:= **Show[circ,parab]**

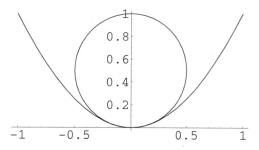

Simply use as the arguments to **Show** the names of the graphics you wish to display (separated as always by commas). It can be two graphics or more. Note that the order in which you list the arguments to the **Show** command can affect the output. In particular, if the various graphics to be displayed each have different settings for a particular option, the graphic listed *first* will pass its value of the option to the resulting display. For example, **ImplicitPlot** will by default set the option **AspectRatio** to **Automatic** (so the scaling on the two axes will be the same), while **Plot** will not. In the above graphic the **AspectRatio** is set to **Automatic** since the **ImplicitPlot** graphic **circ** is listed first. Here's what happens when the order is reversed:

In[82]:= **Show[parab,circ]**

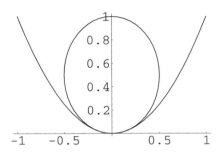

It is worth noting that **Show** can itself accept most of the options that **Plot** can, so you have all the control you need over the final output.

If you do enough superimposing of plots, you will probably want to find a way to get to the final superimposed graphic without first having to produce the individual graphics separately. It is possible to do this, although it's a bit awkward. You essentially have to go through the same process of producing individual graphics and pasting them together with the **Show** command, but you suppress the intermediate graphics with the option **DisplayFunction → Identity**, then reset this option to its default **DisplayFunction → $DisplayFunction** inside the **Show** command. The **DisplayFunction** option can be used with any command that generates graphics:

In[83]:= **Clear[x,y,circ,sine];**
    $\text{circ} = \text{ImplicitPlot}\left[\left(x - \dfrac{\pi}{2}\right)^2 + y^2 == 1, \{x, 0, 3\},\right.$
      DisplayFunction→Identity];
    sine = Plot[Sin[x],{x,0,2π},
      DisplayFunction→Identity];
    Show[circ,sine,
      DisplayFunction→$DisplayFunction]

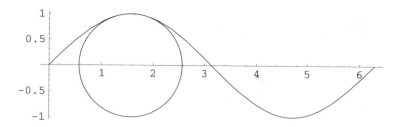

3.9   Animating Plots

It is easy to produce your own *Mathematica* movie. You simply generate a sequence of graphics, then instruct *Mathematica* to "play" them. Here's how:

First use the **Table** command to generate a table whose elements are plots, each of which differs incrementally from the one before it. Use the **PlotRange** option to assure that each plot encompasses the same region of the x–y plane (otherwise the scaling of the y axes may differ from one plot to the next, resulting in a confusing, jerky animation). For example, consider the following input:

```
In[84]:= Table[
         Plot[x Cos[10 x^n],{x,0,2},PlotRange->{-2,2}],
         {n,0,1,.1}]
```

The output in this case will be ten plots, rendered one after the other. Double click on the grouping bracket to the right of the plots to close the group; only the first plot will be shown.

Now double click on the graphic (or go to the **Cell** menu and select **Animate Selected Graphics**) to play the movie. Several buttons will appear at the bottom of your notebook window (see the accompanying figure); use them to slow things down, or speed them up, reverse the order of play, pause the action, etc. The horizontal scroll bar to the right of these buttons can be used to advance the movie frame by frame.

3.10 Working with Data

In situations where you have numerical data for a pair of variables, you will want to enter the data into the computer to study it. How is this most easily accomplished with *Mathematica*? Here is an example. This is data indicating the

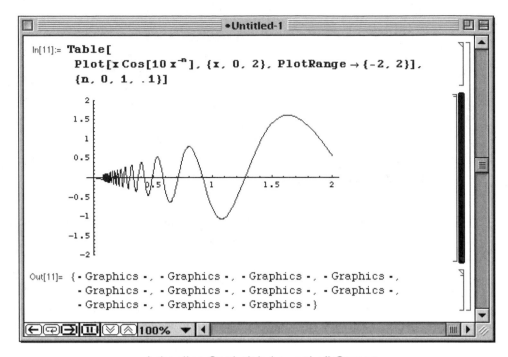

Animation Controls in Lower Left Corner

temperature of a cup of coffee over time. The first column of data indicates the number of minutes that have elapsed. The second column indicates the temperature of the coffee at that time, measured in degrees Fahrenheit:

$In[85] := $ **data =**

0	149.5
2	141.7
4	134.7
6	128.3
8	122.6
10	117.4
12	112.7
14	108.5
16	104.7
18	101.3
20	98.2
22	95.4
24	92.9
26	90.5
28	88.5
30	86.6

;

To enter this data into *Mathematica*, first type **data =**, then select **Create Table/Matrix/Palette...** from the **Input** menu. A dialogue box will appear. In the top field, select **Table**. In the next field specify the number of rows (in this case 16), and the number of columns (in this case 2). Ignore the remaining options in the dialogue box, and hit the **OK** button. A rectangular array of the dimensions you specified will appear in your notebook, and a very long blinking cursor will appear just to the right of the array. Type **;** so that when you eventually enter this cell the output will be suppressed. Now click in the upper left corner of the array and enter the first data value. When you are finished hit the TAB key and enter the next data value. Continue until all the data have been typed in. Now enter the cell.

When you enter data in this way, *Mathematica* stores it as a list of ordered pairs (one pair for each row in the table). Technically, it's a list of lists. If you don't put the semicolon after the cell, you will see the data displayed in this form. Or you can ask for it by name:

```
In[86]:= data
Out[86]= {{0,149.5},{2,141.7},{4,134.7},{6,128.3},
          {8,122.6},{10,117.4},{12,112.7},{14,108.5},
          {16,104.7},{18,101.3},{20,98.2},{22,95.4},
          {24,92.9},{26,90.5},{28,88.5},{30,86.6}}
```

You won't need to work with the data in this form, but it's good to see it once so you know how *Mathematica* interprets it.

The command for plotting a list of points is **ListPlot**:

```
In[87]:= ListPlot[data]
```

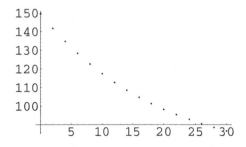

ListPlot takes a single argument: a list of two-tuples. Each two-tuple is interpreted as a point in the plane, and these points are then plotted. If your list of points is short enough, you may find it easiest to type it directly into **ListPlot** rather than first making a data table:

```
In[88]:= ListPlot[{{1,1},{2,3},{3,2},{4,3}}]
```

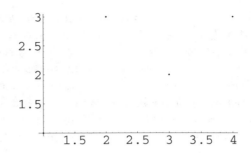

It is an annoying fact of life that **ListPlot** will almost always hide one or more of your points behind the coordinate axes. In the plot above, the point (1, 1) is at the intersection of the two axes! One way to alleviate this is to "connect the dots." The option **PlotJoined → True** accomplishes this:

In[89]:= **ListPlot[{{1,1},{2,3},{3,2},{4,3}},**
            PlotJoined→True]

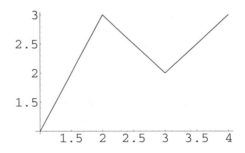

But **ListPlot** also accepts most of the options that the **Plot** command does, so it is a simple matter to produce as elaborate a graph as you desire. Here we assign the name "dots" to our plot so that we can easily refer to it later:

In[90]:= **dots = ListPlot[data,**
          AxesLabel→{"time","temperature"},
          PlotStyle→PointSize[.01],
          AxesOrigin→{-1,80}]

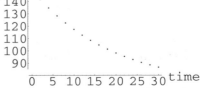

The option **PointSize** is used to set the size of the points as a fraction of the width of the entire plot. In this case, each point is 1% of the width of the plot. The x and y values in **AxesOrigin** were chosen just a bit smaller than the smallest x and y values appearing in the data. This pulls the axes off any data points.

You can have *Mathematica* find the best-fitting polynomial for your data (according to the criteria of least squares) quite easily using the **Fit** command. Here is the best fitting quadratic function. We assign it the name **bestfunction**:

```
In[91]:= Clear[x];
         bestfunction = Fit[data,{1,x,x²},x]
Out[91]= 148.465 - 3.56107 x + 0.0509498 x²
```

The **Fit** command takes three arguments. The first argument is a list of two-tuples (your data). The second argument is a list of powers of the independent variable for which you want coefficients (use **{1,x}** to fit a line, **{1,x,x²}** to fit a quadratic, etc.), and the third argument specifies the name of the independent variable. You can then plot the quadratic. Since we named it **bestfunction**, we don't have to type the awful formula for the quadratic inside the **Plot** command. We assign to our plot the name **bestplot**:

```
In[92]:= bestplot = Plot[bestfunction,{x,0,30}]
```

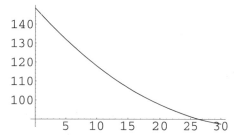

Finally, you can show the plot of the function superimposed on the plot of the data:

```
In[93]:= Show[dots, bestplot]
```

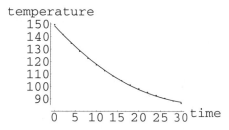

Finding the best-fitting function for a given set of data is a subtle business. Just in case you were thinking that cooling coffee can be accurately modeled by a quadratic function, let's take a look at what the model predicts over a full

60 minutes (note that since **dots** is listed first in the **Show** command, its options are used. Hence there is no need to include **DisplayFunction → $Display Function** as an option for **Show**):

```
In[94]:= bestplot = Plot[bestfunction, {x,0,60},
            DisplayFunction→Identity];
         Show[dots,bestplot]
```

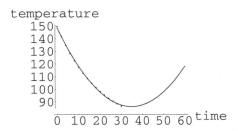

The quadratic model works pretty well for the 30-minute period spanned by the data, but is obviously flawed in the long term, for it projects that the temperature of the coffee will begin to rise again. The moral of the story is this: *Mathematica* can perform difficult calculations painlessly, and provide you with very nice results, but it is up to you to judge the efficacy and relevance of those results.

3.11 Manipulating Data – An Introduction to Lists

You will often need to modify or transform the data with which you started. Here are a few techniques you can use to help with this task.

We mentioned earlier in the chapter that a *list* in *Mathematica* is a collection of items separated by commas and enclosed in curly brackets, such as **{2,5,9,7,4}**. The most fundamental operation that can be performed on a list is the extraction of an item from the list. This is accomplished as follows:

```
In[95]:= mylist = {2,5,9,7,4}
Out[95]= {2,5,9,7,4}

In[96]:= mylist[[3]]
Out[96]= 9
```

You simply type the name of the list followed by **[[3]]** to extract the third item in the list. You can also use the ■**[[□]]** button on the **BasicInput** palette to produce **mylist[[3]]**, which has the same meaning. If it is easier to locate an item by counting its position relative to the end of list, use a negative number inside the double square brackets. For instance, here is the second to last item:

```
In[97]:= mylist[[-2]]
Out[97]= 7
```

Most of *Mathematica*'s arithmetic operations are *listable*. That is, they can be applied to an entire list just as easily as they can be applied to individual numbers:

```
In[98]:= mylist + 3
Out[98]= {5,8,12,10,7}

In[99]:= Log[mylist]
Out[99]= {Log[2],Log[5],Log[9],Log[7],Log[4]}
```

⚠ To find out whether a command has the "listable" attribute, type **??** followed by the command name (this is done for the **Plot** command on page 65). All the attributes of the command, along with its options, will be displayed – see if **Listable** appears among the attributes.

Recall that *Mathematica* stores a table of data as a list of lists. That is, the data table is stored as one long list, the members of which are the rows of the table. Each row of the table is in turn stored as a list:

```
                  1    214
                  11   378
                  21   680
In[100]:= data =
                  31   1215
                  41   2178
                  51   3907
Out[100]= {{1,214},{11,378},{21,680},{31,1215},{41,2178},
           {51,3907}}

In[101]:= data[[3]]
Out[101]= {21,680}
```

To extract the item located in row 3, column 2, do this:

```
In[102]:= data[[3,2]]
Out[102]= 680
```

In version 4 of *Mathematica* you can use **All** in either position. Put **All** in the first position to extract a column from your data:

```
In[103]:= data[[All,2]]
Out[103]= {214,378,680,1215,2178,3907}
```

The importance of these extraction commands manifests itself in situations that call for a transformation of the data. In most cases this will amount to performing some arithmetic operation on every item in a *column* of your data table. The first column of a data table consists of the *x* coordinates of the data points, while the second column contains the *y* coordinates, and typically you will need to transform one coordinate or other. For instance, you may want to take the logarithm of all the *y* coordinates, or subtract 70 from all of the *x* coordinates. How can this be accomplished?

The simplest situation is one in which you perform the same operation on every member of a data table. The *listable* attribute of most arithmetic operators makes this a one-step process. Here, for instance, is how you could take the natural logarithm of every member of a data table:

```
In[104]:= Log[data]//TableForm
Out[104]//TableForm=
            0          Log[214]
            Log[11]    Log[378]
            Log[21]    Log[680]
            Log[31]    Log[1215]
            Log[41]    Log[2178]
            Log[51]    Log[3907]
```

If you want to operate on just one of the columns, and you are using version 4 of *Mathematica*, things are almost as simple. Suppose, for instance, that you want to take the logarithm of only the second column. Here's what you should do:

```
In[105]:= newdata = data;
          newdata[[All,2]] = Log[data[[All,2]]];
          newdata//TableForm
Out[105]//TableForm=
            1     Log[214]
            11    Log[378]
            21    Log[680]
            31    Log[1215]
            41    Log[2178]
            51    Log[3907]
```

Things are not quite as simple if you want to operate on just one of the columns and you are using version 3 of *Mathematica*. Suppose, for instance, that you want to take the logarithm of only the second column. You will need to first *transpose* the table, which will switch the rows and the columns.

```
In[106]:= Transpose[data]
Out[106]= {{1,11,21,31,41,51},{214,378,680,1215,2178,3907}}
```

If you were to apply **Transpose** again, you would get the original data table back. You can give a name to each of the two items in the transposed table like this:

```
In[107]:= {xdata, ydata} = %
Out[107]= {{1,11,21,31,41,51},{214,378,680,1215,2178,3907}}
```

You can now apply **Log** to the list of *y* coordinates in the transposed table, and then transpose the whole thing back again:

```
In[108]:= newdata = Transpose[{xdata, Log[ydata]}]
Out[108]= {{1,Log[214]},{11,Log[378]},{21,Log[680]},
          {31,Log[1215]},{41,Log[2178]},{51,Log[3907]}}
```

```
In[109]:= TableForm[%]
Out[109]//TableForm=
          1    Log[214]
          11   Log[378]
          21   Log[680]
          31   Log[1215]
          41   Log[2178]
          51   Log[3907]
```

The reason for performing operations like this on one column of data is usually to make the data line up better in a list plot. Note how taking the logarithm of the *y* coordinates leads to a good linear fit. Here's the original data:

```
In[110]:= originalDataPlot = ListPlot[data,
              PlotStyle→PointSize[0.01],
              AxesOrigin→{0,100}]
```

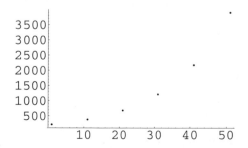

And here's the transformed data:

```
In[111]:= ListPlot[newdata,
              PlotStyle→PointSize[0.01],
              AxesOrigin→{0,5.3}]
```

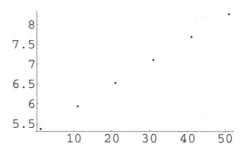

The equation of the linear function relating the log of the **ydata** with the **xdata** can be found with **Fit**:

```
In[112]:= Fit[newdata,{1,x},x]
Out[112]= 5.30146+0.0581627 x
```

This tells us that for the original data

$$\log(y) = 5.30146 + 0.0581627x.$$

It is now a simple matter to solve for y to reveal an exponential relationship in the original data:

$$y = e^{5.30146+0.0581627x} = e^{5.30146}\left(e^{0.0581627}\right)^{x} = 200.63\,(1.05909)^{x}$$

```
In[113]:= p = Plot[200.63 (1.05909)^x,{x,0,52},
            DisplayFunction→Identity];
          Show[originalDataPlot,p]
```

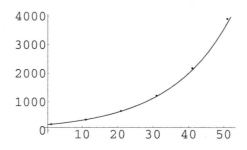

Another common type of transformation is needed if your original table of data contains more than two columns. In such instances, you must produce a new data table consisting of exactly two columns from your original table. The new data table can then be input into the **ListPlot** or **Fit** commands. For instance, here is some data:

$$In[114]:= \textbf{data} = \begin{matrix} 0 & 1.2 & 49 \\ 1 & 1.5 & 46 \\ 2 & 1.9 & 44 \\ 3 & 2.1 & 40 \end{matrix} \; ;$$

If you want to work with the first and third columns, one approach would be to use the **Transpose** command much as we did above:

```
In[115]:= trans = Transpose[data];
          xdata = trans[[1]];
          ydata = trans[[3]];
          newdata = Transpose[{xdata,ydata}];
```

```
In[116]:= newdata// TableForm
```

$Out[116] // TableForm =$

0	49
1	46
2	44
3	40

This approach allows you to transform one column or the other easily; for instance, you could have defined **newdata = Transpose[{xdata, Log[ydata]}]**.

A completely different method for extracting columns is easier in concept, but is no good for applying such transformations to individual columns. You simply copy and paste the desired columns from your original data table into a new table:

$$In[117]:= \textbf{data} = \begin{matrix} 0 & 1.2 & 49 \\ 1 & 1.5 & 46 \\ 2 & 1.9 & 44 \\ 3 & 2.1 & 40 \end{matrix} \; ;$$

To carry this out, type **newdata =** in a new input cell, then scroll up and carefully highlight the first column of the input cell above with your mouse (this is a test of mousing skill; try starting above and to the right of the column, and dragging down and just a little to your left). Now choose **Copy** from the **Edit** menu, then click where you want to paste the column and choose **Paste** from the **Edit** menu. Repeat with the third column:

$$In[118]:= \textbf{newdata} = \begin{matrix} 0 & 49 \\ 1 & 46 \\ 2 & 44 \\ 3 & 40 \end{matrix} \; ;$$

Now enter this cell and proceed to analyze **newdata** to your heart's content.

This technique is also useful for extracting only certain rows of a data table for analysis, for instance to remove an outlier or to study a relationship that appears only among certain cases in your data. To select several rows of data, use your mouse, this time starting at the lower right and dragging upward and to the left. You may then copy and paste your selection as above.

> Now is a good time to review the four types of brackets that are used in *Mathematica*. Parentheses ( ) are used to group terms in algebraic expressions. Square brackets [ ] are used to enclose the arguments of functions. Curly brackets { } are used to enclose lists. And double square brackets ⟦ ⟧ or [[ ]] are used to extract items from lists. Mercifully, that's it for brackets; there are no more that you'll ever need to learn in your future encounters with *Mathematica*.

3.12 Importing Data into *Mathematica*

If you would like to use *Mathematica* to work with data that already exists in electronic form, such as a set of data that you've found on the internet, what is the easiest way to import it into *Mathematica*? If it is a small set of data, go ahead and type it in as described in Section 3.10, "Working with Data." If the data set is large, is there an easy way to import it directly into *Mathematica*? The answer is yes, although the method will vary depending on whether you are using version 3 or version 4 of *Mathematica*.

The first step is to save your data as a plain text file (sometimes called an ascii file) with the suffix ".dat". Saving data in ascii format is a standard option in spreadsheet and statistical software. If you are using version 3 of *Mathematica* and your data has more than one column, save the data using *spaces* to separate columns (spreadsheet and statistical software typically have this as an option). Gathering data from the world wide web is a bit trickier, as data can be presented in many formats. One option is to highlight the data with your mouse in your web browser, copy it, and paste it into a text file. Another is to ask your browser to save the entire web page as a text file (with the suffix ".dat"). In either case, it will be necessary to use a basic text editor to get a look at the raw data file, and to parse it of any spurious text. The file should contain one or more columns of data, and nothing else.

The next step is to place your data file in an appropriate directory on the computer where *Mathematica* resides. If possible, place your data file in the main *Mathematica* directory. If this is not possible (for instance, if you are using computers in a class lab that do not allow you save files on the local hard drive), just save the file to a floppy disk or other removable media.

Finally, import the data into *Mathematica*. Let's assume that you have created the text file *bogusdata.dat* and placed it in the main *Mathematica* directory. If you are using version 4 of *Mathematica*, use the **Import** command. It takes a single argument, the name of the data file enclosed in quotation marks:

```
In[119]:= data = Import["bogusdata.dat"]
Out[119]= {{1,1},{2,2},{3,3},{4,4}}

In[120]:= data// TableForm
Out[120] // TableForm=
        1  1
        2  2
        3  3
        4  4
```

If you are using version 3 of *Mathematica*, you have to do a bit more typing. Data is imported with the **ReadList** command. **ReadList** takes two arguments. The first is the name of the data file, enclosed in quotation marks. The second is **Number**, indicating that the file contains numbers. The option **RecordLists → True** should be used if the data contains more than one column.

```
In[121]:= data = ReadList["bogusdata.dat",Number,
             RecordLists → True]
Out[121]= {{1,1},{2,2},{3,3},{4,4}}
```

If your data file is stored on a floppy disk, the above commands will still be used to bring the data into *Mathematica* from the floppy, but there are subtle differences in their use across platforms. That is, you need to type something slightly different depending on whether you have a Mac, a PC, or something else. The differences occur only in the directory structure of the various operating systems, and manifest themselves in the directory path name that appears as the argument to **Import** or the first argument to **ReadList**.

On a Machine Running the Mac OS

Here's how to read the file named *bogusdata.dat* that is stored on the floppy disk named *MathStuff*. If you have version 4 of *Mathematica*, type:

```
In[122]:= data = Import["MathStuff : bogusdata.dat"];
```

If you have version 3 of *Mathematica*, type:

```
In[123]:= data = ReadList["MathStuff : bogusdata.dat",Number,
             RecordLists → True];
```

On a PC Running Windows

Here's how to read the file named *bogusdata.dat* that is stored on the floppy disk inserted in the A drive. If you have version 4 of *Mathematica*, type:

```
In[124]:= data = Import["A : bogusdata.dat"];
```

If you have version 3 of *Mathematica*, type:

```
In[125]:= data = ReadList["A : bogusdata.dat", Number,
            RecordLists → True];
```

Extracting Columns from the Data (All Platforms)

If the data contains more than two columns (variables), and you want to extract exactly two columns to work with, click once *below* the output cell, and select **Copy Output from Above** from the **Input** menu. The data table will be copied to an input cell that you can edit with the mouse, as described at the end of the previous section in this chapter, "Manipulating Data." In particular, you may extract rows and columns at will.

3.13 Working with Difference Equations

A *sequence* is a function whose domain consists of the positive integers. In other words, it is a function s whose values can be listed: $s[1]$, $s[2]$, $s[3]$, ... A more traditional notation for these values is s_1, s_2, s_3, ...

It is often possible to define a sequence by specifying the value of the first term (say $s[1] = 3$), and giving a *difference equation* (also called a recurrence relation) that expresses every subsequent term as a function of the previous term. For instance, if each term in a sequence is twice the previous term, we get the difference equation $s[n] = 2 \times s[n-1]$ for each $n > 1$. A sequence defined by a difference equation is said to be defined *recursively*. Computers make it easy to calculate many terms of recursively defined sequences. Here's how *Mathematica* can be harnessed for such purposes:

```
In[126]:= Clear[s, n]
In[127]:= s[1] = 3;
          s[n_/; n > 1] := s[n] = 2 * s[n - 1]
```

This probably looks a bit strange. The line **s[1] = 3** specifies the value of the first term of the sequence. The last line contains the difference equation, with some extra features added for safety and efficiency. Starting from the left:

The **/; n > 1** is a safety feature. It guarantees that the function will only accept values of n that exceed one. The **/;** is a conditional operator that can be read as "provided that." The importance of this condition cannot be understated. Without it, imagine what would happen if you inadvertantly asked *Mathematica* to use this difference equation to find $s[-3]$. *Mathematica* would use the equation to find that $s[-3]$ is equal to $2 \times s[-4]$, and would then use the formula again to find $s[-4]$ is equal to $2 \times s[-5]$, and so on. The process would only stop when *Mathematica* eventually would rightly suspect that it had been thrown into an infinite loop. An error message would result. It is our experience that students who generate such error messages are far more likely to crash *Mathematica* in the next few minutes than those who do not. Adding the text **/; n > 1** prevents even the possibility that this might happen.

Continuing across the input line, **:=** is just what we expect in the definition of a function, but the **s[n]=** is not. It is added for efficiency. Without it *Mathematica* would regard s strictly as a rule. Computing $s[6]$ would involve these steps: $s[6]$ is equal to $2 \times s[5]$ is equal to $2 \times (2 \times s[4])$ is equal to $2 \times (2 \times (2 \times s[3]))$ is equal to $2 \times (2 \times (2 \times (2 \times s[2])))$ is equal to $2 \times (2 \times (2 \times (2 \times (2 \times s[1]))))$ is equal to $2^5 \times 3$ is equal to 96. If you then asked for $s[7]$, *Mathematica* would have to do this all over again. By adding the text "**s[n]=**" you are instructing *Mathematica* to view s not only as a rule but also as a name, so that after computing $s[6]$ *Mathematica* would remember in subsequent calculations that $s[6]$ has been assigned the value 96. Now when asked to compute $s[7]$, *Mathematica* simply has to go through one step: $s[7]$ is equal to $2 \times s[6]$, which is 2×96, or 192.

Lastly (continuing across the input line), the text **2 * s[n - 1]** is the difference equation itself.

The three most common things you can do with such a sequence are: compute an individual term, make a table of values, or make a plot. These are easy. More difficult is the task of trying to find a *solution* to a difference equation–an explicit representation of $s[n]$ as a function of n. The task of solving difference equations is discussed in Section 4.7 on page 124.

Any individual term in a sequence is found by plugging in the appropriate value of n:

```
In[128]:= s[3]
Out[128]= 12
```

A table of values allows you to see many terms of the sequence at once:

In[129]:= **Table[{n, s[n]}, {n, 1, 10}] // TableForm**

Out[129] // TableForm =

1	3
2	6
3	12
4	24
5	48
6	96
7	192
8	384
9	768
10	1536

In order to see a little further out in the sequence without generating a mile-long table, you might want to calculate only every tenth term. The table below does this by modifying the iterator. It also uses the **TableHeadings** option for the **TableForm** command to add column labels (the **None** indicates that we don't want row labels):

In[130]:= **TableForm[**
        Table[{n, s[n]}, {n, 1, 101, 10}],
        TableHeadings → {None, {"n", "s[n]"}}]

Out[130] // TableForm =

n	s[n]
1	3
11	3072
21	3145728
31	3221225472
41	3298534883328
51	3377699720527872
61	3458764513820540928
71	3541774862152233910272
81	3626777458843887524118528
91	3713820117856140824697372672
101	3802951800684688204490109616128

Here is a plot of *s*[*n*] versus *n*:

In[131]:= **ListPlot[Table[{n, s[n]}, {n, 1, 10}],**
        AxesLabel → {"n", "s[n]"},
        AxesOrigin → {0, -20}]

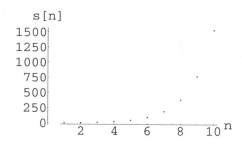

Here is another example, this time of a sequence defined by a *logistic growth* difference equation. Such sequences often have interesting behavior that is difficult to investigate without a computer (the difference equation has no solution). Note that the **Clear** command is important when moving from one example to the next, for we need to erase all those values $s[2], s[3], \ldots, s[101]$ that we generated with the last example:

```
In[132]:= Clear[s,n];
          s[1] = 2;
          s[n_] := s[n] = 3 s[n - 1] - 0.05 s[n - 1]^2 /; n > 1
In[133]:= t = Table[{n, s[n]}, {n, 1, 50}];

In[134]:= ListPlot[t, PlotRange -> {{0, 50}, {0, 45}}]
```

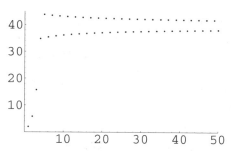

Adding the **PlotJoined → True** option can help you make sense of plots such as this:

```
In[135]:= ListPlot[t, PlotRange -> {{0, 50}, {0, 45}},
              PlotJoined -> True]
```

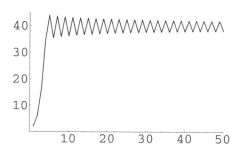

Chapter 4

Algebra

4.1 Factoring and Expanding Polynomials

A *polynomial* in the variable x is function of the form:

$$f(x) = a_0 + a_1x + a_2x^2 + \cdots + a_nx^n,$$

where the coefficients $a_0, a_1, \ldots, a_n$ are real numbers. Polynomials may be expressed in expanded or in factored form. Without a computer algebra system, moving from one form to the other is a tedious and often difficult process. With *Mathematica*, it is quite easy; the commands needed to transform a polynomial are called **Expand** and **Factor**.

Consider:

```
In[1]:= Clear[f, x];
        f[x_] := 12 - 3x - 12x³ + 3x⁴
In[2]:= Plot[f[x], {x, -2, 5}]
```

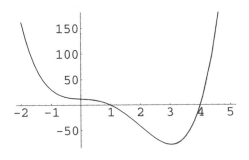

Here is a polynomial that appears to have *roots* at $x = 1$ and $x = 4$ (that is, the function appears to assume the value 0 when $x = 1$ and $x = 4$). We can confirm this by factoring the polynomial:

```
In[3]:= Factor[f[x]]
Out[3]= 3 (-4 + x) (-1 + x) (1 + x + x²)
```

Observe that when x assumes the value 4, the linear factor $-4 + x$ is zero, making the entire product equal to zero. If $x = 1$, the linear factor $-1 + x$ is zero, and again the product is zero. Rational roots of a polynomial can be spotted by looking for linear factors in the factored form of the polynomial.

The task of finding the roots of a given function f is a vitally important one. Suppose, for instance, that you need to solve an equation in one variable, say $-12x^3 + 3x^4 = 3x - 12$. Equations such as this arise in a wide variety of applied contexts, and their solution is often of great importance. But solving such an equation is equivalent to finding the roots of a function – just subtract from each side of the given equation everything on the right hand side. In this case we get $12 - 3x - 12x^3 + 3x^4 = 0$, so the solutions of the equation are the roots of the function $f(x) = 12 - 3x - 12x^3 + 3x^4$, which we have just found (via factoring) to be 4 and 1. Solving equations and finding roots are essentially the same task.

You can expand a factored polynomial with the **Expand** command. This will essentially "undo" the factoring. One way to use this command is to open the **AlgebraicManipulation** palette (look for palettes in the **File** menu), then use your mouse to highlight the factored output above, then push the $\boxed{\textbf{Expand[}\blacksquare\textbf{]}}$ button. Another way is to type:

```
In[4]:= Expand[%]
Out[4]= 12 - 3 x - 12 x³ + 3 x⁴
```

The expanded form is handy too. The constant term (in this case 12) represents the y intercept of the polynomial's graph. It's simply the value of the function when $x = 0$. The leading coefficient (in this case 3, the coefficient of x^4) is positive. Since the $3x^4$ summand will dominate the others for large values of x, a positive leading coefficient tells us that the function values will get large as x gets large.

It is important to note that some polynomials have real roots that will not be revealed by the **Factor** command:

```
In[5]:= Plot[-1 + 3x + x², {x, -5, 3}]
```

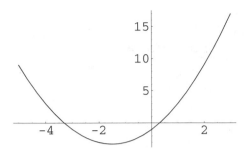

$In[6]:=$ **Factor[-1 + 3x + x^2]**
$Out[6]=$ $-1 + 3 x + x^2$

The graph clearly indicates two real roots, the x intercepts, yet there are no linear factors present in the factored form of the polynomial. Why? The **Factor** command will not extract factors that involve irrational or complex numbers unless such numbers appear as coefficients in the polynomial being factored. Since the coefficients in the above polynomial are all integers, only factors with integer coefficients will be extracted. To get *approximations* to the real roots, simply replace one of the integer coefficients in the original polynomial by its decimal equivalent by placing a decimal point after it. In doing this you are telling *Mathematica* that decimals are acceptable in the output:

$In[7]:=$ **Factor[-1. + 3x + x^2]**
$Out[7]=$ $1. (-0.302776 + x) (3.30278 + x)$

The real roots are approximately 0.302776 and -3.30278. You can easily check that this is consistent with the graph (and of course, you should).

Lastly, note that as always *Mathematica* makes a distinction between decimals and fractions when factoring:

$In[8]:=$ **Factor[x^2 - 0.25]**
$Out[8]=$ $1. (-0.5 + x) (0.5 + x)$

$In[9]:=$ **Factor$\left[x^2 - \dfrac{1}{4}\right]$**
$Out[9]=$ $\dfrac{1}{4} (-1 + 2 x) (1 + 2 x)$

4.2 Finding Roots of Polynomials with **Solve** and **NSolve**

The **Factor** command together with the **Plot** command are a powerful set of tools for discovering the real roots of polynomials. But there are a few shortcommings. Notice, for instance, that we can only *approximate* real roots that happen to be irrational (inexpressible as a quotient of integers). In addition, complex roots (involving the imaginary number i, the square root of -1) are completely inaccessible. For these reasons we introduce the **NSolve** and **Solve** commands.

Let's take another look at the polynomial $-1 + 3x + x^2$ from the previous section:

In[10]:= **NSolve[-1 + 3x + x^2 == 0, x]**
Out[10]= {{x → -3.30278}, {x → 0.302776}}

NSolve provides approximate numerical solutions to equations. It takes two arguments, separated as always by a comma. The first argument is an *equation*. (Note that the double equal sign **==** is used for equations; this is because the single equal sign **=** is used to assign values to expressions, an essentially different operation. You may also use the ▣▣ button on the **BasicInput** palette.) The second argument in the **NSolve** command (**x** in the example above) specifies the variable to be solved for. It may be obvious to you that you wish to solve for x, but it's not to the computer. For instance, there may be occasions when the equation you are solving involves more than one variable (we'll see an example later in this section). Lastly, the **NSolve** command can take an optional third argument which specifies the number of digits of precision that you desire:

In[11]:= **NSolve[-1 + 3x + x^2 == 0, x, 15]**
Out[11]= {{x → -3.30277563773199}, {x → 0.302775637731995}}

Now what about the output? First notice that it is in the form a *list* (a sequence of items separated by commas with a set of curly brackets around the whole thing). This is because there are typically numerous solutions to a given equation, so it is sensible to present them in a list. Now let's focus on the items in this list. Each is of the form {x → *solution*}. This looks strange at first, but it is easy enough to interpret. It is an example of a structure called a *replacement rule*, which will be explored later in this section.

You can smarten the appearance of the list of solutions by appending the postfix command **//TableForm**. As discussed in the last chapter (Section 3.3, see page 48) **TableForm** is applied to a list and produces a neatly formated column, the rows of which are the members of the list:

In[12]:= **NSolve[-1 + 3x + x² == 0, x, 35] //TableForm**

Out[12] // TableForm =

$$x \rightarrow -3.3027756377319946465596106337352480$$

$$x \rightarrow 0.3027756377319946465596106337352480$$

Can *Mathematica* produce *exact* solutions to polynomial equations? The answer is sometimes. Some polynomial equations involving powers of x that exceed 4 cannot be solved algebraically. However, if such an equation can be solved algebraically, the **Solve** command is the ticket. Here are the precise roots of the polynomial above:

In[13]:= **Solve[-1 + 3x + x² == 0, x] //TableForm**

Out[13] // TableForm =

$$x \rightarrow \tfrac{1}{2} \left(-3-\sqrt{13}\right)$$

$$x \rightarrow \tfrac{1}{2} \left(-3+\sqrt{13}\right)$$

Remember the quadratic formula? That's all that's happening here. In fact, if you ever forget the quadratic formula, you can have *Mathematica* derive it for you:

In[14]:= **Clear[a, b, c, x];**
       Solve[a x² + b x + c == 0, x] //TableForm

Out[14] // TableForm =

$$x \rightarrow \frac{-b-\sqrt{b^2-4\,a\,c}}{2\,a}$$

$$x \rightarrow \frac{-b+\sqrt{b^2-4\,a\,c}}{2\,a}$$

Note the spaces between the **a** and **x²**, and between the **b** and the **x** in the last input line; they are needed to indicate multiplication. This example also makes it clear why the second argument to the **Solve** command is so important; this is an equation that could be solved for a, for b, for c, or for x. You have to specify the variable for which you wish to solve.

Let's look a few more examples of these commands in action. We'll start with the **NSolve** command and later address some special considerations for using the

`Solve` command:

In[15]:= **Plot[x + 3x² + x³, {x, -3, 1}]**

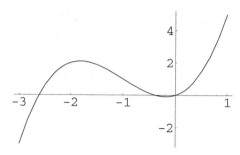

In[16]:= **Factor[x + 3x² + x³]**

Out[16]= x (1 + 3 x + x²)

In[17]:= **NSolve[x + 3x² + x³ == 0, x] //TableForm**

Out[17] // TableForm =
$$x \rightarrow -2.61803$$
$$x \rightarrow -0.381966$$
$$x \rightarrow 0.$$

Note how the factor x indicates the root $x = 0$, but that the other roots are not revealed by the **Factor** command (although they would have been found had we replaced the **x** by **1.*x** in the polynomial). The **NSolve** command reveals all roots, always.

Now let's tweak things a little. We can shift the graph of this function up by one unit by adding 1 to its formula, and the resulting function should have only one real root (the dip on the right of the graph will be entirely above the x axis):

In[18]:= **Plot[1 + x + 3x² + x³, {x, -3, 1}]**

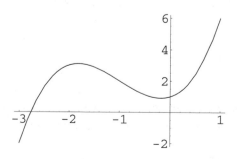

In[19]:= **Factor[1 + x + 3x² + x³]**

Out[19]= 1 + x + 3 x² + x³

This didn't do a thing; the new function has no rational roots. What happens if we replace one of the integer coefficients with its decimal equivalent?

```
In[20]:= Factor[1. + x + 3x² + x³]
Out[20]= 1. (2.76929 + x) (0.361103 + 0.230708 x + x²)
```

This reveals a real root near $x = -2.76929$. But what about the quadratic factor?

```
In[21]:= NSolve[1 + x + 3x² + x³ == 0, x] //TableForm
Out[21] // TableForm =
        x → -2.76929
        x → -0.115354 - 0.589743 I
        x → -0.115354 + 0.589743 I
```

Mathematica is reporting three roots. The first root reported is the x-intercept that we see in the plot. The second two are complex numbers; they are each expressions involving i, the square root of -1. They are purely algebraic solutions to the polynomial equation, bearing no obvious geometric relationship to its graph. Although you may not care about complex roots of equations, the **Solve** and **NSolve** commands will always display them if they exist. It is a fact that every polynomial whose highest power of x is n will have exactly n roots, some of which may be complex numbers. It is also true that complex roots, when they appear, come in *conjugate pairs*; one will be of the form $a + bi$, the other $a - bi$, as in the output above. If you would rather that *Mathematica* not show you any complex output, see Section 4.3 of this chapter on page 104.

How can you extract one solution from a list of solutions? For instance, you may only need a real solution, or the context of the problem may dictate that only positive solutions be considered. You can extract a single solution from the list of solutions using double brackets. Here's an example to illustrate:

```
In[22]:= sols = Solve[x² - 225 == 0, x]
Out[22]= {{x → -15}, {x → 15}}
```

We have given the list of solutions the name **sols** (note the assignment operator = assigns the name **sols** to the output, while the equation operator == is used to produce equations). Here's how to extract the first element from a list:

```
In[23]:= sols[[1]]
Out[23]= {x → -15}
```

and the second element:

```
In[24]:= sols[[2]]
Out[24]= {x → 15}
```

This method works for any list:

```
In[25]:= {a, b, c, d, e}[[2]]
Out[25]= b
```

You may also use the ▪❲▫❳ button on the **BasicInput** palette to extract an item from a list.

To use one of the solutions provided by the **NSolve** or **Solve** command in a subsequent calculation, you need to understand the syntax of *replacement rules*. The symbol **/.** tells *Mathematica* to make a replacement. You first write an expression involving **x**, then write **/.** and then write a replacement rule of the form **x→** *solution*. The arrow → is found on the **BasicInput** palette. You may type **->** (the "minus" sign followed by the "greater than" sign) in place of the arrow if you wish:

```
In[26]:= x² /. x → 3
Out[26]= 9
```

This last input line can be read as "Evaluate the expression x^2, replacing x by 3." Here's how you can use replacement rules to extract solutions generated by the **Solve** command:

```
In[27]:= x /. sols[[1]]
Out[27]= -15
In[28]:= x /. sols[[2]]
Out[28]= 15
In[29]:= x² /. sols[[2]]
Out[29]= 225
```

If you don't specify which solution you want, you will get a list where x is replaced by each solution in turn:

```
In[30]:= x /. sols
Out[30]= {-15, 15}
```

You could do all of this in one step, generating output that is a list of solutions rather than a list of replacement rules:

In[31]:= **x /. Solve[x² - 225 == 0, x]**
Out[31]= {-15, 15}

You may also use replacement rules to test whether an equation holds for a particular value of x:

In[32]:= **x² - 225 == 0 /. sols[[1]]**
Out[32]= True

In[33]:= **x² - 225 == 0 /. x → 10**
Out[33]= False

Another example will illustrate how you might proceed in practice to find the real root of a cubic equation:

In[34]:= **NSolve[x³ - x + 2 == 0, x] //TableForm**
Out[34] // TableForm =
$$x \to -1.52138$$
$$x \to 0.76069 - 0.857874 \, I$$
$$x \to 0.76069 + 0.857874 \, I$$

In[35]:= **x /. %[[1]]**
Out[35]= -1.52138

Now let's look at the **Solve** command in greater detail. Note that you can find the exact solutions to the polynomial above:

In[36]:= **Solve[x³ - x + 2 == 0, x] //TableForm**
Out[36] // TableForm =

$$x \to -\frac{\left(9-\sqrt{78}\right)^{1/3}}{3^{2/3}} - \frac{1}{\left(3\left(9-\sqrt{78}\right)\right)^{1/3}}$$

$$x \to \frac{\left(1+I\sqrt{3}\right)\left(9-\sqrt{78}\right)^{1/3}}{2\ 3^{2/3}} + \frac{1-I\sqrt{3}}{2\left(3\left(9-\sqrt{78}\right)\right)^{1/3}}$$

$$x \to \frac{\left(1-I\sqrt{3}\right)\left(9-\sqrt{78}\right)^{1/3}}{2\ 3^{2/3}} + \frac{1+I\sqrt{3}}{2\left(3\left(9-\sqrt{78}\right)\right)^{1/3}}$$

Wow, this is powerful stuff! But be careful when using the **Solve** command. If you just need an approximate decimal solution to an equation you will be better served using **NSolve**. In particular, if you want a numerical approximation to a solution generated by the **Solve** command, as you might with the output generated above, it is *not* a good idea to apply the **N** command to the result. In some cases, for instance, you may end up with complex numbers approximating real roots (try solving $x^3 - 15x + 2 = 0$; it has three real roots, yet applying **N** to the output of the **Solve** command produces complex numbers). The moral of the story: Use **Solve** only to generate exact answers; use **NSolve** to generate numerical solutions to any required degree of accuracy.

Another consideration to be aware of when using the **Solve** command is that equations involving polynomials of degree 5 or more (i.e., where the highest power of x is 5 or more) may not have explicit algebraic solutions. This is a mathematical fact; no software package on the planet now or ever will be able to provide exact algebraic solutions to such equations. Here is what the output will look like in these situations:

In[37]:= **Solve[x^5 - x + 1 == 0, x]**

Out[37]=

$$\{\{x \to \text{Root}[1 - \#1 + \#1^5\&, 1]\}, \{x \to \text{Root}[1 - \#1 + \#1^5\&, 2]\},$$
$$\{x \to \text{Root}[1 - \#1 + \#1^5\&, 3]\}, \{x \to \text{Root}[1 - \#1 + \#1^5\&, 4]\},$$
$$\{x \to \text{Root}[1 - \#1 + \#1^5\&, 5]\}\}$$

Don't waste time trying to make sense of the output. Note, however, that **NSolve** can approximate such solutions with ease:

In[38]:= **NSolve[x^5 - x + 1 == 0, x] //TableForm**

Out[38] // TableForm=

$$x \to -1.1673$$
$$x \to -0.181232 - 1.08395 \text{ I}$$
$$x \to -0.181232 + 1.08395 \text{ I}$$
$$x \to 0.764884 - 0.352472 \text{ I}$$
$$x \to 0.764884 + 0.352472 \text{ I}$$

After all this you may wonder why the **Solve** command is ever used, since **NSolve** seems to be more versatile and robust. The answer is that it depends on your purposes. For numerical solutions to specific problems, **NSolve** is probably all you need. But for exact algebraic solutions or the derivation of general formulae, **Solve** is indispensable. Here are two more examples to illustrate the power of this command. The first provides the general solution for the roots of a cubic equation of the form $x^3 + bx + c$, where b and c may be any numbers:

$In[39]:=$ **Clear[b, c, x];**
        Solve[x^3 + b x + c == 0, x] //TableForm

$Out[39] //TableForm=$

$$x \rightarrow -\frac{2^{1/3}\,b}{\left(-27\,c+\sqrt{108\,b^3+729\,c^2}\right)^{1/3}} + \frac{\left(-27\,c+\sqrt{108\,b^3+729\,c^2}\right)^{1/3}}{3\;2^{1/3}}$$

$$x \rightarrow \frac{\left(1+I\sqrt{3}\right)\,b}{2^{2/3}\,\left(-27\,c+\sqrt{108\,b^3+729\,c^2}\right)^{1/3}} - \frac{\left(1-I\sqrt{3}\right)\,\left(-27\,c+\sqrt{108\,b^3+729\,c^2}\right)^{1/3}}{6\;2^{1/3}}$$

$$x \rightarrow \frac{\left(1-I\sqrt{3}\right)\,b}{2^{2/3}\,\left(-27\,c+\sqrt{108\,b^3+729\,c^2}\right)^{1/3}} - \frac{\left(1+I\sqrt{3}\right)\,\left(-27\,c+\sqrt{108\,b^3+729\,c^2}\right)^{1/3}}{6\;2^{1/3}}$$

The next example illustrates how **Solve** may be used to put a given formula into a different form. It is a rather trite computation, but it illustrates the versatility of the **Solve** command:

$In[40]:=$ **Clear[e, m, c];**
        Solve[e == m c^2, m] //TableForm

$Out[40] //TableForm=$
        $$m \rightarrow \frac{e}{c^2}$$

One last comment about the **Solve** command is in order. As you may expect, it will distinguish between decimals and fractions in the input, and adjust its output to match:

$In[41]:=$ **Solve[x^2 - 0.25 == 0, x]**
$Out[41]=$ $\{\{x \rightarrow -0.5\}, \{x \rightarrow 0.5\}\}$

$In[42]:=$ **Solve$\left[x^2 - \dfrac{1}{4} == 0, x\right]$**

$Out[42]=$ $\left\{\left\{x \rightarrow -\dfrac{1}{2}\right\}, \left\{x \rightarrow \dfrac{1}{2}\right\}\right\}$

4.3 Suppressing Complex Output

You've noticed by now that complex numbers sometimes appear in *Mathematica*'s output. They can pop up in a variety of places. Here, for instance is an attempt at a plot of the cube root function, to be plotted on the domain $-5 \leq x \leq 5$:

```
In[43]:= Plot[x^(1/3), {x, -5, 5}]
        Plot::plnr:
          x^(1/3) is not a machine-size real number at x=-5.
        Plot::plnr:
          x^(1/3) is not a machine-size real number at x=-4.59433.
        Plot::plnr:
          x^(1/3) is not a machine-size real number at x=-4.15191.
        General::stop: Further output of Plot will be
          suppressed during this calculation.
```

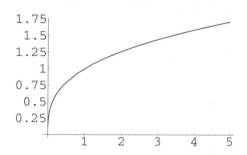

No negative numbers appear in the output. That seems odd – don't negative numbers have cube roots? We know that $(-2)^3 = -8$, so the cube root of -8 should be -2, shouldn't it?

```
In[44]:= (-8.0)^(1/3)
Out[44]= 1.+1.73205 I
```

What's happening is this: all nonzero real numbers, including negative numbers, have three cube roots, two of which are complex (involving $i = I = \sqrt{-1}$) and one of which is real. *Mathematica* is doing the right thing by reporting a complex number when you ask for *the* cube root of -8; it reports the principal value, the complex number with the smallest positive argument from among the three possible answers. This behavior is quite useful for people who understand and appreciate the complex number system, but can be annoying for those who do not. Here are a few other instances where complex numbers can pop up in the context of a real computation:

```
In[45]:= Log[-2]
Out[45]= I π + Log[2]
```

In[46]:= **Solve[x² == -4, x]**

Out[46]= {{x → -2 I}, {x → 2 I}}

Now this sort of output ought to make you hungry to learn about the complex numbers. If you are even a bit curious, please ask about them (great way to send your teacher off on a big old tangent during class time), or look them up. However, if it doesn't and you aren't, and you wish that they would please just go away, that can be arranged too. All you need to do is load a package:

In[47]:= **Needs["Miscellaneous`RealOnly`"]**

That's it – no new commands to learn, nothing else needs doing. By loading this package, you have instructed *Mathematica* to do two things: suppress all complex output, and report only real roots of real numbers. That cube root plot will work fine now:

In[48]:= **Plot[x^(1/3), {x, -5, 5}]**

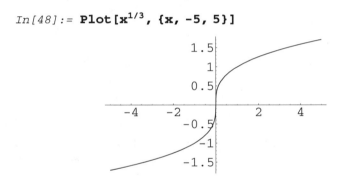

In[49]:= **(-8.0)^(1/3)**

Out[49]= -2.

In[50]:= **Log[-2]**

Nonreal::warning : Nonreal number encountered.

Out[50]= Nonreal

In[51]:= **Solve[x² == -4, x]**

Nonreal::warning : Nonreal number encountered.

Out[51]= {{x → Nonreal}, {x → Nonreal}}

⚠ If this is the way you want things to work always, it is possible to set up your *Mathematica* system to automatically load this package every time you start a session. It involves moving a file on your computer from one directory to another. Use your computer's file finding utility to find the file `RealOnly.m`. Now move the file into the **Autoload** subdirectory of the **AddOns** directory (**AddOns** lives in *Mathematica*'s main directory). This technique can be used to automatically load any package at startup.

4.4 Simplifying and Manipulating Rational Functions

Solving Equations

The **Solve** and **NSolve** commands are built for polynomials, but they will also work for equations involving *rational functions* (quotients of polynomials). Essentially, the roots of the numerator that are not also roots of the denominator will be reported:

$In[52]:=$ **Solve$\left[\dfrac{(x+3)(x-1)}{(x-1)} == 0, x \right]$ //TableForm**

$Out[52] // TableForm =$
$$x \to -3$$

Thus all the remarks in Section 4.2 apply to equations involving rational functions as well to those involving only polynomials.

Simplifying Rational Expressions

When you are working with a rational function, you may want to use the **Simplify** command to, well ... simplify things:

$In[53]:=$ **Simplify$\left[\dfrac{1-x^5}{1-x} \right]$**

$Out[53] = 1 + x + x^2 + x^3 + x^4$

The **Simplify** command, like **Expand** and **Factor**, takes an expression as input and returns an equivalent expression as output. **Simplify** attempts a number of transformations and returns what it believes is the most simple form. In the case of rational functions, **Simplify** will cancel the common factors appearing in the numerator and denominator. In the example above, the linear expression $1 - x$ can be factored out of the numerator. You can easily check the result:

$In[54]:=$ **Expand[(1 - x) (1 + x + x^2 + x^3 + x^4)]**
$Out[54] = 1 - x^5$

You can also guide *Mathematica* through such a simplification step by step. The best way to do this is by opening the **AlgebraicManipulation** palette (look for palettes in the **File** menu). Use your mouse to highlight a certain portion of an algebraic expression, and then feed that portion of the expression to one of the algebraic manipulation commands. This essentially allows you to drive *Mathematica* step by step through an algebraic manipulation. Here, for instance, is a rational function:

$$\frac{3 + 7\,x + 8\,x^2 + 5\,x^3 + x^4}{3 + 10\,x + 18\,x^2 + 14\,x^3 + 3\,x^4}$$

Rather than simplify it with the **Simplify** command, let's drive through it step by step. First, use the mouse to highlight the numerator, then push the **Factor[■]** button on the **AlgebraicManipulation** palette. The cell will then look like this:

$$\frac{((1+x)\,(3+x)\,(1+x+x^2))}{3 + 10\,x + 18\,x^2 + 14\,x^3 + 3\,x^4}$$

Now repeat the process to factor the denominator:

$$\frac{((1+x)\,(3+x)\,(1+x+x^2))}{((1+x)\,(3+x)\,(1+2\,x+3\,x^2))}$$

There is clearly some cancellation that can be done. Highlight the entire expression and push the **Cancel[■]** button:

$$\frac{1 + x + x^2}{1 + 2\,x + 3\,x^2}$$

The results are the same as if you had simplified the original expression using the **Simplify** command. The difference is that you know exactly how the simplification took place:

$$In[55] := \mathbf{Simplify}\left[\frac{3 + 7\,x + 8\,x^2 + 5\,x^3 + x^4}{3 + 10\,x + 18\,x^2 + 14\,x^3 + 3\,x^4}\right]$$

$$Out[55] = \frac{1 + x + x^2}{1 + 2\,x + 3\,x^2}$$

This sort of interactive manipulation puts you in the driver's seat. You will sharpen your algebraic skills without falling into the abyss of tedium and silly mistakes (such as dropped minus signs) that can occur when performing algebraic manipulations by hand.

A rational function and the function that results from its simplification are identical, except that the original rational function will not be defined at those values of x that are roots of both the numerator and denominator. In the example above, the original function is not defined at $x = -1$ and $x = -3$, while the simplified function is defined. For all other values of x the two functions are identical.

Vertical Asymptotes

Roots of the denominator that are not also roots of the numerator will yield vertical asymptotes in the graph of a rational function. Here, for example, is a function with vertical asymptotes at $x = 3$ and $x = -3$:

$$In[56]:= \ \textbf{f[x\_] := } \frac{\textbf{x}^4 + \textbf{3x}^3 - \textbf{x}^2 + \textbf{5x} - \textbf{4}}{\textbf{x}^2 - \textbf{9}}$$

$In[57]:= \textbf{Solve[x}^2 \textbf{- 9 == 0, x]}$

$Out[57]= \{\{x \to -3\}, \{x \to 3\}\}$

$In[58]:= \textbf{Plot[f[x], \{x, -10, 10\}]}$

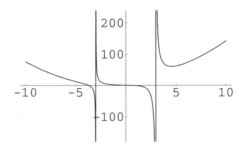

Long Division

Another manipulation that is useful when working with rational functions is long division. It can be done by hand, and you may have discovered that it is a tedious process. Every rational function $\frac{f(x)}{h(x)}$ can be expressed in the form $q(x) + \frac{r(x)}{h(x)}$, where $q(x)$ and $r(x)$ are polynomials, and $r(x)$ has degree less than $h(x)$. The term $q(x)$ is called the *quotient*, and the numerator $r(x)$ is called the *remainder*. When x gets sufficiently large, $\frac{r(x)}{h(x)}$ assumes values close to zero (since $r(x)$ has lesser degree than $h(x)$), so the rational function $\frac{f(x)}{h(x)}$ and the polynomial $q(x)$ are asymptotic to each other. Here's how to get *Mathematica* to calculate the quotient and remainder:

$$In[59]:= \ \textbf{k[x\_] := } \frac{\textbf{x}^4 + \textbf{3x}^3 - \textbf{x}^2 + \textbf{5x} - \textbf{4}}{\textbf{x}^2 - \textbf{9}}$$

The commands **Numerator** and **Denominator** can be used to isolate the numerator and denominator of any fraction. You can then use these to find the quotient $q(x)$ and the remainder $r(x)$ with the commands **PolynomialQuotient** and **PolynomialRemainder**:

$In[60]:= \textbf{num = Numerator[k[x]]}$

$Out[60]= -4 + 5\,x - x^2 + 3\,x^3 + x^4$

In[61]:= **den = Denominator[k[x]]**
Out[61]= $-9 + x^2$

In[62]:= **q[x_] := PolynomialQuotient[num, den, x]**
Out[62]= $8 + 3\,x + x^2$

In[63]:= **r[x_] := PolynomialRemainder[num, den, x]**
Out[63]= $68 + 32\,x$

The commands **PolynomialQuotient** and **PolynomialRemainder** each take three arguments. The first and second are polynomials representing the numerator and denominator of a rational function, respectively. The third is the name of the independent variable. In this example we have computed that:

$$\frac{-4 + 5\,x - x^2 + 3\,x^3 + x^4}{-9 + x^2} = 8 + 3\,x + x^2 + \frac{68 + 32\,x}{-9 + x^2}.$$

You can check that *Mathematica* has done things correctly. The following computation accomplishes this. Can you see why?

In[64]:= **Expand[(8 + 3x + x²)(-9 + x²) + (68 + 32x)]**
Out[64]= $-4 + 5\,x - x^2 + 3\,x^3 + x^4$

Here is a plot of *k* together with the quotient polynomial, which in this case is a parabola. We see that the graph of *k* is asymptotic to the parabola as *x* approaches $\pm\infty$:

In[65]:= **Plot[{k[x], q[x]}, {x, -15, 15}]**

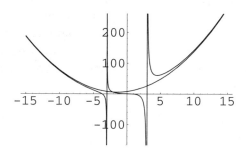

Partial Fractions

One final manipulation that is sometimes useful when working with rational functions is known as *partial fraction* decomposition. It is a fact that every rational function can be expressed as a sum of simpler rational functions. The *Mathematica* command that can accomplish this decomposition is called **Apart**:

$$In[66]:= \text{Apart}\left[\frac{x^4 + 3x^3 - x^2 + 5x - 4}{x^2 - 9}\right]$$

$$Out[66]= 8 + \frac{82}{3\ (-3+x)} + 3\ x + x^2 + \frac{14}{3\ (3+x)}$$

The command that puts sums of rational expressions over a common denominator (i.e., the command that does what **Apart** undoes) is called **Together**. Both can be found in the **AlgebraicManipulation** palette. If you take your mouse and highlight the output cell above, and then push the Together [■] button, a new cell will be created that will look like this:

$$\frac{-4 + 5\ x - x^2 + 3\ x^3 + x^4}{(-3+x)\ (3+x)}$$

4.5   Simplifying and Manipulating Other Expressions

The commands found in the **AgebraicManipulation** palette can be applied to all sorts of expressions other than polynomials and rational functions. Like **Expand** and **Factor**, the commands in this palette are given an algebraic expression as input, and return an equivalent algebraic expression as output. In this section we give examples how some of these commands can be used.

Simplifying Things

The **Simplify** command can handle all types of expressions as input. Any time you have a messy expression, it won't hurt to attempt a simplification. The worst that can happen is nothing; in such cases the output will simply match the input:

$$In[67]:= \text{Simplify}[1 - \text{Tan}[x]^4]$$

$$Out[67]= \text{Cos}[2\ x]\ \text{Sec}[x]^4$$

$$In[68]:= \text{Simplify}[1 + \text{Tan}[x]^4]$$

$$Out[68]= 1 + \text{Tan}[x]^4$$

In version 4 of *Mathematica*, the **Simplify** command can also accept a second argument specifying the domain of any variable in the expression to be simplified. For instance, consider the following example:

$$In[69]:= \text{Simplify}[\text{Log}[e^x]]$$

$$Out[69]= \text{Log}[e^x]$$

This seems odd; you may recall having been taught that the natural logarithm function and the exponential function are *inverses* of one another – their composition should simply yield **x**. The problem is that this is not necessarily true if **x** is a complex number, and *Mathematica* does not preclude this possibility. If you are using version 4 of *Mathematica* and would like to have the domain of **x** restricted to real numbers, do this:

In[70]:= **Simplify[Log[e^x], x∈Reals]**

Out[70]= x

The ∈ character can be read "is an element of". It can be found on the **BasicInput** palette. To learn about other choices for this second argument, look up **Assumptions** in the Help Browser.

Here is another example of how the **Simplify** command might be used. Note carefully the distinct uses of **:=** (for defining functions), **==** (for writing equations), and **=** (for assigning names):

In[71]:= **Clear[f, x];**
    f[x_] := x^3 – 2x + 9

In[72]:= **Solve[f[x] == 0, x] //TableForm**

Out[72] // TableForm =

$$x \to -2 \left(\frac{2}{3\,(81-\sqrt{6465})} \right)^{1/3} - \frac{\left(\frac{1}{2}\,(81-\sqrt{6465}) \right)^{1/3}}{3^{2/3}}$$

$$x \to (1+I\sqrt{3}) \left(\frac{2}{3\,(81-\sqrt{6465})} \right)^{1/3} + \frac{(1-I\sqrt{3})\,\left(\frac{1}{2}\,(81-\sqrt{6465}) \right)^{1/3}}{2\cdot3^{2/3}}$$

$$x \to (1-I\sqrt{3}) \left(\frac{2}{3\,(81-\sqrt{6465})} \right)^{1/3} + \frac{(1+I\sqrt{3})\,\left(\frac{1}{2}\,(81-\sqrt{6465}) \right)^{1/3}}{2\cdot3^{2/3}}$$

In[73]:= **realroot = x /. %〚1〛**

$$Out[73]= -2 \left(\frac{2}{3\,(81-\sqrt{6465})} \right)^{1/3} - \frac{\left(\frac{1}{2}\,(81-\sqrt{6465}) \right)^{1/3}}{3^{2/3}}$$

When you plug a root of a function into the function, you had better get zero:

In[74]:= **f[realroot]**

Out[74]=

$$9-2\left(-2\left(\frac{2}{3\,(81-\sqrt{6465})} \right)^{1/3} - \frac{\left(\frac{1}{2}\,(81-\sqrt{6465}) \right)^{1/3}}{3^{2/3}} \right) +$$

$$\left(-2\left(\frac{2}{3\,(81-\sqrt{6465})} \right)^{1/3} - \frac{\left(\frac{1}{2}\,(81-\sqrt{6465}) \right)^{1/3}}{3^{2/3}} \right)^3$$

Really?

```
In[75]:= Simplify[%]
Out[75]= 0
```

That's better.

Another example will illustrate a method for simplifying real roots of polynomials when they are reported as complex numbers. Just as the real number -1 can be written as i^2, *Mathematica*'s **Solve** command will sometimes express real roots in a way that involves the imaginary number i (it will appear as I in StandardForm output). How can you simplify such output to make the i's go away? For instance, here is a cubic with three real roots.

```
In[76]:= Plot[x³ - 15x + 2, {x, -5, 5}]
```

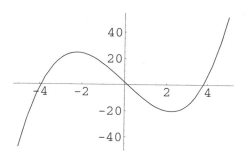

You can use **NSolve** to get numerical approximations to the roots of this cubic, but *Mathematica*'s **Solve** command expresses these real numbers in a form that makes use of imaginary numbers.

```
In[77]:= NSolve[x³ - 15x + 2 == 0, x]
Out[77]= {{x → -3.938}, {x → 0.133492}, {x → 3.80451}}
```

```
In[78]:= sols = x/.Solve[x³ - 15x + 2 == 0, x]
Out[78]=
```

$$\left\{ \frac{5}{\left(-1+2\,I\,\sqrt{31}\right)^{1/3}} + \left(-1+2\,I\,\sqrt{31}\right)^{1/3}, \right.$$

$$-\frac{5\,(1+I\,\sqrt{3})}{2\,\left(-1+2\,I\,\sqrt{31}\right)^{1/3}} - \frac{1}{2}\,(1-I\,\sqrt{3})\,\left(-1+2\,I\,\sqrt{31}\right)^{1/3},$$

$$\left.-\frac{5\,(1-I\,\sqrt{3})}{2\,\left(-1+2\,I\,\sqrt{31}\right)^{1/3}} - \frac{1}{2}\,(1+I\,\sqrt{3})\,\left(-1+2\,I\,\sqrt{31}\right)^{1/3} \right\}$$

Note that **Simplify** will not change a thing:

In[79]:= **Simplify[sols]**

Out[79]=

$$\left\{ \frac{5}{\left(-1+2\ I\ \sqrt{31}\right)^{1/3}} + \left(-1+2\ I\ \sqrt{31}\right)^{1/3}, \right.$$

$$-\frac{5\ (1+I\ \sqrt{3})}{2\ (-1+2\ I\ \sqrt{31})^{1/3}} - \frac{1}{2}\ (1-I\ \sqrt{3})\ (-1+2\ I\ \sqrt{31})^{1/3},$$

$$\left. -\frac{5\ (1-I\ \sqrt{3})}{2\ (-1+2\ I\ \sqrt{31})^{1/3}} - \frac{1}{2}\ (1+I\ \sqrt{3})\ (-1+2\ I\ \sqrt{31})^{1/3} \right\}$$

The command that can help is called **ComplexExpand**. It works like **Simplify**. Note how all the I's disappear. (In certain instances, you may need to apply **Simplify** after applying **ComplexExpand** to get the output into its most simple form.) We have:

In[80]:= **ComplexExpand[sols]//TableForm**

Out[80] // TableForm =

$$2\ \sqrt{5}\ \text{Cos}\left[\frac{1}{3}\ \left(\pi - \text{ArcTan}\left[2\ \sqrt{31}\right]\right)\right]$$

$$-\sqrt{5}\ \text{Cos}\left[\frac{1}{3}\ \left(\pi - \text{ArcTan}\left[2\ \sqrt{31}\right]\right)\right] - \sqrt{15}\ \text{Sin}\left[\frac{1}{3}\ \left(\pi - \text{ArcTan}\left[2\ \sqrt{31}\right]\right)\right]$$

$$-\sqrt{5}\ \text{Cos}\left[\frac{1}{3}\ \left(\pi - \text{ArcTan}\left[2\ \sqrt{31}\right]\right)\right] + \sqrt{15}\ \text{Sin}\left[\frac{1}{3}\ \left(\pi - \text{ArcTan}\left[2\ \sqrt{31}\right]\right)\right]$$

In[81]:= **N[%]**

Out[81]= {3.80451, -3.938, 0.133492}

Neat, huh?

The command **FullSimplify** works like **Simplify**, but it applies more transformations to the expression (and consequently takes longer to execute). In certain instances, it will be able to reduce an expression that **Simplify** cannot.

Manipulating Trigonometric Expressions

There is a suite of commands specifically designed to deal with trigonometric expressions. They are **TrigExpand**, **TrigFactor**, **TrigReduce**, **ExpToTrig**, and **TrigToExp**. They really shine when you're working with trigonometric functions, and they're great for helping you remember your trigonometric identities:

In[82]:= **Clear[α, β, γ, x];**
            TrigExpand[Cos[α + β]]

Out[82]= Cos[α] Cos[β] - Sin[α] Sin[β]

Of course we all know that identity. But what about this one?

```
In[83]:= TrigExpand[Cos[α +β +γ]]
```
$$Out[83]= \; Cos[\alpha] \; Cos[\beta] \; Cos[\gamma] - Cos[\gamma] \; Sin[\alpha] \; Sin[\beta] -$$
$$Cos[\beta] \; Sin[\alpha] \; Sin[\gamma] - Cos[\alpha] \; Sin[\beta] \; Sin[\gamma]$$

Here are examples of some other commands:

```
In[84]:= TrigFactor[Cos[α] +Cos[β]]
```
$$Out[84]= \; 2 \; Cos\left[\frac{\alpha}{2}-\frac{\beta}{2}\right] \; Cos\left[\frac{\alpha}{2}+\frac{\beta}{2}\right]$$

```
In[85]:= TrigReduce[1+Tan[x]⁴]
```
$$Out[85]= \; \frac{1}{4} \; (3 \; Sec[x]^4 + Cos[4 \; x] \; Sec[x]^4)$$

TrigExpand and **TrigFactor** are analogous to **Expand** and **Factor**, but they are designed to deal with trigonometric expressions. **TrigReduce** will rewrite products and powers of trigonometric functions in terms of trigonometric functions with more complicated arguments.

Any of the commands on the **AlgebraicManipulation** palette can be used in an interactive manner as explained in the previous section, where a method for individually factoring the numerator and denominator in a rational expression was discussed. Here's another example:

Cos[x]² +2 Cos[2x] +3

Highlight the first summand, **Cos[x]²**, and push the $\boxed{\textbf{TrigReduce[∎]}}$ button on the **AlgebraicManipulation** palette. The cell will then look like this:

$\frac{1}{2}$ **(1 + Cos[2x]) +2 Cos[2x] +3**

There is now clearly some combining of like terms that can occur. Do it in your head, or else highlight the entire expression and push the $\boxed{\textbf{Simplify[∎]}}$ button. The cell will then look like this:

$\frac{1}{2}$ **(7 +5 Cos[2x])**

You can keep manipulating an expression as much as you like. For instance, if you highlight the entire expression and push the $\boxed{\textbf{TrigExpand[∎]}}$ button you will have this:

$\frac{1}{2}$ **(7 +5 Cos[x]² - 5 Sin[x]²)**

The point is that you have a great degree of control in manipulating expressions. You might continue to operate on an expression until it reaches a form that reveals some interesting property that was less than obvious before the expression was put in that form.

As useful as these commands are, it is important to realize that they are not a panacea. Most algebraic identities are at best difficult to uncover through blind application of the suite of commands provided in the **AlgebraicManipulation** palette. For instance, it is true that

$$\frac{\pi}{4} = \arctan\left(\frac{1}{2}\right) + \arctan\left(\frac{1}{3}\right),$$

yet no amount of manipulation of the right hand side using only the tools in the **AlgebraicManipulation** palette will produce the value $\frac{\pi}{4}$. How can these tools be used to explore, or to uncover, such an identity? The answer is subtle. First, recognize that they are only tools. They must be used carefully, with due deliberation and forethought. Owning a hammer doesn't make one a carpenter. That's the bad news. The process is much like traditional pencil-and-paper mathematics in that you pursue an idea and see if it bears fruit. The good news is that the pursuit is made less tedious with *Mathematica* working for you.

Let's explore the identity above. First, for sanity's sake, let's see if it can possibly be true:

In[86]:= **ArcTan $\left[\frac{1}{2}\right]$ + ArcTan $\left[\frac{1}{3}\right]$//N**

Out[86]= 0.785398

In[87]:= $\frac{\pi}{4}$**//N**

Out[87]= 0.785398

Okay, it's believable. Now can we derive a general formula, for which the above identity is but a special case? As a first attempt, we might try commands such as **TrigExpand**, **TrigFactor**, and **TrigReduce** on the expression **ArcTan[a] + ArcTan[b]**. We find that none has any effect. For instance:

In[88]:= **Clear[a, b];**
          TrigExpand[ArcTan[a]+ArcTan[b]]
Out[88]= ArcTan[a] + ArcTan[b]

Now we are at a critical juncture in our investigation. We have made no progress, except to learn that *Mathematica* does not appear to have the magic command that will provide us with the type of formula we seek. It is at this point that we need to stop and *think*. What else might we try? Well, what if we took the tangent of the expression **ArcTan[a]+ArcTan[b]**, then tried to expand that? Believe it or not, this gets us somewhere:

In[89]:= **Clear[a, b];**
TrigExpand[Tan[ArcTan[a]+ArcTan[b]]]

$$\textit{Out[89]=} \quad \frac{a}{\sqrt{1+a^2}\,\sqrt{1+b^2}\left(\dfrac{1}{\sqrt{1+a^2}\,\sqrt{1+b^2}} - \dfrac{a\,b}{\sqrt{1+a^2}\,\sqrt{1+b^2}}\right)}$$
$$+\frac{b}{\sqrt{1+a^2}\,\sqrt{1+b^2}\left(\dfrac{1}{\sqrt{1+a^2}\,\sqrt{1+b^2}} - \dfrac{a\,b}{\sqrt{1+a^2}\,\sqrt{1+b^2}}\right)}$$

In[90]:= **%//Simplify**

$$\textit{Out[90]=} \quad \frac{a+b}{1-a\,b}$$

This tells us that

$$\frac{a+b}{1-ab} = \tan(\arctan a + \arctan b),$$

or, taking the inverse tangent of each side, that

$$\arctan\left(\frac{a+b}{1-ab}\right) = \arctan a + \arctan b.$$

It is a simple matter to see that when $a = \frac{1}{2}$ and $b = \frac{1}{3}$, the left-hand side is equal to arctan(1), which is $\frac{\pi}{4}$, and so this reduces to the identity mentioned previously. This formula is a generalization of that identity. The final task is determining for which values of a and b the formula is valid. We leave this task to the reader.

4.6 Solving General Equations

The **Solve** and **NSolve** commands are built for polynomials. They will also work for equations involving rational functions, and they will sometimes work with equations involving other types of functions. They are the commands to start with when you need to solve an equation. However, there are still a few things you can do if you don't get the answer you need. We'll address some of these issues in this section.

Often **Solve** and **NSolve** can be effectively used to solve equations involving powers that are rational numbers. For instance, since raising a quantity to the power $\frac{1}{2}$ is the same as taking its square root, equations involving square roots fall into this category:

$In[91]:=$ **Solve$\left[\sqrt{1+x+x^2} \ == \ 2, \ x\right]$ //TableForm**

$Out[91]$ // $TableForm=$

$$x \to \frac{1}{2}\left(-1-\sqrt{13}\right)$$

$$x \to \frac{1}{2}\left(-1+\sqrt{13}\right)$$

$In[92]:=$ **Solve$\left[x^{1/3} \ == \ 2x, \ x\right]$ //TableForm**

$Out[92]$ // $TableForm=$

$$x \to 0$$

$$x \to \frac{1}{16}$$

Solve and **NSolve** can find solutions to simple equations with the variable appearing inside a logarithm or as an exponent:

$In[93]:=$ **Solve[400 Log[10, x] == 2, x]**

$Out[93]=$ $\{\{x \to 10^{1/200}\}\}$

$In[94]:=$ **Solve[200(1.05)^x == 300, x]**

> Solve::ifun : Inverse functions are being used by Solve,
> so some solutions may not be found.

$Out[94]=$ $\{\{x \to 8.31039\}\}$

Here we are warned that although one solution was found, there may be more. In fact, for this example no other solution exists, but we have no way of knowing that on the basis of this output. In many other instances where this warning message is displayed, an infinite number of solutions may exist. This often happens in equations involving trigonometric functions:

$In[95]:=$ **Solve[Sin[x] == Cos[x], x]**

> Solve::ifun : Inverse functions are being used by Solve,
> so some solutions may not be found.

$Out[95]=$ $\left\{\left\{x \to -\frac{3\pi}{4}\right\}, \ \left\{x \to \frac{\pi}{4}\right\}\right\}$

On occasion these commands will come up empty even when a unique solution exists:

$In[96]:=$ **Solve[Sin[x] == x - 1, x]**

> Solve::tdep : The equations appear to involve
> transcendental functions of the variables in an
> essentially non-algebraic way.

$Out[96]=$ Solve[Sin[x] == -1+x, x]

When dealing with equations involving these types of functions, the first order of business is the construction of a plot. Make things easy for yourself by plotting two functions, the left side and right side of the equation you wish to solve. The solution occurs at the **x** coordinate of the point where the curves intersect. For instance, here's a view of the equation above:

In[97]:= **Plot[{Sin[x], x - 1}, {x, -6, 6}]**

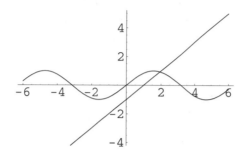

Ah, so there is a solution near $x = 2$. To zero in on a solution once you know roughly where it is, use the **FindRoot** command:

In[98]:= **FindRoot[Sin[x] == x - 1, {x, 2}]**
Out[98]= {x → 1.93456}

The first argument of the **FindRoot** command is an equation, the second is a list whose first member is the variable to be solved for, and whose second member is a rough guess at the true root. To get *n*-digit precision, you must use the optional argument **WorkingPrecision**:

In[99]:= **FindRoot[Sin[x] == x - 1, {x, 2},**
        WorkingPrecision → 400]
Out[99]= {x →
        1.93456321075202426756326145376885002762330 28 ·.
        49353341290328231795513512694459272831007787 ·.
        22332410744341080757905541787599986842515285 ·.
        69101190209020202566373790063657058661502567 ·.
        58548630871697407033723117057902857867803814 ·.
        96546568856912163498139653316125699027169973 ·.
        34104665669369056060455985930485417707162013 ·.
        03999749328685654102947765594946692790583978 ·.
        26085956460925384302125068722567683980548742 ·.
        549}

This technique of first estimating a solution with a plot and then using **Find-Root** to zero in on it is very robust in that it will work on almost any equation you wish to solve (provided that a solution exists). It does have a few drawbacks, however. First, it is sometimes difficult (or at least tedious) to find the appropriate domain for a plot, one in which a point of intersection resides. Second, it is often difficult to discern whether or not other intersection points might be present to the left or right of those you have already found. And third, for some equations the algorithm will fail altogether. For instance, **FindRoot** relies in part on a well-known algorithm, Newton's method, in producing its solutions. It is also well known that Newton's method doesn't work for all combinations of equations and initial guesses, even when a unique solution exists:

In[100]:= **FindRoot[200 (1.05)^x == 300, {x, 270}]**

> FindRoot::cvnwt : Newton's method failed to converge
> to the prescribed accuracy after 15 iterations.

Out[100]= {x → 8.35144}

The output here is not correct. On page 118, the **Solve** command has already told us that the root is 8.31039. In most cases, you can avoid this sort of thing if you make a reasonable initial guess. The problem is eliminated if you follow our advice and make a few plots first, using the plots to get reasonable initial guesses for **FindRoot**. However, the example suggests another strategy that is also useful. We looked for a root near $x = 270$, and found that one might exist near $x = 8$. To make use of this information, edit and reenter the last cell, using 8 as the initial guess:

In[101]:= **FindRoot[200 (1.05)^x == 300, {x, 8}]**
Out[101]= {x → 8.31039}

Good. *Mathematica* didn't complain, and the output matches that of the **Solve** command for this same equation, found earlier. In your dealings with computers, you should live by the maxim made famous by Ronald Reagan: "Trust, but verify." In that spirit, we finish this example with a pair of plots:

In[102]:= **Plot[{200 (1.05)^x, 300}, {x, 0, 15}]**

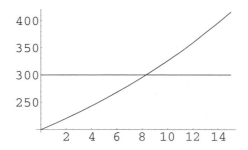

We can zoom in to verify the accuracy of our solution:

In[103]:= **Plot[{200 (1.05)^x, 300}, {x, 8.31, 8.311}]**

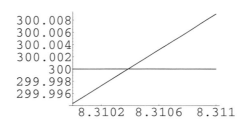

Let's look at another example: solve the equation $\log x = x^3 - 1$:

In[104]:= **Solve[Log[x] == x^3 - 1, x]**

> InverseFunction::ifun:Warning: Inverse functions
> are being used. Values may be lost for multivalued
> inverses.

> Solve::ifun: Inverse functions are being used by
> Solve, so some solutions may not be found.

Out[104]= $\left\{ \left\{ x \to -(-1)^{2/3} \left(\frac{1}{3} \mathrm{ProductLog}\left[-\frac{3}{E^3}\right] \right)^{1/3} \right\}, \right.$

$\left. \left\{ x \to -(-1)^{2/3} \left(\frac{1}{3} \mathrm{ProductLog}\left[-1, -\frac{3}{E^3}\right] \right)^{1/3} \right\} \right\}$

Mathematica has found two solutions, but is reporting them in terms of a function it calls **ProductLog**. Don't fret. *Mathematica* is just telling you this on the off chance that you might have heard of it. In doing the best it can, it will occasionally throw stuff at you that's a little over your head. You might try educating yourself by asking about **ProductLog**:

In[105]:= **?ProductLog**

> ProductLog[z] gives the principal solution for w in
>   z = w e^w. ProductLog[k, z] gives the kth solution.

Oh well, it was worth a try. If you ever get output expressed in terms of a function that you do not understand, regard it as a cue that perhaps you should try another approach. Let's try **NSolve**:

In[106]:= **NSolve[Log[x] == x^3 - 1, x]**

> InverseFunction::ifun:Warning: Inverse functions
>   are being used. Values may be lost for multivalued
>   inverses.

> Solve::ifun:Inverse functions are being used by
>   Solve, so some solutions may not be found.

Out[106]= {{x → 0.39044+0. I}, {x → 1.+0. I}}

Now we have two approximate solutions being reported, both real (or possibly complex with very small imaginary components). You shouldn't be satisfied with this output. Let's make a plot and use **FindRoot** to confirm these results:

In[107]:= **Plot[{Log[x], x^3 - 1}, {x, 0, 10}]**

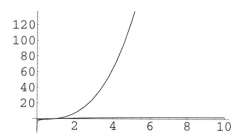

One of the functions is barely visible. If you are unsure which, make the **Log** function blue (**Hue[.5]**) and the cubic red (**Hue[1]**) on your screen. In the graphic below, the **Log** function is shown in light gray:

In[108]:= **Plot[{Log[x], x^3 - 1}, {x, 0, 10},**
            PlotStyle → {Hue[0.5], Hue[1]}]

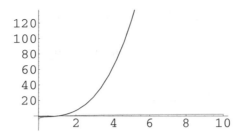

Suspicion confirmed: the **Log** function is quite flat compared to the cubic on this domain. Perhaps they intersect over there on the left, somewhere between 0 and 2. Try again: edit the iterator above, specifying the new plot domain, and reenter the cell:

```
In[109]:= Plot[{Log[x], x³ - 1}, {x, 0, 2},
            PlotStyle → Hue[0.5], Hue[1]}]
```

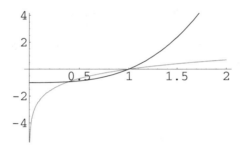

Bingo! Let's zero in on these babies:

```
In[110]:= FindRoot[Log[x] == x³ - 1, {x, 0.4}]
Out[110]= {x → 0.39044}

In[111]:= FindRoot[Log[x] == x³ - 1, {x, 1}]
Out[111]= {x → 1.}
```

Is $x = 1$ an exact solution? Try it. Do it by hand, or do this:

```
In[112]:= Log[x] == x³ - 1 /. x → 1
Out[112]= True
```

It is worth noting that you can manipulate any equation into the form *expression==0* simply by subtracting the original quantity on the right from each side of the equation. Solving the resulting equation is then a matter of finding the roots of *expression*. The obvious advantages to this approach are that there is only one function to plot, and the roots are easy to read, since they fall directly on the labeled x axis. Here is the graph for the last example when presented this way:

In[113]:= **Plot[Log[x] - x³+1, {x, 0, 2}]**

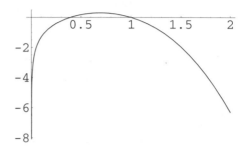

The roots, of course, are the same as the solutions we found earlier. **FindRoot** will report the same output regardless of whether you input the equation **Log[x] == x³ - 1** or the equation **Log[x] - x³ + 1 == 0**. In fact, you can simply type **Log[x] - x³+1** (and forgo the **== 0**) when using **FindRoot**. The name "FindRoot" makes good sense in this light. You can use whichever approach seems easier to you.

4.7 Solving Difference Equations

Difference equations (also called recurrence relations) were discussed in Chapter 3 (Section 3.13, see page 90). Suppose we are given a difference equation for a sequence a. Let's say that the nth term of the sequence is always twice the previous term, so the difference equation is $a[n] = 2a[n-1]$. How can we find an explicit formula for $a[n]$, not in terms of $a[n-1]$, but as a function of n? It is not difficult in this example to find a solution by hand, but how can *Mathematica* be employed for the purpose of solving this or any other difference equation? The command that you need is called **RSolve**, and it is found in the package **DiscreteMath-'RSolve'**:

In[114]:= **Needs["DiscreteMath'RSolve'"]**

RSolve takes three arguments. The first is a difference equation (such as **a[n] == 2a[n-1]**, the second is the name of the term for which a solution is sought (in this case **a[n]**), and the third is the name of the independent variable (in this case **n**):

```
In[115]:= Clear[a, n];
          RSolve[a[n] == 2 a[n - 1], a[n], n]
Out[115]= {{a[n] → 2ⁿ C[1]}}
```

Here the output includes the term $C[1]$, which stands for an arbitrary constant. This indicates that there are an infinite number of solutions, one for each value of $C[1]$. The sequence will be uniquely determined if we indicate an initial condition – a numerical value for the first term of the sequence. This is accomplished by putting a *list* of equations as the first argument to **RSolve**. Below we add the initial condition $a[0] = 11$. Note also that you can enter either of the mathematically equivalent difference equations $a[n] = 2a[n-1]$ or $a[n+1] = 2a[n]$ when using **RSolve**:

```
In[116]:= RSolve[{a[n + 1] == 2 a[n], a[0] == 11}, a[n], n]
Out[116]= {{a[n] → 11 2ⁿ}}
```

RSolve is most useful when dealing with somewhat more complicated difference equations. It can easily handle *second-order* difference equations – difference equations that describe the nth term as a function of the *two* previous terms. Here, for example, is an expression for the nth *Fibonacci number* (defined by the difference equation $a[n] = a[n-1] + a[n-2]$ and the initial condition $a[0] = a[1] = 1$)[1]:

```
In[117]:= RSolve[{a[n] == a[n - 1] + a[n - 2], a[0] == 1,
              a[1] == 1}, a[n], n]
```

$$Out[117]= \left\{\left\{a[n] \rightarrow \frac{(\frac{1}{2}(1-\sqrt{5}))^n(-1+\sqrt{5}) + 2^{-n}(1+\sqrt{5})^{1+n}}{2\sqrt{5}}\right\}\right\}$$

It is important to note that some difference equations do not admit solutions that can be written in terms of elementary functions. So there will be difference equations that **RSolve** cannot handle. In such situations, the output will simply

---

[1] Leonardo Fibonacci lived from approximately 1170 to 1250. He was born in Pisa, Italy, and was the most prominant mathematician of the thirteenth century. His work *Liber abaci*, in which the sequence that now bears his name was first studied, was instrumental in advocating the use of the Arabic number system, which gradually became the standard.

match your input. Here, for instance, is what happens when **RSolve** is fed a logistic growth difference equation:

$In[118]:=$ **RSolve[{a[n+1] == 3 a[n] − 0.05 a[n]^2, a[1] == 2},**
            a[n], n]

$Out[118]=$ RSolve[{a[n+1] == 3 a[n] − 0.05 a[n]^2, a[1] == 2},
            a[n], n]

4.8 Solving Systems of Equations

It is sometimes necessary to solve several equations simultaneously. For instance, what values of x and y satisfy both $2x - 39y = 79$ and $7x + 5y = 800$? To find out, use **Solve** (or **NSolve**), with a list of equations as the first argument and a list of variables to be solved for (such as **{x, y}**) as the second argument:

$In[119]:=$ **Solve[{2x − 39y == 79, 7x + 5y == 800}, {x, y}]**

$$Out[119]= \left\{ \left\{ x \to \frac{31595}{283}, \ y \to \frac{1047}{283} \right\} \right\}$$

You can leave out the second argument entirely if you want to solve for *all* the variables appearing in the equations:

$In[120]:=$ **Solve[{2x − 39y == 79, 7x + 5y == 800}]**

$$Out[120]= \left\{ \left\{ x \to \frac{31595}{283}, \ y \to \frac{1047}{283} \right\} \right\}$$

You can easily use generic coefficients to generate a general formula for solving similar systems:

$In[121]:=$ **Clear[a, b, c, d, e, f, x, y];**
            Solve[a * x + b * y == c, d * x + e * y == f}, {x, y}]

$$Out[121]= \left\{ \left\{ x \to -\frac{-ce+b\,f}{-b\,d+a\,e}, \ y \to -\frac{cd-a\,f}{-b\,d+a\,e} \right\} \right\}$$

The **Solve** command works very well for linear equations (where no exponent is greater than 1). It also does a good job with many polynomials. Here is an example showing the points of intersection of a circle and a parabola:

In[122]:= **Needs["Graphics`ImplicitPlot`"]**
In[123]:= **ImplicitPlot[{x² + y² == 4, y + 1 == (x − 1)²}, {x, −2, 2}]**

It turns out that there are two real solutions (you can see them on the plot) and two complex ones. One of the real ones is the point (2, 0). The other is:

In[124]:= **Solve[{x² + y² == 4, y + 1 == (x − 1)²}]〚2〛 //TableForm**

Out[124] // TableForm =

$$y \to \frac{1}{9}\left(-6 + \frac{1}{\left(28 - 3\sqrt{87}\right)^{2/3}} + \frac{2}{\left(28 - 3\sqrt{87}\right)^{1/3}}\right.$$
$$\left. + 2\left(28 - 3\sqrt{87}\right)^{1/3} + \left(28 - 3\sqrt{87}\right)^{2/3}\right)$$

$$x \to \frac{2}{3} - \frac{1}{3\left(28 - 3\sqrt{87}\right)^{1/3}} - \frac{1}{3}\left(28 - 3\sqrt{87}\right)^{1/3}$$

We won't list the complex solutions, as they're even nastier.

Just as there are single equations that can foil the **Solve** and **NSolve** commands, there are systems of equations that can as well:

In[125]:= **ImplicitPlot[{y == x², y⁷ + 2x² == 1}, {x, −2, 2}]**

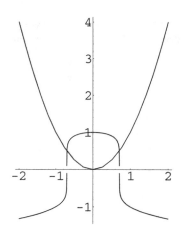

In[126]:= **Solve[{y == x^2, y^7 + 2x^2 == 1}]**

Out[126]=

$$\left\{\left\{x \to -\sqrt{\text{Root}[-1+2\,\#1+\#1^7\&,\ 1]},\ y \to \text{Root}[-1+2\,\#1+\#1^7\&,\ 1]\right\},\right.$$

$$\left\{x \to \sqrt{\text{Root}[-1+2\,\#1+\#1^7\&,\ 1]},\ y \to \text{Root}[-1+2\,\#1+\#1^7\&,\ 1]\right\},$$

$$\left\{x \to -\sqrt{\text{Root}[-1+2\,\#1+\#1^7\&,\ 2]},\ y \to \text{Root}[-1+2\,\#1+\#1^7\&,\ 2]\right\},$$

$$\left\{x \to \sqrt{\text{Root}[-1+2\,\#1+\#1^7\&,\ 2]},\ y \to \text{Root}[-1+2\,\#1+\#1^7\&,\ 2]\right\},$$

$$\left\{x \to -\sqrt{\text{Root}[-1+2\,\#1+\#1^7\&,\ 3]},\ y \to \text{Root}[-1+2\,\#1+\#1^7\&,\ 3]\right\},$$

$$\left\{x \to \sqrt{\text{Root}[-1+2\,\#1+\#1^7\&,\ 3]},\ y \to \text{Root}[-1+2\,\#1+\#1^7\&,\ 3]\right\},$$

$$\left\{x \to -\sqrt{\text{Root}[-1+2\,\#1+\#1^7\&,\ 4]},\ y \to \text{Root}[-1+2\,\#1+\#1^7\&,\ 4]\right\},$$

$$\left\{x \to \sqrt{\text{Root}[-1+2\,\#1+\#1^7\&,\ 4]},\ y \to \text{Root}[-1+2\,\#1+\#1^7\&,\ 4]\right\},$$

$$\left\{x \to -\sqrt{\text{Root}[-1+2\,\#1+\#1^7\&,\ 5]},\ y \to \text{Root}[-1+2\,\#1+\#1^7\&,\ 5]\right\},$$

$$\left\{x \to \sqrt{\text{Root}[-1+2\,\#1+\#1^7\&,\ 5]},\ y \to \text{Root}[-1+2\,\#1+\#1^7\&,\ 5]\right\},$$

$$\left\{x \to -\sqrt{\text{Root}[-1+2\,\#1+\#1^7\&,\ 6]},\ y \to \text{Root}[-1+2\,\#1+\#1^7\&,\ 6]\right\},$$

$$\left\{x \to \sqrt{\text{Root}[-1+2\,\#1+\#1^7\&,\ 6]},\ y \to \text{Root}[-1+2\,\#1+\#1^7\&,\ 6]\right\},$$

$$\left\{x \to -\sqrt{\text{Root}[-1+2\,\#1+\#1^7\&,\ 7]},\ y \to \text{Root}[-1+2\,\#1+\#1^7\&,\ 7]\right\},$$

$$\left.\left\{x \to \sqrt{\text{Root}[-1+2\,\#1+\#1^7\&,\ 7]},\ y \to \text{Root}[-1+2\,\#1+\#1^7\&,\ 7]\right\}\right\}$$

—which is impenetrable. In such situations, **NSolve** will often be able to provide you with a good approximation. The two real solutions correspond to the points of intersection in the plot:

$In[127]:=$ **NSolve[{y == x^2, y^7+2x^2 == 1}]//TableForm**

$Out[127]//TableForm=$

x → −0.978813−0.298975 I	y → 0.868688+0.585282 I
x → −0.978813+0.298975 I	y → 0.868688−0.585282 I
x → −0.73046−0.780978 I	y → −0.0763556+1.14095 I
x → −0.73046+0.780978 I	y → −0.0763556−1.14095 I
x → −0.70448	y → 0.496292
x → −0.268914−1.05489 I	y → −1.04048+0.56735 I
x → −0.268914+1.05489 I	y → −1.04048−0.56735 I
x → 0.268914−1.05489 I	y → −1.04048−0.56735 I
x → 0.268914+1.05489 I	y → −1.04048+0.56735 I
x → 0.70448	y → 0.496292
x → 0.73046−0.780978 I	y → −0.0763556−1.14095 I
x → 0.73046+0.780978 I	y → −0.0763556+1.14095 I
x → 0.978813−0.298975 I	y → 0.868688−0.585282 I
x → 0.978813+0.298975 I	y → 0.868688+0.585282 I

Another option is to use **FindRoot**. Give as the first argument the list of equations. Follow that with an additional argument for each variable. Each of these arguments is of the form {*variable*, *guess*}, where the guess is your best estimate of the actual value for that variable. Use a plot to help you make your guess:

$In[128]:=$ **FindRoot[{y == x^2, y^7 +2x^2 == 1}, {x, 1}, {y, 0.5}]**

$Out[128]=$ {x → 0.70448, y → 0.496292}

Chapter 5

Calculus

5.1 Computing Limits

An understanding of limits is fundamental to an understanding of calculus. Let's start by defining a few functions:

```
In[1]:= Clear[f,g,x];
        f[x_] := Sin[x]/x ;
        g[x_] := 1/x
```

Note that $x = 0$ is not in the domain of either these functions. How do they behave as x approaches 0, that is, as x assumes values very close to 0? A plot is a sensible way to approach this question:

```
In[2]:= Plot[f[x],{x,-10,10}]
```

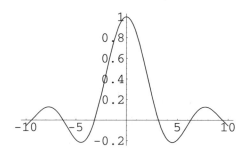

In[3]:= **Plot[g[x],{x,-1,1}]**

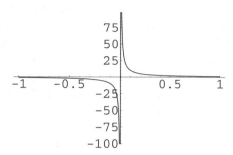

The two outcomes are strikingly different, and they illustrate the likely possibilities for similar investigations. The function f assumes values that approach 1 as x approaches 0. The function g has a vertical asymptote at $x = 0$; as x approaches 0 from the right, g assumes values that approach ∞, while as x approaches 0 from the left, g assumes values that approach $-\infty$.

We can check this numerically by making a table of values. Here is a table of values for f as x approaches 0 from the right:

In[4]:= **TableForm[**
Table[{N[10^-n],N[f[10^-n],20]},{n,1,5}],
TableHeadings → {None,{"x","f[x]"}}]

Out[4]//TableForm=

x	f[x]
0.1	0.998334166468281523
0.01	0.999983333416666468
0.001	0.999999833333341667
0.0001	0.999999998333333334
0.00001	0.999999999983333333

The **Limit** command provides an easy way to investigate the behavior of functions as the independent variable approaches some particular value (such as 0):

In[5]:= **Limit[f[x], x → 0]**
Out[5]= 1

In[6]:= **Limit[g[x], x → 0]**
Out[6]= ∞

The first argument to the **Limit** command is the expression for which you wish to find a limiting value. The second argument ($x → 0$ in these examples) specifies the independent variable and the value which it will approach. You may use the

→ symbol from the **BasicInput** palette or the keyboard equivalent `->` by hitting the "minus" sign followed by the "greater than" sign.

It is important to note that the **Limit** command by default computes one-sided limits, and these are limits *from the right*. That is, the expression is examined with x values chosen slightly to the *right* of the value that x approaches. In the limit for g as $x \to 0$, for instance, the output was ∞. You can take limits from the left by adding the option **Direction → 1**. You can think of this as the direction in which you need to move on a number line to get to the number 1 from the origin.

```
In[7]:= Limit[g[x], x → 0, Direction → 1]
Out[7]= -∞
```

In a strictly mathematical sense, a limit exists if and only if the limits from the left and right agree. So the limit of the function g as x approaches 0 *does not exist* since the limit from the right is ∞ while the limit from the left is $-\infty$. In *Mathematica,* the **Limit** command defaults to the limit from the right to increase the likelihood of being able to find a limiting value. It is crucial to check that the limit from the left matches the limit from the right before concluding that a limit exists. A plot is usually helpful in this regard. The only exception to this convention is a limit as x approaches infinity (where the **Limit** command will by default compute limits from the left).

```
In[8]:= Limit[g[x], x → ∞]
Out[8]= 0
```

Taking another glance at the graph of g, you can see that as the value of x gets large, the value of $g(x)$ approaches 0. A table of values is also useful in this regard:

```
In[9]:= TableForm[
          Table[{10ⁿ, g[10ⁿ]} // N, {n, 1, 5}],
          TableHeadings → {None, {"x", "g[x]"}}]
```
```
Out[9] // TableForm =
         x         g[x]
         10.       0.1
         100.      0.01
         1000.     0.001
         10000.    0.0001
         100000.   0.00001
```

Note that you may use the ∞ symbol from the **BasicInput** palette, or type **Infinity**. Note also that some functions will not have one-sided limits:

In[10]:= **Limit[Sin[x],x → ∞]**

Out[10]= Interval[{-1,1}]

The output here indicates that the sine function assumes values in the interval from −1 to 1 without approaching a single limiting value as x approaches infinity. This is consistent with our knowledge of the sine function; a plot provides additional confirmation:

In[11]:= **Plot[Sin[x],{x,0,30}]**

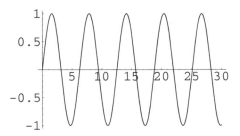

5.2 Working with Difference Quotients

Producing and Simplifying Difference Quotients

It is easy to simplify difference quotients with *Mathematica*. (Get the Δ character from the **BasicInput** palette, and do not put a space between it and **x**, for you are creating a new symbol whose name is **Δx**, rather than multiplying Δ by **x**.)

In[12]:= **Clear[diffquot,x,Δx];**

$$\textbf{diffquot[f\_] := } \frac{\textbf{f[x + Δx] - f[x]}}{\textbf{Δx}}$$

This is much more fun to do than to read about, so if possible get yourself started in a *Mathematica* session. You first define a function, and then produce the difference quotient:

In[13]:= **h[x_] := x³;**

diffquot[h]

Out[13]= $\dfrac{-x^3 + (x + Δx)^3}{Δx}$

You can now simplify it by typing and entering **Simplify[%]**, but its much more fun (and informative) to "drive" *Mathematica* through it step by step. First use your mouse to highlight $(x + \triangle x)^3$ in the last output, and then hit the Expand[■] button on the **AlgebraicManipulation** palette (found in the **File** menu). You will then have this:

$$\frac{-x^3 + x^3 + 3x^2 \triangle x + 3x \triangle x^2 + \triangle x^3}{\triangle x}$$

Now highlight the entire numerator, and hit the Simplify[■] button. The x^3 cancels with the $-x^3$, and $\triangle x$ is factored out of the remaining three summands. You will have:

$$\frac{(\triangle x(3x^2 + 3x \triangle x + \triangle x^2))}{\triangle x}$$

Lastly, select the entire output and hit the Simplify[■] button again. The $\triangle x$'s cancel and you are left with:

$$3x^2 + 3x \triangle x + \triangle x^2$$

That's it! You've just simplified an algebraic expression painlessly, with no dropped minus signs, and without skipping a step. We encourage you to do this for five or six functions of your choosing; you might even find it fun.

Average Rate of Change

Once you have entered the cell defining the **diffquot** command, you can work with specific values of x and $\triangle x$ to find the average rate of change of a function as the independent variable ranges from x to $x + \triangle x$:

$In[14]:=$ **Clear[f,x,$\triangle$x];**

$$\mathbf{f[x\_]} := \frac{\mathbf{Sin[\pi x]}}{\mathbf{x}}$$

$In[15]:=$ **diffquot[f]**

$$Out[15]= \frac{-\dfrac{Sin[\pi x]}{x} + \dfrac{Sin[\pi(x + \triangle x)]}{x + \triangle x}}{\triangle x}$$

You can find the rate of change of f from $x = 2$ to $x = 2.5$ as follows:

$In[16]:=$ **diffquot[f]/.{x $\rightarrow$ 2,$\triangle$x $\rightarrow$ 0.5}**
$Out[16]=$ 0.8

Recall from the last chapter (Section 4.2, page 101) that the replacement rule **/.{x $\rightarrow$ 2,$\triangle$x $\rightarrow$ 0.5}** instructs *Mathematica* to replace x by 2 and $\triangle x$ by 0.5. You can find the rate of change of f from $x = 2$ to $x = 2.1$ as follows:

```
In[17]:= diffquot[f]/.{x → 2, Δx → 0.1}
Out[17]= 1.47151
```

Here is a table of values for the difference quotient of f at $x = 2$ for various small values of Δx:

```
In[18]:= TableForm[
           Table[{Δx,diffquot[f]}/.{x→2,Δx→N[10^-n]},
             {n,1,5}],
           TableHeadings → {None,{"Δx","diffquot"}}]
Out[18]//TableForm=
             Δx        diffquot
             0.1       1.47151
             0.01      1.56272
             0.001     1.57001
             0.0001    1.57072
             0.00001   1.57079
```

Instantaneous Rate of Change

The *instantaneous* rate of change at $x = 2$ is found by taking the limit as Δx approaches 0 of the difference quotient at $x = 2$:

```
In[19]:= diffquot[f]/. x → 2
```
$$Out[19]= \frac{Sin[\pi(2 + \Delta x)]}{\Delta x(2 + \Delta x)}$$

```
In[20]:= Limit[%,Δx → 0]
```
$$Out[20]= \frac{\pi}{2}$$

```
In[21]:= N[%,10]
Out[21]= 1.570796327
```

Note that this result is consistent with the table that we computed above.

5.3 The Derivative

Of course there is a simpler way to take derivatives than to compute the instantaneous rate of change as above. This is an instance where the *Mathematica* syntax matches that of traditional mathematical notation. For the function f defined above, the derivative can be found as follows:

$In[22]:=$ **f'[x]**

$Out[22]= \dfrac{\pi \cos[\pi x]}{x} - \dfrac{\sin[\pi x]}{x^2}$

If you check this using the quotient rule, your answer may look slightly different. You can simplify the output above by highlighting it and pushing the `Simplify[■]` button on the **AlgebraicManipulation** palette, or by typing:

$In[23]:=$ **Simplify[%]**

$Out[23]= \dfrac{\pi x \cos[\pi x] - \sin[\pi x]}{x^2}$

This is exactly what you would obtain if you worked by hand using the quotient rule. We can evaluate the derivative at any value of x:

$In[24]:=$ **f'[2]**

$Out[24]= \dfrac{\pi}{2}$

A plot of a function and the tangent line to the function at a point (at $x = 2$, for example) can be produced as follows. The expression representing the line is obtained from the *point–slope* formula for a line, where the point on the line is $(2, f(2))$, and the slope of the line is $f'(2)$. You can zoom in (or out) by changing the bounds on the iterator. Try **{x,1.9,2.1}** to zoom in on the two graphs near $x = 2$.

$In[25]:=$ **Plot[{f[x], f[2] + f'[2]*(x-2)}, {x,1.5,2.5}]**

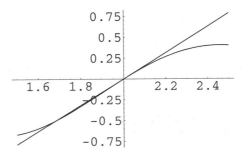

You may also find it instructive to study the graph of a function and its derivative on the same set of axes. Here the graph of f is black, while its derivative is gray. You can replace **GrayLevel** with **Hue** to get a full color version:

In[26]:= **Plot[{f[x],f'[x]},{x,0,3},**
           PlotStyle → {GrayLevel[0],GrayLevel[0.5]}]

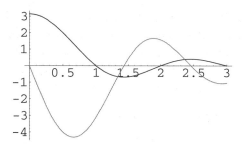

There is another way to take derivatives of expressions with *Mathematica* that is useful in many situations. The command is called **D**, and it takes two arguments; the first is an expression to be differentiated, and the second is name of the variable with respect to which the differentiation is to be performed:

In[27]:= **D$\left[\dfrac{\text{Sin}[\pi \text{x}]}{\text{x}}, \text{x}\right]$**

Out[27]= $\dfrac{\pi \, \text{Cos}[\pi \, \text{x}]}{\text{x}} - \dfrac{\text{Sin}[\pi \, \text{x}]}{\text{x}^2}$

A palette version of the **D** command exists and is sometimes useful. Go to the **BasicInput** palette, and find the $\boxed{\partial_\square \blacksquare}$ button. Type and highlight the expression you wish to differentiate, *then* push this button. Now type **x** (as the subscript) to indicate that you wish to differentiate with respect to *x*:

In[28]:= **∂_x Sin[x]**
Out[28]= Cos[x]

The palette approach is most useful when the expression you wish to differentiate already exists on your screen (as the output of some former computation, for instance). You can then highlight it and push the button.

A word of warning regarding the palette button is in order. If you *first* hit the palette button and *then* enter an expression to be differentiated in the position of the placeholder, you should put grouping parentheses around the expression. Here's an example of what can happen if you don't:

In[29]:= **∂_x x^2 +x^3**
Out[29]= 2x + x^3

You certainly don't want to report that the derivative of $x^2 + x^3$ is $2x + x^3$! With parentheses things are fine:

$$In[30] := \partial_x (x^2 + x^3)$$
$$Out[30] = 2x + 3x^2$$

When you first highlight the expression to be differentiated, and then push the palette button, *Mathematica* will add the grouping parentheses automatically.

D can be used to easily derive just about any differentiation rule. You just need to ask it to derive an expression involving "dummy" functions (functions which have been given no specific definition). Here is the product rule, for instance:

```
In[31] := Clear[f,g,x];
          D[f[x] * g[x],x]
```
$$Out[31] = g[x] f'[x] + f[x] g'[x]$$

There are two points to remember about the **D** command. First, it is imperative that the variable (**x** in the example above) be cleared of any value before it is used in the **D** command. Second, if you plan to plot a derivative generated by the **D** command, you need to wrap it in the **Evaluate** command before plotting:

```
In[32] := Plot[Evaluate[{x^2, D[x^2,x]}],{x, -1,1}]
```

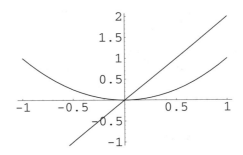

As a general rule of thumb, **D** is useful for differentiating unnamed expressions and for deriving general formulae. For functions to which you have already given names (such as f), the "prime" command **f'[x]** is generally easier to use than **D**.

5.4 Higher Derivatives

```
In[33] := Clear[f,x];
          f[x_] := Sin[πx]
                   ─────────
                       x
```

The easiest way to take a second derivative is to do this:

$In[34]:=$ **f''[x]**

$Out[34]= -\dfrac{2\pi \cos[\pi x]}{x^2} + \dfrac{2\sin[\pi x]}{x^3} - \dfrac{\pi^2 \sin[\pi x]}{x}$

You must use two *single* quotation marks.

Third derivatives?

$In[35]:=$ **f'''[x]**

$Out[35]= \dfrac{6\pi \cos[\pi x]}{x^3} - \dfrac{\pi^3 \cos[\pi x]}{x} - \dfrac{6\sin[\pi x]}{x^4} + \dfrac{3\pi^2 \sin[\pi x]}{x^2}$

Another way to take a third derivative is to use the **D** command as follows:

$In[36]:=$ **D[f[x], {x, 3}]**

$Out[36]= \dfrac{6\pi \cos[\pi x]}{x^3} - \dfrac{\pi^3 \cos[\pi x]}{x} - \dfrac{6\sin[\pi x]}{x^4} + \dfrac{3\pi^2 \sin[\pi x]}{x^2}$

The **D** command is useful for producing general formulae as in the last section. For example, here is the (seldom seen) second-derivative product rule:

$In[37]:=$ **Clear[f,g,x];**
          D[f[x] * g[x], {x,2}]

$Out[37]=$ 2 f'[x]g'[x] + g[x]f''[x] + f[x]g''[x]

5.5   Maxima and Minima

A function can only attain its relative maximum and minimum values at *critical points*, points where its graph has horizontal tangents, or where no tangent line exists (due to a sharp corner in the graph, for instance). For a differentiable function there is a unique tangent line at each point in the domain, so the critical points are all of the first type. To find a value of x for which f has a horizontal tangent, one must set the derivative equal to 0 and solve for x. Having experience with taking derivatives and solving equations with *Mathematica*, this shouldn't be too difficult. In many cases it's not. Here's an example:

$In[38]:=$ **Clear[f,x];**
          f[x_] := x³ - 9x + 5
$In[39]:=$ **Solve[f'[x] == 0,x]**
$Out[39]= \left\{\left\{x \to -\sqrt{3}\right\}, \left\{x \to \sqrt{3}\right\}\right\}$

Recall from Section 4.2 (page 101) that the **Solve** command returns a list of *replacement rules*. Here is how to use that output to get a list of the two critical points, each of the form $\{x, f[x]\}$. These are the points in the plane where the graph of f assumes its extreme values:

```
In[40]:= extrema = {x, f[x]}/.%
Out[40]= {{-√3, 5 + 6 √3}, {√3, 5 - 6 √3}}
```

And here is a plot of f, with the extreme points superimposed as large dots. They will appear as large red dots on a color monitor:

```
In[41]:= Plot[f[x],{x, -4,4},
            Epilog → {PointSize[0.03],Hue[1],
              Map[Point,extrema]}
         ]
```

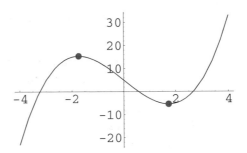

The **Epilog** option can be used with any command that produces graphics, such as **Plot**. It allows you to overlay "graphics primitives," such as points, on the graphic after it has been rendered. In this case, the **PointSize[.03]** makes the points big enough to see (they are each 3% of the width of the graphic), the **Hue[1]** makes them red (on a color monitor), and the **Map[Point,extrema]** produces a list of primitive point objects, one for each point in the list we named **extrema**. Here's what that list looks like:

```
In[42]:= Map[Point,extrema]
Out[42]= {Point[{-√3, 5 + 6√3}], Point[{√3, 5 - 6√3}]}
```

⚠ The **Map** command provides a means for applying a command to each of several arguments in a list. For instance the command **Map[f,{1,2,3}]** would produce the list {f[1],f[2],f[3]}. For more information, type **Map** in a notebook, then go to the **Help** menu and choose **Find in Help...** (version 3 of *Mathematica*), or **Find Selected Function...** (version 4 of *Mathematica*).

In any event, that little bit of technical typing produces a satisfying plot, and allows you to verify visually that the points you found using the **Solve** command are really the extrema you sought.

We can confirm that an extreme point is a maximum or a minimum by using the second derivative:

In[43]:= **f''$\left[-\sqrt{3}\right]$ < 0**

Out[43]= True

The function is concave down at $x = -\sqrt{3}$ and so has a maximum at $x = -\sqrt{3}$. Similarly, the second derivative confirms that f has a minimum at $x = \sqrt{3}$:

In[44]:= **f''$\left[\sqrt{3}\right]$ > 0**

Out[44]= True

Returning to the task at hand, the strategy that we followed above will fail precisely when the **Solve** (or **NSolve**) command is unable to solve the equation $f'(x) = 0$, typically when f is something other than a polynomial of low degree:

In[45]:= **f[x_] := $\dfrac{\text{Sin}[\pi x]}{x}$**

In[46]:= **NSolve[f'[x] == 0,x]**

      Solve : tdep :

         The equations appear to involve transcendental
         functions of the variables in an essentially
         non-algebraic way.

Out[46]= NSolve$\left[\dfrac{\pi \text{Cos}[\pi x]}{x} - \dfrac{\text{Sin}[\pi x]}{x^2} == 0, x\right]$

This is a clue that you need to follow an alternate strategy. One approach is to stare hard at the equation $f'(x) = 0$ and see if you can find a solution by hand. Sometimes there is an obvious solution that *Mathematica* will miss (there's an example at the end of this section). Try a few values of x, such as 0 or 1, and see if they work. If the **Solve** (or **NSolve**) command does produce a solution, but warns you that inverse functions were used, work by hand to see if you can find other solutions. Bear in mind that this process of finding extrema cannot be reduced to a single, simple, automated procedure; you have to remain fully engaged at every step. If your efforts in solving $f'(x) = 0$ bear no fruit (as will probably be the case with the example above), don't despair. In such cases we resort to attacking the extreme points one at a time, using **Plot** and **FindRoot**, and settle for approximations to the actual extreme points.

The first step in this strategy is to produce a graph of f. In this example, we'll look at the graph of f between $x = 0$ and $x = 3$. If you are working on an applied problem, there is probably some specified domain. That would be a good choice for your plot:

In[47]:= **Plot[f[x],{x,0,3}]**

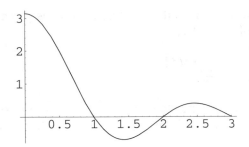

There appears to be a relative minimum near $x = 1.5$. Use that as an initial guess, and let **FindRoot** do the rest:

```
In[48]:= FindRoot[f'[x] == 0,{x,1.5}]
Out[48]= {x → 1.4303}
```

The coordinates of the relative minimum can be easily recovered using replacement rules:

```
In[49]:= minpoint = {x, f[x]}/.%
Out[49]= {1.4303, -0.68246}
```

Note that this is an approximate, rather than an exact solution. This is the best that *Mathematica* can do in such situations. Note also that when you use **FindRoot**, you can almost always get an answer, but you have to settle for one solution at a time. If you need to find six extreme points, you need to run **FindRoot** six times, each with a different initial guess (suggested by a plot).

Here's how to produce a plot with the relative minimum shown. It will appear as a red dot on a color monitor:

```
In[50]:= Plot[f[x],{x,0,3},
          Epilog → {PointSize[0.03],Hue[1],Point[minpoint]}
          ]
```

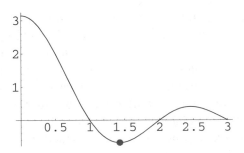

Be mindful that a plot of some sort is important. For although relative extrema for a function f must occur at values of x that satisfy $f'(x) = 0$, satisfying this equation is no guarantee that the point in question is in fact a relative maximum or minimum. This will often happen when the equation $f'(x) = 0$ has repeated roots:

```
In[51]:= f[x_] := 8.01 + 12x - 6x² + x³
```

```
In[52]:= NSolve[f'[x] == 0, x]
Out[52]= {{x→2.}, {x→2.}}
```

```
In[53]:= Plot[f[x], {x,1,3},
            Epilog → {PointSize[0.03], Hue[1], Point[{2, f[2]}]}
            ]
```

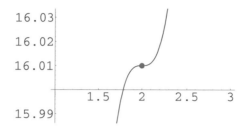

The plot suggests that even though f has a horizontal tangent when $x = 2$, f takes points immediately to the left of 2 to values smaller than $f(2)$, and f takes points immediately to the right of 2 to values greater than $f(2)$. In other words, f has no relative maximum or minimum at $x = 2$. Without a plot (or some careful mathematical reasoning) it is unclear whether a function f has extrema at those values of x satisfying $f'(x) = 0$. Note that the second derivative confirms that the function is neither concave up nor concave down at $x = 2$:

```
In[54]:= f''[2]
Out[54]= 0
```

We end the section with an example of a function f for which *Mathematica*'s **Solve** command cannot produce a real solution for the equation $f'(x) = 0$, but for which an exact solution can be found by hand:

```
In[55]:= f[x_] := Cos[πeˣ]
```

```
In[56]:= f'[x]
Out[56]= -Eˣ π Sin[Eˣ π]
```

```
In[57]:= Solve[f'[x] == 0, x]
        Solve :: ifun : Inverse functions are being used by
            Solve, so some solutions may not be found.
Out[57]= {{x→ -∞}, {x→ -∞}}
```

Now since $e^0 = 1$ and $\sin \pi = 0$, it isn't hard to see that $x = 0$ is a solution to the equation $f'(x) = 0$. A plot will verify this, and will suggest the existence of infinitely many other solutions:

```
In[58]:= Plot[f[x],{x,-3,3},
            Epilog → {PointSize[0.03], Hue[1], Point[{0, f[0]}]}
            ]
```

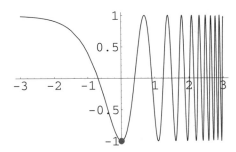

Can you find the other solutions to the equation $f'(x) = 0$ by hand? *Mathematica* can't, but it's really not too hard.

The moral is that you should always try to find solutions by hand, even when the computer cannot. You'll sharpen your skills, and in some instances you will certainly be successful.

5.6   Inflection Points

```
In[59]:= Clear[f,x];
         f[x_] := Sin[πx]
                  ────────
                     x
```

The procedure for finding points of inflection mirrors that for finding relative extrema outlined in the last section, except that second derivatives are used. A glance at the graph of f in the preceding section on page 142, suggests that f has an inflection point near $x = 2$. Let's zero in on it with **FindRoot**:

```
In[60]:= FindRoot[f''[x] == 0,{x,2}]
Out[60]= {x→ 1.89088}
```

```
In[61]:= infpt = {x, f[x]}/.%
Out[61]= {1.89088, -0.177769}
```

```
In[62]:= Plot[f[x], {x,1,3},
            Epilog → {PointSize[0.03],Hue[1],Point[infpt]}
            ]
```

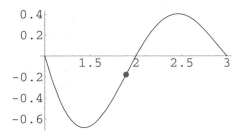

The plot confirms that f has an inflection point at approximately $x = 1.89088$.

You may find it instructive to study the graph of a function and its derivatives on the same set of axes. Here the graph of f is black, while its first two derivatives appear in successively lighter shades of gray (you can replace **GrayLevel** with **Hue** to get a full-color version). Note how the zeros of f' correspond to the relative extrema of f, while the zeros of f'' correspond to the inflection points of f:

```
In[63]:= Plot[{f[x],f'[x],f''[x]},{x,1,3},
            AspectRatio →1.5,
            PlotStyle → {GrayLevel[0],GrayLevel[0.4],
              GrayLevel[0.7]}
            ]
```

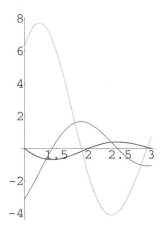

5.7 Implicit Differentiation

For an implicitly defined function described by a simple equation, it is probably easier to work by hand than to use a computer algebra system to differentiate. However, it is satisfying to have *Mathematica* verify your work. For complicated expressions, on the other hand, the computer is good for maintaining your sanity.

To produce plots of implicitly defined functions, see Section 3.7, on page 68.

Here's how to find $\frac{dy}{dx}$ for the implicit equation $\cos(x^2) = \sin(y^2)$. First, rewrite the equation with every nonzero term on the left-hand side, so that it is of the form *expression* $= 0$. In this case we get $\cos(x^2) - \sin(y^2) = 0$. The key to implicit differentiation is to tell *Mathematica* that y is to be regarded as a function of x. This is accomplished by simply typing **y[x]** in place of **y**. We can now differentiate the expression on the left-hand side with respect to x. For convenience, we name it **lhs**:

```
In[64]:= Clear[x, y];
         lhs = D[Cos[x^2] - Sin[y[x]^2],x]
Out[64]= -2x Sin[x^2] - 2 Cos[y[x]^2]y[x]y'[x]
```

It is important to remember that this derivative is equal to the derivative of 0 (the right-hand side of our implicit equation), which is also 0. We can get an expression for $\frac{dy}{dx}$ by solving this equation:

```
In[65]:= Solve[lhs == 0,y'[x]]
Out[65]= {{y'[x] → - (x Sec[y[x]^2] Sin[x^2]) / y[x] }}
```

In traditional notation we replace $y[x]$ by y, yielding

$$\frac{dy}{dx} = -\frac{x \sec(y^2) \sin(x^2)}{y}$$

In some instances, you may be asked to differentiate an equation such as $\cos(x^2) = \sin(y^2)$ with respect to a third variable, such as t. In this case we assume that each of x and y are functions of t, and type **x[t]** and **y[t]** in place of **x** and **y**, respectively. The differentiation is carried out with respect to t:

```
In[66]:= Clear[x,y,t];
         lhs = D[Cos[x[t]^2] - Sin[y[t]^2],t]
Out[66]= -2 Sin[x[t]^2]x[t]x'[t] - 2Cos[y[t]^2]y[t]y'[t]
```

Since this expression is equal to 0, we can find $\frac{dx}{dt}$ and $\frac{dy}{dt}$ as in the previous example:

```
In[67]:= Solve[lhs == 0, x'[t]]
```
$$Out[67]= \left\{\left\{x'[t] \rightarrow -\frac{Cos[y[t]^2]Csc[x[t]^2]y[t]y'[t]}{x[t]}\right\}\right\}$$

```
In[68]:= Solve[lhs == 0, y'[t]]
```
$$Out[68]= \left\{\left\{y'[t] \rightarrow -\frac{Sec[y[t]^2]Sin[x[t]^2]x[t]x'[t]}{y[t]}\right\}\right\}$$

5.8   Differential Equations

There are many applied situations in which you can observe a relationship between a function and one or more of its derivatives, even when an explicit algebraic formula for the function is unknown. In such situations, it is often possible
to find the algebraic formula for the function in question by solving the *differential equation* that relates the function to its derivative(s). For instance, suppose
there is a function $y(t)$ whose derivative is equal to $\frac{1}{3}$ times $y(t)$ for each value of t.
This sort of situation can exist, for instance, in modeling population growth: the
population at time t is denoted by $y(t)$, and the rate of growth $y'(t)$ is proportional
to the population at time t. As the population gets larger, it grows faster, since
there are more people available to engage in reproduction. What kind of function
is $y(t)$? What is its algebraic formula? You can solve a differential equation such
as this with the **DSolve** command:

```
In[69]:= Clear[y,t];
```
$$DSolve\left[y'[t] == \frac{1}{3}y[t], y[t], t\right]$$
```
Out[69]= {{y[t] → E^{t/3} C[1]}}
```

The **DSolve** command takes three arguments. The first is a differential equation, an equation that includes a derivative. The second is the function whose
algebraic formula you wish to find, and the third is the name of the independent
variable. The second and third arguments appear redundant in an example like
this one, but in more complex situations they are needed to avoid ambiguity. In
any event, you need to use them, always.

The output to **DSolve** is a list of replacement rules, exactly like those produced
by the **Solve** command (see Section 4.2 in the previous chapter for a detailed
description of the **Solve** command and replacement rules). The C[1] in the

output represents a constant. It can be replaced by any number to produce an explicit solution. In applied settings, some other information is usually given that will enable you to find the value of such a constant. For instance, if we use our population growth model, we might have been told that initially, at time $t = 0$, the population was 400. Then we see that $400 = y(0) = e^0 C[1] = C[1]$. Thus we conclude that the algebraic formula for $y(t)$ is $y(t) = 400 e^{t/3}$.

```
In[70]:= y[t] /. %[[1]] /. C[1] → 400
Out[70]= 400 E^{t/3}
```

You can also use **DSolve** by giving a list of equations as the first argument. You can, for instance, put the differential equation *and* an initial condition in the list. This makes life very easy indeed:

```
In[71]:= Clear [y,t];
         DSolve[{ y'[t] == 1/3 y[t], y[0] == 400 }, y[t], t]
Out[71]= {{y[t] → 400 E^{t/3}}}
```

```
In[72]:= Plot[y[t] /. %, {t, 0, 10}]
```

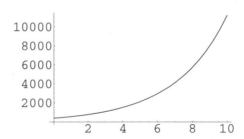

Here's another example:

```
In[73]:= Clear[y,t];
         DSolve[y'[t] == -1/5 y[t] + 100, y[t], t]
Out[73]= {{y[t] → 500 + E^{-t/5} C[1]}}
```

Here we have a family of solutions, with individual solutions determined by the values of the constant $C[1]$. Here is how to plot several solutions for values of $C[1]$ ranging from -500 to 500 in increments of 50:

In[74]:= **sols =**
      Table[y[t]/.%〚1〛/.C[1] → n,{n,-500,500,50}]

Out[74]= $\{500 - 500 E^{-t/5}, 500 - 450 E^{-t/5}, 500 - 400 E^{-t/5},$
      $500 - 350 E^{-t/5}, 500 - 300 E^{-t/5}, 500 - 250 E^{-t/5},$
      $500 - 200 E^{-t/5}, 500 - 150 E^{-t/5}, 500 - 100 E^{-t/5},$
      $500 - 50 E^{-t/5}, 500, 500 + 50 E^{-t/5},$
      $500 + 100 E^{-t/5}, 500 + 150 E^{-t/5}, 500 + 200 E^{-t/5},$
      $500 + 250 E^{-t/5}, 500 + 300 E^{-t/5}, 500 + 350 E^{-t/5},$
      $500 + 400 E^{-t/5}, 500 + 450 E^{-t/5}, 500 + 500 E^{-t/5}\}$

We now have a list consisting of twenty-one functions, each a solution of our differential equation, and each corresponding to a different numerical value of C[1]. Let's plot these functions on the same set of axes. Remember to **Evaluate** lists generated by the **Table** command before plotting:

In[75]:= **Plot[Evaluate[sols], {t, 0, 15}]**

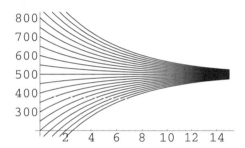

Just as there is the **NSolve** command to complement the **Solve** command, there is the **NDSolve** command to complement the **DSolve** command. Use **NDSolve** in situations where the **DSolve** command is unable to provide an exact algebraic solution (or if **DSolve** seems to be taking all day). Choose **Abort Evaluation** in the **Kernel** menu to get *Mathematica* to stop a computation.

To use **NDSolve**, you need to specify both a differential equation *and* an initial condition in a list for the first argument. The second argument is the function to be solved for, as with **DSolve**. The third argument is an iterator, specifying the name of the independent variable and the range of values it is to assume. As for the output, you will not get an explicit algebraic formula – only **DSolve** can provide that. Rather, you get a nebulous object known as an *interpolating function*. It is a numerical approximation to the true solution of the differential equation on the specified domain. It behaves like an ordinary function in that it can be plotted, and can be used in calculations:

```
In[76]:= sol =
           NDSolve[{y'[t] == 0.05y[t] - 0.0001y[t]², y[0] == 10},
           y[t], {t, 0, 200}]
Out[76]= {{y[t] → InterpolatingFunction[{{0., 200.}}]}
```

```
In[77]:= Plot[y[t]/.sol〚1〛, {t, 0, 200}]
```

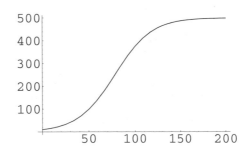

You can also produce a table of values for such a function:

```
In[78]:= Table[{t, y[t]/.sol〚1〛}, {t, 0, 200, 20}]
           // TableForm
Out[78]//TableForm=
```

0	10.
20	26.2797
40	65.5183
60	145.367
80	263.509
100	375.894
120	445.848
140	478.614
160	491.914
180	496.995
200	498.89

5.9 Integration

If you haven't been impressed thus far, this is where *Mathematica* finally pays for itself. Unlike differentiation, which with perseverance can always be completed by hand, integration can be exceedingly difficult. In most cases, however, if a function has an antiderivative, *Mathematica* can find it:

$$In[79]:= \int \frac{1}{1-x^3} \, dx$$

$$Out[79]= \frac{ArcTan\left[\frac{1+2x}{\sqrt{3}}\right]}{\sqrt{3}} - \frac{1}{3}Log[-1+x] + \frac{1}{6}Log[1+x+x^2]$$

The integration button can be found on the **BasicInput** palette. First type a function ($\frac{1}{1-x^3}$ in the example above), then highlight it with your mouse. Now press the $\boxed{\int \blacksquare \, d\square}$ button on the **BasicInput** palette. Your function will be pasted inside the integral at the position of the black square, and the cursor will be at the second placeholder. Here you type the variable with respect to which the integration will be performed (**x** in the example above). Now enter the cell.

If the function you wish to integrate is already on your screen (in either an input or an output cell), highlight it using the mouse, then push the integration button. It will be pasted inside the integral in a new input cell. You then enter the variable with respect to which the integration is to be performed and enter the cell.

Some people find it more natural to use the palette in a slightly different way, *first* pushing the integral button, and *then* typing the function in the position delimited by the first placeholder. This is okay, but be careful. If the expression you want to integrate is a sum, you need to put grouping parentheses around the whole thing. Here's what happens if you don't:

$$In[80]:= \int 1 - x^2 \, dx$$

$$\text{Integrate :: nodiffd : } \int 1 \text{ cannot be interpreted.}$$
$$\text{Integrals are entered in the form } \int f \, dx \text{ where } d \text{ is}$$
$$\text{entered as } \boxed{ESC} dd \boxed{ESC}.$$

$$Out[80]= \int 1 - x^2 \, dx$$

You can probably make sense of this message: *Mathematica* sees the incomplete expression $\int 1$ from which it is supposed to subtract the quantity $x^2 dx$. With the parentheses things work fine:

$$In[81]:= \int (1+x^2) \, dx$$

$$Out[81]= x + \frac{x^3}{3}$$

You can produce the $\int$ symbol without the palette by typing $\boxed{\text{ESCAPE}}$**int**$\boxed{\text{ESCAPE}}$, and you can produce the d symbol by typing $\boxed{\text{ESCAPE}}$**dd**$\boxed{\text{ESCAPE}}$. Alternatively, you can use the **Integrate** command. It does the same thing as the palette button described above; in fact the palette button simply invokes the **Integrate** command:

$In[82]:=$ **Integrate[ArcTan[x], x]**

$Out[82]=$ $\mathrm{x\,ArcTan[x]} - \dfrac{1}{2}\mathrm{Log[1 + x^2]}$

The first argument is the expression you wish to integrate, the second is the variable with respect to which the integration will be performed.

It is important to remember that if a function has one antiderivative, it has infinitely many others. But given one, any other can be obtained by adding a constant to it. *Mathematica* always gives the most simple antiderivative, the one whose constant term is zero.

It is also worth noting that there are numerous "special" functions that cannot be defined in terms of such elementary functions as polynomials, trigonometric functions, inverse trigonometric functions, logarithms, or exponential functions, but that can be described in terms of antiderivatives of such functions. If you use *Mathematica* to integrate a function and see in the output something you've never heard of, chances are that *Mathematica* is expressing the integral in terms of one of these special functions. Here's an example:

$In[83]:=$ $\displaystyle\int$ **Cos[x^2]dx**

$Out[83]=$ $\sqrt{\dfrac{\pi}{2}}\ \mathrm{FresnelC}\Big[\sqrt{\dfrac{2}{\pi}}\mathrm{x}\Big]$

Let's inquire about **FresnelC**:

$In[84]:=$ **?FresnelC**

FresnelC[x] gives the Fresnel integral C[x]=
Integrate[Cos[Pi t^2/2], {t, 0, x}].

Don't be intimidated by such output. It simply says the integral you asked for cannot be expressed in terms of elementary functions. It expresses the answer in terms of another such integral, one so famous that it has its own name (like **FresnelC**).[1]

---

[1] Augustin Fresnel (1788–1827), a French mathematical physicist, studied this and similar integrals extensively in the early nineteenth century. There is a **FresnelS** integral as well; it uses sine in place of cosine.

There is also the possibility that *Mathematica* will evaluate an integral producing an expression that involves complex numbers. Such numbers can be recognized by the presence of the character I in the output, which denotes i, the square root of -1.

$In[85]:= \int (\sqrt{x} + x^3)\, dx$

$$Out[85]= \frac{2}{5} x \sqrt{x + x^3}$$
$$+ \frac{4\, I \sqrt{(-I + x)\,(I + x)}\, \sqrt{x + x^3}\ \text{EllipticE}\left[\text{ArcSin}\left[\frac{\sqrt{-I\,(I + x)}}{\sqrt{2}}\right], 2\right]}{5\sqrt{Ix}\,(1 + x^2)}$$

In this example we also have an appearance by the special function **EllipticE**. What's that?

$In[86]:= $ **?EllipticE**

> EllipticE[m] gives the complete elliptic integral E(m).
> EllipticE[phi,m] gives the elliptic integral of the
> second kind E(phi|m).

If that's not helpful, don't worry about it. Suffice it to say that there is a whole world of advanced mathematics out there, and you've just caught a glimpse of a small piece of it. The point is that integration is difficult by nature. *Mathematica* doesn't know whether or not you hold a Ph.D. in mathematics. It does the best it can. You shouldn't be surprised or discouraged if you occasionally get a bit more back than you expected.

Another possibility when integrating is that *Mathematica* simply won't be able to arrive at an answer. Alas, some integrals are just that way. In such situations, the output will match the input exactly:

$In[87]:= \int \sqrt{\textbf{ArcTan[t]}}\, dt$

$Out[87]= \int \sqrt{\text{ArcTan[t]}}\, dt$

5.10 Definite and Improper Integrals

Computing Definite Integrals

You've probably already found the $\int_{\square}^{\square} \blacksquare\, d\square$ button on the **BasicInput** palette. Use the TAB key to move from one placeholder to the next:

$$In[88]:= \int_{-2}^{2} (1 - x^2)\,dx$$

$$Out[88]= -\frac{4}{3}$$

The same comments made in the last section with regard to grouping parentheses apply here as well; in particular, if you push the palette button *before* typing the expression you wish to integrate, be sure to put grouping parentheses around that expression when you type it. If you prefer typing to palettes, the command you need is **Integrate**. It works as it did in the last section, but the second argument is now an iterator giving the name of the variable and the bounds of integration:

$$In[89]:= \textbf{Integrate}[1 - x^2, \{x, -2, 2\}]$$

$$Out[89]= -\frac{4}{3}$$

Riemann Sums

Mathematica makes the computation of Riemann sums easy with the **Sum** command. **Sum** works very much like **Table**, but rather than producing a list of the specified items, it adds them:

$$In[90]:= \textbf{Sum}[i^2, \{i, 1, 4\}]$$

$$Out[90]= 30$$

This is the same as adding $1 + 4 + 9 + 16$. The advantage of using the **Sum** command for such additions can be seen when you want to add lots of numbers:

$$In[91]:= \textbf{Sum}[i^2, \{i, 1, 100\}]$$

$$Out[91]= 338350$$

There is a palette version of the **Sum** command on the **BasicInput** palette that allows you to employ the traditional summation notation. Use the $\boxed{\sum_{\square=\square}^{\square} \blacksquare}$ button, and then use the TAB key to move from one placeholder to the next:

$$In[92]:= \sum_{i=1}^{100} i^2$$

$$Out[92]= 338350$$

The cells below provide an example of a Riemann sum computation for a function f over the interval from a to b, with n rectangles and f evaluated at the left endpoint of each subinterval. The first cell sets the values of f, a, and b. It needs to be edited every time you move from one example to the next:

```
In[93]:= Clear[f,a,b,n,x,Δx,i];
         f[x_] :=Cos[x];
         a = 0;
         b = 2;
```

The following cell makes use of the values above and defines the appropriate Riemann sum as a function of n. It does not need to be edited as you move from one example to the next:

$$In[94]:= \ \Delta\mathbf{x[n\_]} \ := \frac{b-a}{n};$$

$$\mathbf{x[i\_,n\_]} := a+i*\Delta\mathbf{x[n]};$$

$$\mathbf{leftRsum[n\_]} := \sum_{i=0}^{n-1} \mathbf{f[x[i,n]]} * \Delta\mathbf{x[n]} // \mathbf{N}$$

The function $\Delta\mathbf{x}$ returns the width of an individual rectangle – it is a function of n because its value depends on the number of subintervals between a and b. The function $\mathbf{x}$ returns the right endpoint of the ith subinterval. It is a function of both i and n. Lastly, **leftRsum** returns the Riemann sum for your function between a and b, with the function evaluated at the left endpoint of each subinterval. It is a function of n, for its value depends on the number of rectangles used. Here is the Riemann sum for $\cos(x)$ on the interval $[0, 2]$ with 50 rectangles:

```
In[95]:= leftRsum[50]
Out[95]= 0.937499
```

Note that the values of i in the summation (from 0 to $n - 1$) dictate that f be evaluated at the *left* endpoint of each subinterval. To compute a Riemann sum with f evaluated at the *right* endpoint of each subinterval you can change the bounds of the summation to 1 and n:

$$In[96]:= \ \mathbf{rightRsum[n\_]} := \sum_{i=1}^{n} \mathbf{f[x[i,n]]} * \Delta\mathbf{x[n]} // \mathbf{N}$$

```
In[97]:= rightRsum[50]
Out[97]= 0.880853
```

Either sum can be viewed as an approximation to the definite integral of f over the interval from a to b. It is not hard to modify the process to generate other approximations such as those employing the trapezoidal rule or Simpson's rule. The approximations tend to get better as the value of n increases, as the following table shows:

```
In[98]:= t = Table[{n,rightRsum[n]},{n,50,250,50}];
         TableForm[t,
           TableHeadings → {None,{"n","Riemann sum"}}]
Out[98]//TableForm=
         n     Riemann sum
         50    0.880853
         100   0.895106
         150   0.899843
         200   0.902209
         250   0.903628
```

Curious about the actual value of the integral?

$$In[99]:= \int_0^2 f[x]\,dx\,//\,N$$

```
Out[99]= 0.909297
```

Producing Filled Plots

It is easy to produce a plot of the function you integrate, with the area between the function and the horizontal axis shaded. The shaded area provides a geometric interpretation for the definite integral: the shaded area above the x axis minus the shaded area below it is the value of the integral. You first need to load a package called **FilledPlot**, which is located in the **Graphics** directory. Here's what you need to type to load the package (see Section 2.8 on page 36 if you have problems):

```
In[100]:= Needs["Graphics`FilledPlot`"]
```

Now you can use the command **FilledPlot**. It works just like **Plot**:

```
In[101]:= FilledPlot[1 - x², {x,-2,2}]
```

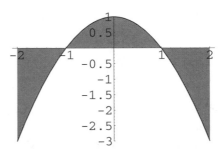

FilledPlot produces a plot exactly as the **Plot** command does, but shades the region(s) bounded above and below by the function and the x axis. You can find the areas of individual regions by integrating over the appropriate intervals:

$In[102]:= \displaystyle\int_{-2}^{-1} (1 - x^2)\, dx$

$Out[102]= -\dfrac{4}{3}$

$In[103]:= \displaystyle\int_{-1}^{1} (1 - x^2)\, dx$

$Out[103]= \dfrac{4}{3}$

$In[104]:= \displaystyle\int_{1}^{2} (1 - x^2)\, dx$

$Out[104]= -\dfrac{4}{3}$

It is worth noting that you will sometimes have to use the **PlotRange** option to **FilledPlot** to see the entire shaded region. This is necessary in those situations where the function lies too far above or below the x axis for both to appear by default in the plot over the entire domain. You can set **PlotRange** to **All**, or to a list of the form {*ymin*, *ymax*}:

$In[105]:=$ **FilledPlot[1-x^2,{x,-1,2}]**

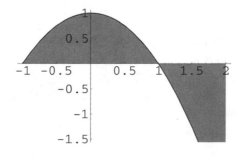

$In[106]:=$ **FilledPlot[1 - x^2, {x, -1, 2}, PlotRange → {-3,1}]**

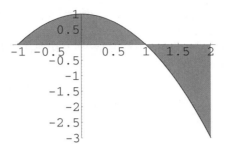

Note that in this plot the two regions have exactly the same area: $\frac{4}{3}$.

FilledPlot can also accept a list of functions for its first argument. In this case it will shade the regions between the functions:

In[107]:= **FilledPlot[{Sin[x],1 - x^2},{x,-2,2}]**

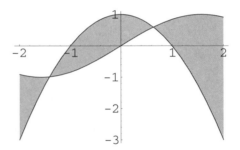

In[108]:= $\int_{-2}^{2} (1 - x^2 - Sin[x]) dx$

Out[108]= $-\dfrac{4}{3}$

You can change the color of the shaded regions using the **Fills** option. On a color monitor, the hues of the various regions will be shaded according to settings you choose. Note that two functions produce one shaded region, while three functions produce two shaded regions, etc. The shaded region between each successive pair of functions in your list will be superimposed over the regions determined by previous pairs of functions:

In[109]:= **FilledPlot[{-1 + x^2, 1 - x^2, Sin[x]}, {x, -2, 2},**
        Fills → {Hue[0.7], Hue[0.1]}]

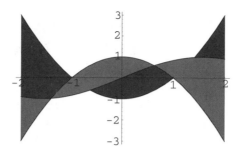

Computing Improper Integrals

Just use ∞ as a bound of integration. You may use the $\boxed{\infty}$ button on the **BasicInput** palette, or type $\boxed{\text{ESCAPE}}\,\textbf{inf}\,\boxed{\text{ESCAPE}}$, or type the word **Infinity**:

$In[110]:=$ $\displaystyle\int_{-\infty}^{\infty} e^{-x^2}\,dx$

$Out[110]=$ $\sqrt{\pi}$

$In[111]:=$ **Integrate$\left[\dfrac{1}{x^3}, \{x, 1, \infty\}\right]$**

$Out[111]=$ $\dfrac{1}{2}$

Of course there is the possibility that an improper integral will fail to converge. *Mathematica* will warn you in such circumstances:

$In[112]:=$ $\displaystyle\int_{1}^{\infty} \dfrac{1}{x}\,dx$

Integrate :: idiv : Integral of $\frac{1}{x}$ does not converge on

$\{1, \infty\}$.

$Out[112]=$ $\displaystyle\int_{1}^{\infty} \dfrac{1}{x}\,dx$

Defining Functions with Integrals

It is possible to define functions by integrating dummy variables:

$In[113]:=$ **a[t_] := -32**

$In[114]:=$ **v[t_] :=** $\displaystyle\int_{0}^{t}$ **a[u] du + 20**

$$In[115]:= \mathbf{h[t\_]} := \int_0^t \mathbf{v[u]} \, \mathbf{du} + \mathbf{4}$$

$$In[116]:= \mathbf{h[t]}$$
$$Out[116]= 4 + 20\,t - 16\,t^2$$

You simply need to remember that **Integrate** always returns the antideriva-tive whose constant term is equal to zero, so constants need to be included in such definitions. The function $v(t)$ above satisfies the condition that $v(0) = 20$, while the function $h(t)$ satisfies $h(0) = 4$. In the example above, $h(t)$ represents the height in feet above ground level of an object after t seconds if it is thrown vertically upward at an initial velocity of 20 feet per second and from an initial height of 4 feet; $v(t)$ is the velocity of the object at time t, and $a(t)$ is the object's acceleration. Air resistance is ignored.

Integrands with Discontinuities

Integrate is often, but not always, able to deal with integrands that have dis-continuities. A common class of examples is provided by rational functions whose denominators have roots between the bounds of integration:

$$In[117]:= \int_{-2}^2 \frac{1}{x^2} \, dx$$

$$Out[117]= \infty$$

$$In[118]:= \mathbf{FilledPlot}\Big[\frac{1}{x^2}, \{x, -2, 2\}, \mathbf{PlotRange} \to \{0, 50\}\Big]$$

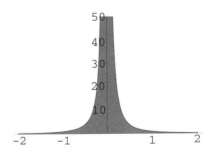

Mathematica is rightly reporting that the shaded area (were it not cut off at $y = 50$) is infinite. But here is another integral whose value is infinite, yet *Mathematica* does not tell us directly:

$In[119]:= \int_2^3 \frac{1}{(x-1)(x-2)} \, dx$

Integrate :: idiv : Integral of $\frac{1}{(-2+x)(-1+x)}$ does not
converge on {2, 3}.

$Out[119]= \int_2^3 \frac{1}{(-2+x)(-1+x)} \, dx$

$In[120]:= \mathbf{FilledPlot}\Big[\frac{1}{(x-1)(x-2)}, \{x, 2, 3\}\Big]$

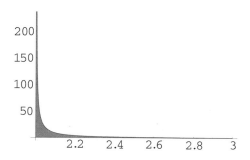

On the basis of *Mathematica*'s output above it is difficult to discern whether the integral converges to a finite number. A plot of an antiderivative confirms that it does not (if it did, the value of integral would be the difference in height between the left and right endpoints on the graph below; but the left endpoint is at $-\infty$):

$In[121]:= \mathbf{Integrate}\Big[\frac{1}{(x-1)(x-2)}, x\Big]$

$Out[121]= \text{Log}[-2+x] - \text{Log}[-1+x]$

$In[122]:= \mathbf{Plot}[\%, \{x, 2, 3\}]$

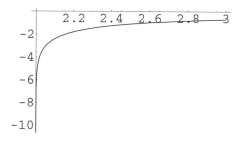

In[123]:= **Limit[%%, x → 2, Direction → -1]**
Out[123]= $-\infty$

Some Integrals Are Bad

And as is the case with indefinite integrals, there are functions for which there is no way to express an antiderivative in closed form, and consequently no way to evaluate the definite integral exactly:

In[124]:= $\int_0^1 \sqrt{\texttt{ArcTan[t]}} \ dt$
Out[124]= $\int_0^1 \sqrt{\mathrm{ArcTan}[t]} \ dt$

Even in cases like this, you will often be able to get numerical approximations:

In[125]:= **N[%]**
Out[125]= 0.629823

The next section explores another way to get numerical approximations to definite integrals.

5.11 Numerical Integration

Mathematica has a numerical integration command, **NIntegrate**, which is often quite effective at providing numerical approximations to the values of definite integrals, even those (indeed, especially those) that the **Integrate** command can't handle:

In[126]:= **Integrate$\left[\sqrt{\texttt{ArcTan[t]}}, \{t, 0, 1\}\right]$**
Out[126]= $\int_0^1 \sqrt{\mathrm{ArcTan}[t]} \ dt$

In[127]:= **NIntegrate$\left[\sqrt{\texttt{ArcTan[t]}}, \{t, 0, 1\}\right]$**
Out[127]= 0.629823

Note that the plot is consistent with this result:

In[128]:= **Needs["Graphics`FilledPlot`"]**

In[129]:= **FilledPlot$\left[\sqrt{\texttt{ArcTan[t]}}, \{t, 0, 1\}\right]$**

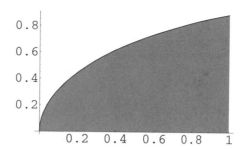

NIntegrate accepts arguments exactly as Integrate does for handling definite integrals. There is no palette version of NIntegrate. It is important to understand that NIntegrate works in an entirely different way from Integrate. Rather than attempt symbolic manipulation, NIntegrate produces a sequence of numerical values for the integrand over the specified interval, and uses these values to produce a numerical estimate for the integral. Although the algorithm used is quite sophisticated, you can think of NIntegrate as producing something analogous to a Riemann sum. The good news is that you now have at your disposal a means for estimating some very messy integrals. The bad news is that NIntegrate can occasionally produce poor estimates. Just as the Plot command can miss features of the graph of a function that are "narrow" relative to the domain over which it is plotted, NIntegrate can miss such features also. Problems arise if points near the narrow feature are not sampled (for a discussion of the Plot command in this context, see Section 3.4 on page 51). Here is an example:

$In[130]:=$ **Plot$\left[e^{-(x-2)^2}, \{x, -5, 5\}, \text{PlotRange} \rightarrow \{0, 1\}\right]$**

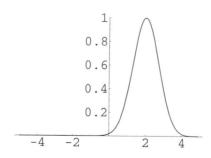

Here is the same function plotted over a much larger domain – so much larger that the bump disappears from view:

$In[131]:=$ **Plot$\left[e^{-(x-2)^2}, \{x, -5000, 5000\}, \text{PlotRange} \rightarrow \{0, 1\}\right]$**

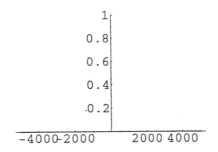

$In[132]:=$ **NIntegrate$\left[e^{-(x-2)^2}, \{x, -5, 5\}\right]$**

$Out[132]=$ 1.77243

When **NIntegrate** is applied to this function over the larger domain, it also misses the bump:

$In[133]:=$ **NIntegrate$\left[e^{-(x-2)^2}, \{x, -5000, 5000\}\right]$**

> NIntegrate :: ploss :
>   Numerical integration stopping due to loss of
>   precision. Achieved neither the requested
>   PrecisionGoal nor AccuracyGoal; suspect highly
>   oscillatory integrand, or the true value of the
>   integral is 0. If your integrand is oscillatory
>   try using the option Method-> Oscillatory in
>   NIntegrate.

$Out[133]=$ $8.50601998124 \times 10^{-619}$

The warning message provides only a hint that something might not be right, yet an incorrect output is generated. This phenomenon can be even worse if the integrand has discontinuities, for in such situations the actual definite integral may not have a real value, yet **NIntegrate** may report one. The following integral, for example, does not converge:

$In[134]:=$ **NIntegrate$\left[\dfrac{1}{(x-2)(x-1)}, \{x, 0, 3\}\right]$**

> NIntegrate :: slwcon :
>   Numerical integration converging too slowly;
>   suspect singularity, value of the integration is 0,
>   oscillatory integrand, or insufficient
>   WorkingPrecision. If your integrand is
>   oscillatory try using the option Method->
>   Oscillatory in NIntegrate.

```
NIntegrate :: ncvb : NIntegrate failed to converge to
    prescribed accuracy after 7 recursive bisections
    in x near x = 0.99609375. `
```
Out[134]= 7.35313

If you know that the integrand has discontinuities in the interval over which you are integrating (vertical asymptotes in the graph are a giveaway), you can instruct **NIntegrate** to look out for them by replacing the iterator {*x*, *xmin*, *xmax* } with {*x*, *xmin*, x_1, x_2, x_3, ..., *xmax* }, where $x_1, x_2, x_3, \ldots$ are the points of discontinuity. Sometimes this won't help, certainly not in those cases when the integral does not have a real value:

In[135]:= **NIntegrate** $\left[\dfrac{1}{(\mathbf{x-1})\,(\mathbf{x-2})}, \{\mathbf{x}, 0, 1, 2, 3\}\right]$

```
NIntegrate :: slwcon :
    Numerical integration converging too slowly;
    suspect singularity, value of the integration
    is 0, oscillatory integrand, or insufficient
    WorkingPrecision. If your integrand is oscillatory
    try using the option Method-> Oscillatory
    in NIntegrate.

NIntegrate :: ncvb : NIntegrate failed to converge to
    prescribed accuracy after 7 recursive bisections
    in x near x = 1.
```
Out[135]= −23950.1

But if the integral has a value, **NIntegrate** will usually produce a very good approximation to it:

In[136]:= **NIntegrate** $\left[\dfrac{1}{\sqrt[4]{(\mathbf{x-1})^2}}, \{\mathbf{x}, 0, 1, 3\}\right]$

Out[136]= 4.82843

In[137]:= **FilledPlot** $\left[\dfrac{1}{\sqrt[4]{(\mathbf{x-1})^2}}, \{\mathbf{x}, 0, 3\}\right]$

One strategy to help you determine if **NIntegrate** is providing an accurate answer is to examine carefully the plot of the integrand. If the numerical value provided by **NIntegrate** appears consistent with the area in the plot, but you still have your doubts, you might try breaking up your integral as a sum of integrals over various disjoint intervals whose union is the interval over which you are integrating. Place short intervals around any discontinuities:

$$In[138]:= \textbf{NIntegrate}\Big[\frac{1}{\sqrt[4]{(x-1)^2}}, \{x, 0, 0.9\}\Big]+$$

$$\textbf{NIntegrate}\Big[\frac{1}{\sqrt[4]{(x-1)^2}}, \{x, 0.9, 1, 1.1\}\Big]+$$

$$\textbf{NIntegrate}\Big[\frac{1}{\sqrt[4]{(x-1)^2}}, \{x, 1.1, 3\}\Big]$$

$$Out[138]= 4.82843$$

Good. This is consistent with the previous output. As usual, it is up to you to test and decide on the efficacy of results produced with the computer.

5.12 Series

There are several powerful commands for dealing with series. The first and most simple is the **Sum** command, discussed earlier in this chapter – the subsection "Riemann Sums" in Section 5.10, see page 154. If you haven't yet used this command (to compute a Riemann sum, for instance), it's not hard. It works like the **Table** command, but rather than creating a list of the specified items, it adds them.

The really amazing thing about this command is that it can accept ∞ as a bound, meaning that it can find the value of an infinite series. You can either type **Infinity** or use the symbol ∞ from the **BasicInput** palette, or type ESCAPE **inf** ESCAPE.

$$In[139]:= \sum_{n=1}^{\infty}\frac{1}{n^2}$$

$$Out[139]= \frac{\pi^2}{6}$$

$$In[140]:= \textbf{N[\%]}$$
$$Out[140]= 1.64493$$

Of course some series fail to converge, and others have solutions that *Mathematica* will not be able to find. Solutions to the latter type can be approximated by summing a large number of terms. Here is a sequence that doesn't converge:

$$In[141]:= \sum_{n=1}^{\infty} \texttt{Cos[n]}$$

Sum :: div : Sum does not converge.

$$Out[141]= \sum_{n=1}^{\infty} \text{Cos[n]}$$

Here is an example of a series involving an independent variable x. Note that the nonpalette version of the **Sum** command is more flexible than its palette counterpart in that the iterator can be adjusted to skip certain terms. Here is the sum $1 + x^2 + x^4 + \cdots$:

```
In[142]:= Clear[x];
          Sum[x^n, {n, 0, ∞, 2}]
```

$$Out[142]= \frac{1}{1 - x^2}$$

In this example *Mathematica* reported a solution, but did not specify which values of the independent variable x are acceptable. In particular, note that if $x = \pm 1$ the denominator will be zero, and the solution makes no sense. *Mathematica* reports the solution you most probably need in such situations, but it is up to you to determine the *region of convergence*, those values of the independent variable for which the solution is valid. In the example above, x must fall between -1 and 1 for the solution to be valid.

The *Mathematica* command that more or less undoes what the **Sum** command does is the **Series** command. Here are the first few terms (those with degree not exceeding five) of the Taylor series expansion of $1/(1 - x^2)$:

$$In[143]:= \texttt{Series}\left[\frac{1}{1 - x^2}, \{x, 0, 5\}\right]$$

$$Out[143]= 1 + x^2 + x^4 + O[x]^6$$

The **Series** command requires two arguments. The first is the function for which you wish to find a power series expansion. The second is a special iterator, one whose form is {*variable*, x_0, *power*}, where *variable* names the independent variable, x_0 is the point about which the series is produced, and *power* specifies the highest power of the variable to be included in the output. The output includes a *big O* term, indicating that there are more terms in the series than those being shown. To get rid of the big O term, use the **Normal** command:

```
In[144]:= Normal[%]
```

$$Out[144]= 1 + x^2 + x^4$$

You can produce a plot of the power series and the function. Note that the series provides a good approximation to the function when x is near x_0 ($x_0 = 0$ in this example):

$$In[145]:= \text{Plot}\left[\left\{\text{\%}, \frac{1}{1-x^2}\right\}, \{x, -1, 1\}\right]$$

Note that you can get the formula for a Taylor series expansion for an arbitrary function (such as f) about an arbitrary point (such as a). Here are the first four terms of such a series:

$$In[146]:= \text{Clear[a, f];}$$
$$\text{Normal[Series[f[x], \{x, a, 3\}]]}$$

$$Out[146]= \text{f[a]} + (-a + x)\ \text{f'[a]} + \frac{1}{2}(-a+x)^2\ \text{f''[a]} + \frac{1}{6}(-a+x)^3\ f^{(3)}\text{[a]}$$

In fact it is a simple matter to design a custom command for generating Taylor polynomials of degree n for the function f about the point x_0:

$$In[147]:= \text{taylor[f\_, \{x\_, x0\_\}, n\_] :=}$$
$$\text{Normal[Series[f[x], \{x, x0, n\}]]}$$

For example, we can now easily compute the eleventh-degree Taylor polynomial for the sine function, expanded around the point $x = 0$:

$$In[148]:= \text{taylor[Sin, \{x, 0\}, 11]}$$

$$Out[148]= x - \frac{x^3}{6} + \frac{x^5}{120} - \frac{x^7}{5040} + \frac{x^9}{362880} - \frac{x^{11}}{39916800}$$

Here is another example. The fourth-degree Taylor polynomial for $\cos(x)$, expanded about the point $x = \frac{\pi}{4}$, is given below:

$$In[149]:= \text{taylor}\left[\text{Cos}, \left\{x, \frac{\pi}{4}\right\}, 4\right]$$

$$Out[149]= \frac{1}{\sqrt{2}} - \frac{-\frac{\pi}{4} + x}{\sqrt{2}} - \frac{\left(-\frac{\pi}{4} + x\right)^2}{2\sqrt{2}} + \frac{\left(-\frac{\pi}{4} + x\right)^3}{6\sqrt{2}} + \frac{\left(-\frac{\pi}{4} + x\right)^4}{24\sqrt{2}}$$

And here is a list of the first six Taylor polynomials for $\cos(x)$, again expanded about the point $x = \frac{\pi}{4}$:

$In[150]:=$ `Table`$\left[\text{taylor}\left[\text{Cos}, \left\{x, \frac{\pi}{4}\right\}, n\right], \{n, 6\}\right]$`//TableForm`

$Out[150] // TableForm =$

$$\frac{1}{\sqrt{2}} - \frac{-\frac{\pi}{4} + x}{\sqrt{2}}$$

$$\frac{1}{\sqrt{2}} - \frac{-\frac{\pi}{4} + x}{\sqrt{2}} - \frac{\left(-\frac{\pi}{4} + x\right)^2}{2\sqrt{2}}$$

$$\frac{1}{\sqrt{2}} - \frac{-\frac{\pi}{4} + x}{\sqrt{2}} - \frac{\left(-\frac{\pi}{4} + x\right)^2}{2\sqrt{2}} + \frac{\left(-\frac{\pi}{4} + x\right)^3}{6\sqrt{2}}$$

$$\frac{1}{\sqrt{2}} - \frac{-\frac{\pi}{4} + x}{\sqrt{2}} - \frac{\left(-\frac{\pi}{4} + x\right)^2}{2\sqrt{2}} + \frac{\left(-\frac{\pi}{4} + x\right)^3}{6\sqrt{2}} + \frac{\left(-\frac{\pi}{4} + x\right)^4}{24\sqrt{2}}$$

$$\frac{1}{\sqrt{2}} - \frac{-\frac{\pi}{4} + x}{\sqrt{2}} - \frac{\left(-\frac{\pi}{4} + x\right)^2}{2\sqrt{2}} + \frac{\left(-\frac{\pi}{4} + x\right)^3}{6\sqrt{2}} + \frac{\left(-\frac{\pi}{4} + x\right)^4}{24\sqrt{2}} - \frac{\left(-\frac{\pi}{4} + x\right)^5}{120\sqrt{2}}$$

$$\frac{1}{\sqrt{2}} - \frac{-\frac{\pi}{4} + x}{\sqrt{2}} - \frac{\left(-\frac{\pi}{4} + x\right)^2}{2\sqrt{2}} + \frac{\left(-\frac{\pi}{4} + x\right)^3}{6\sqrt{2}} + \frac{\left(-\frac{\pi}{4} + x\right)^4}{24\sqrt{2}} - \frac{\left(-\frac{\pi}{4} + x\right)^5}{120\sqrt{2}} - \frac{\left(-\frac{\pi}{4} + x\right)^6}{720\sqrt{2}}$$

Finally, let's produce a sequence of graphics, one for each of the first twelve Taylor polynomials for the cosine function, expanded about the point $\frac{\pi}{4}$. Each plot will show the cosine function in light gray, with the Taylor polynomial in black, and with the point $(\frac{\pi}{4}, \cos(\frac{\pi}{4})) = (\frac{\pi}{4}, \frac{1}{\sqrt{2}})$ highlighted. The resulting sequence of graphics can be animated (see Section 3.9 on page 77 for information on playing the animation). It's best to advance it frame by frame to see plots of sequentially higher degree Taylor polynomials. The individual frames are displayed below, and should be read from left to right across the rows:

$In[151]:=$ `tList = Table`$\left[\text{taylor}\left[\text{Cos}, \left\{x, \frac{\pi}{4}\right\}, n\right], \{n, 12\}\right]$`;`

$In[152]:=$ `plots=`
```
    Map[
      Plot[{#, Cos[x]}, {x, -2π, 2π},
        PlotRange → {-3, 3},
        PlotStyle → {GrayLevel[0], GrayLevel[0.5]},
          Epilog → { PointSize[0.03], Point[{ π/4, 1/√2 }]}}
      ]&, tList
    ];
```

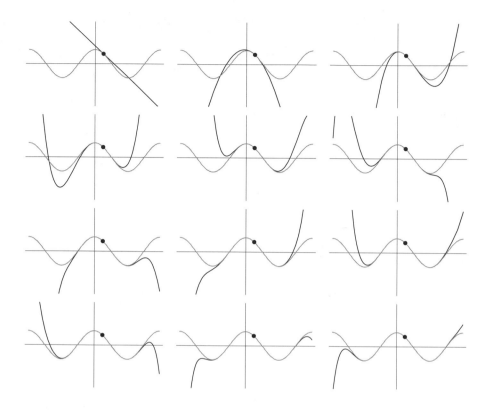

⚠ The symbols **#** and **&** appearing in the last command together constitute an example of something called a *pure function* – a slick way to perform an operation without explicitly defining a new command for it. In this case, each Taylor polynomial in the list **tList** was placed in turn into the position marked **#** in the **Plot** command. For the curious, pure functions are discussed in the first subsection of Section 7.1, see page 234.

Chapter 6

Multivariable Calculus

6.1 Vectors

Vectors and the Dot Product

A standard notation for a vector in the plane is a coordinate pair, such as $(2, 5)$. This represents the vector that has its tail at the origin and its head at the point with x coordinate 2 and y coordinate 5. Another standard notation for this vector is $2\vec{\imath} + 5\vec{\jmath}$. Here $\vec{\imath}$ and $\vec{\jmath}$ denote the unit vectors in the x and y directions, respectively.

In *Mathematica*, a vector in the plane is expressed as a *list* of length two, such as {2, 5}. Vector addition and scalar multiplication work exactly as you would expect:

```
In[1]:= {2, 5} + {17, -4}
Out[1]= {19, 1}
```

```
In[2]:= -4{2, 5}
Out[2]= {-8, -20}
```

```
In[3]:= i = {1, 0};
        j = {0, 1};
        2i + 5j
Out[3]= {2, 5}
```

Higher-dimensional vectors are simply given as longer lists. Here is the sum of two vectors in three-space:

$$In[4]:= \{3, -57, 8\} + \left\{57, -3, \frac{\pi}{4}\right\}$$

$$Out[4]= \left\{60, -60, 8 + \frac{\pi}{4}\right\}$$

The *dot product* of the vectors $(x_1, x_2, \ldots, x_n)$ and $(y_1, y_2, \ldots, y_n)$ is the scalar $x_1 y_1 + x_2 y_2 + \cdots + x_n y_n$. You can compute the dot product of vectors with *Mathematica* by placing a dot (a period) between them:

```
In[5]:= {x₁, y₁}.{x₂, y₂}
Out[5]= x₁ x₂ + y₁ y₂
```

You can calculate the magnitude (i.e., the length) of a vector $\vec{v}$ by taking the square root of the dot product $\vec{v} \cdot \vec{v}$. This is really just a way of applying the distance formula:

```
In[6]:= √{2, 3}.{2, 3}
Out[6]= √13
```

```
In[7]:= √(2 - 0)² + (3 - 0)²
Out[7]= √13
```

You may find yourself calculating the length of vectors so often that you want to automate the process. Here is a simple command that you can define for this purpose:

```
In[8]:= norm[v_List] := √v.v
```

The underscore followed by **List** directs *Mathematica* to only apply this definition if the argument is a vector, that is, a list:

```
In[9]:= norm[{x₁, x₂}]
Out[9]= √x₁² + x₂²
```

```
In[10]:= norm[{12, -57, 10}]
Out[10]= √3493
```

The dot product can also be employed to find the angle between a pair of vectors. You may recall that the cosine of the angle θ between vectors $\vec{u}$ and $\vec{v}$ is given by the formula:

$$\cos\theta = \frac{\vec{u} \cdot \vec{v}}{\|\vec{u}\|\|\vec{v}\|}$$

where $\|\vec{u}\|$ denotes the magnitude of $\vec{u}$. You can find the angle between vectors (in radians) this way:

```
In[11]:= u = {2, 4};
         v = {9, -13};
         θ = ArcCos[─────u . v─────]
                     norm[u] norm[v]
```
$$Out[11]= ArcCos\left[-\frac{17}{25\sqrt{2}}\right]$$

An approximation of the radian measure of this angle is easily extracted:

```
In[12]:= N [%]
Out[12]= 2.0724
```

Conversion to degrees requires multiplying by the conversion factor $\frac{180}{\pi}$, or dividing by the built-in constant **Degree**:

```
In[13]:= ───%────
         Degree
Out[13]= 118.74
```

Rendering Vectors in the Plane

With just a bit of work you can make nice plots showing vectors, at least in two dimensions. You'll first need to load the package **Graphics`Arrow`**. This makes it easy to render decent-looking arrowheads regardless of the scaling of the axes. Next, create the **vector** command:

```
In[14]:= Needs ["Graphics`Arrow`"]

In[15]:= vector[coords_, tailat_]:=
             Graphics[{Hue[1], Arrow[tailat, coords +tailat]}]
```

To create a graphic of the vector $a\vec{\imath} + b\vec{\jmath}$ with its tail positioned at the point (c, d), you will simply type **vector[{a, b}, {c, d}]**.

And let's add this second definition. After it is entered, the **vector** command will also accept a single point as its argument. When used this way it will produce a vector whose tail is at the origin, and whose head is at the specified point. Since such vectors are common, this second definition will save you from having to type **{0,0}** as the second argument to the **vector** command:

```
In[16]:= vector[coords_]:= vector[coords, {0, 0}]
```

⚠ Note that we are essentially defining *two* commands whose name is **vector**; one accepts a single argument, while the other accepts a pair of arguments. This is legal. In fact, it provides you with a very powerful tool, allowing you to extend the definition of an existing command. It also illustrates why it's such a good idea to use the **Clear** command to get rid of your constructions when you're through with them. For it is possible to inadvertently *extend* (rather than overwrite) an existing definition when you create a new one with the same name.

Here are some examples illustrating the **vector** command. Use **Show** to render the vectors, adding any options you like. Axes will only be included if you add the option **Axes → True**. Here we display the vector $-\vec{\imath} + \vec{\jmath}$ with its tail at the point $(2, 1)$. It will be shown in red on a color monitor:

In[17]:= **Show[vector[{-1, 1}, {2, 1}],**
          Axes → True, PlotRange → {{0, 3}, {0, 3}}]

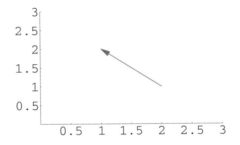

And here are some vectors with their tails at the origin. Be mindful that unless the setting **AspectRatio → Automatic** is included (so that the axes have the same scale), the angles between vectors will be distorted:

In[18]:= **Show[vector[{1, 2}], vector[{2, 1}],**
          Axes → True, PlotRange → {{0, 3}, {0, 3}}]

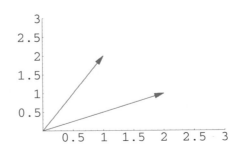

Now let's show the same pair of vectors, but translate the vector (2, 1) so that its tail is shown at the point (1, 2):

```
In[19]:= Show[
           vector[{1, 2}],
           vector[{2, 1}, {1, 2}],
           Axes → True, PlotRange → {{0, 3}, {0, 3}}]
```

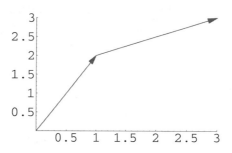

And finally, let's produce a graphic illustrating that the sum of (1, 2) and (2, 1) is (3, 3):

```
In[20]:= Show[
           vector[{1, 2}],
           vector[{2, 1}, {1, 2}],
           vector[{3, 3}],
           Axes → True, PlotRange → {{0, 3}, {0, 3}}]
```

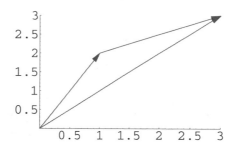

The Cross Product

Imagine a pair of vectors $\vec{u}$ and $\vec{v}$ in three-space drawn so that their tails are placed at the same point. The *cross product* of $\vec{u}$ and $\vec{v}$ is a vector whose direction is orthogonal to the plane spanned by $\vec{u}$ and $\vec{v}$, and whose magnitude is equal to the area of the parallelogram determined by $\vec{u}$ and $\vec{v}$.

You can easily take the cross product of a pair of vectors with the command **Cross**. Here that command is used to give the general formula for the cross product of any two vectors:

$In[21]:=$ **Cross[{u_1, u_2, u_3}, {v_1, v_2, v_3}]**
$Out[21]=$ $\{-u_3\,v_2 + u_2\,v_3,\ u_3\,v_1 - u_1\,v_3,\ -u_2\,v_1 + u_1\,v_2\}$

You can also use the small ⊠ button on the **BasicInput** palette to calculate cross products. It's the button under the i near the middle of the palette. Don't confuse it with the larger ⊠ button to its left; that one is used for ordinary multiplication:

$In[22]:=$ **{1, 3, 5} × {7, 9, 11}**
$Out[22]=$ $\{-12, 24, -12\}$

6.2   Real-Valued Functions of Two or More Variables

Defining a Real-Valued Function of Two or More Variables

You define a real-valued function with two or more variables exactly as you might expect:

$In[23]:=$ **f[x_-, y_-] := Sin[$x^2 - y^2$]**
$In[24]:=$ **g[x_-, y_-, z_-] := $x^2 y^3 - 3x\,z$**

> When defining a function, remember to leave a space (or to place a *) between variables that you intend to multiply, otherwise *Mathematica* will interpret the multiletter combination as a single new variable. For example, note the space between the **x** and the **z** in the definition of **g** above.
>
> One may use multiletter variables when defining a function. A common choice involves the variable names **x1, x2, ...**

You can find the value of a function at any point in its domain by plugging the point into the function:

```
In[25]:= f[1 - π, 1 + π]
Out[25]= Sin[(1 - π)² - (1 + π)²]

In[26]:= Simplify[%]
Out[26]= 0
```

Plotting Functions of Two Variables

The plotting of functions of two variables can be performed with the command **Plot3D**. It works pretty much like **Plot**, but you will need an iterator specifying the span of values assumed by each of *two* variables. The plot will be shown over the rectangle in the plane that is determined by the two iterators. Thus plots produced by **Plot3D** will always have rectangular domains.[1] By default the positive x direction is to the right along the front of the plot, the positive y direction is to the back along the side of the plot, and the positive z direction is up:

```
In[27]:= Plot3D[f[x, y], {x, -2, 2}, {y, -1, 1}]
```

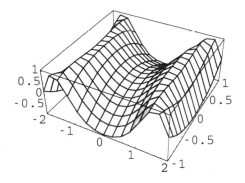

There are a host of options that will allow you to tweak the output of **Plot3D**. A discussion of the various options is contained in the next subsection, beginning on page 183.

---

[1] The graphs of some functions, such as $f(x, y) = x^2 + y^2$, look better when plotted over a circular domain. To plot over a circular domain, use the command **CylindricalPlot3D**, described in the subsection "Cylindrical and Spherical Coordinates" of Section 6.4 on page 213. Its use requires conversion to cylindrical coordinates.

Another commonly used command for visualizing a real-valued function of two variables is **ContourPlot**:

In[28]:= **ContourPlot[f[x,y], {x,-2,2}, {y,-1,1}]**

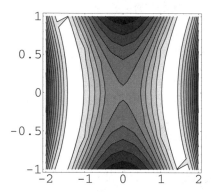

A contour plot is a two-dimensional rendering of a three-dimensional surface. Imagine looking at the surface from above, and placing *contour lines* (also called level curves) on the surface, each one a curve that is level in the sense that its height above (or below) the *x–y* plane is constant. The contour plot is much like a topographical map – it consists of the vertical projections of the contour lines onto the *x–y* plane. By default, **ContourPlot** will produce eleven regions separated by ten contour lines. The function assumes its lowest values (in the specified domain) in the dark regions, and its highest values in the light regions. The height increments between any pair of adjacent contour lines are constant (just as adjacent contour lines on a topographical map indicate equal altitude gains). Thus closely spaced contour lines indicate a steep region of the surface, while wide areas with no contour lines indicate relatively flat regions on the surface.

Options for **ContourPlot** are discussed below.

Three-Dimensional Plotting Tips

Memory Management

Graphics produced with the commands **ContourPlot**, **Plot3D**, and other 3D plotting commands (to be introduced later in the chapter) make significant demands on system resources and take up lots of storage space. This can lead to problems; you might run out of memory and crash *Mathematica* if you generate too many plots in one session, or you might not be able to save a notebook to a floppy disk (because it's too big to fit on one). The solution: delete graphics cells from your notebook when you are done with them. You can keep the input cell that generates a graphic, but get rid of the cell containing the graphic itself, enabling you to re-create the images with little effort. To purge your notebook of *all* output, including graphics, do this: go to the **Kernel** menu and select **Delete All Output**. You will be left with a relatively tiny notebook file consisting of only input, text, and heading cells. You can later reconstitute your notebook by going again to the **Kernel** menu, but now choosing **Evaluate Notebook** from the **Evaluation** submenu.

Options for Contour Plots

Contour plots are two-dimensional renderings of three-dimensional objects, so most of the familiar plotting options that work with the **Plot** command (discussed in Section 3.5, see page 55) will also work with **ContourPlot**. The most common of these are **AspectRatio** and **PlotPoints**. Recall that **AspectRatio** is the ratio of height to width; it is set to 1 by default, producing a square plot. Add the option **AspectRatio → Automatic** to give both axes the same scale. **PlotPoints** is set to 15 by default. Set it to a higher value to reduce the jaggies in a contour plot. *Mathematica* will sample more points when producing the plot, but it will take longer and use more memory to generate the output. It's usually best to bump up the value of **PlotPoints** only after you've produced a jagged plot and know that you need a better one:

In[29]:= **ContourPlot[e^{Sin[xy]}, {x, -2π, 2π}, {y, -π, π}]**

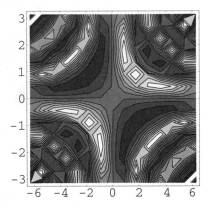

In[30]:= **ContourPlot[e^{Sin[xy]}, {x, -2π, 2π}, {y, -π, π},**
     AspectRatio → Automatic, PlotPoints → 100]

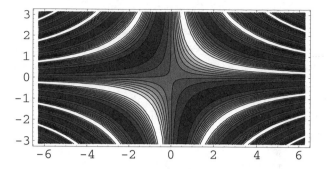

Another option that is sometimes essential and that is shared with **Plot** is **PlotRange**. You can add the option **PlotRange→All** if you suspect that *Mathematica* has "chopped off" an unusually high or low portion of your graph. This can happen if the function you are graphing grows quickly over some portion of the specified domain. In the example below, the upper left and right corners are chopped off; the true graph does *not* level off there as the contour plot suggests:

In[31]:= **ContourPlot[x²eʸ, {x, -3, 3}, {y, 0, 3}, AspectRatio→Automatic]**

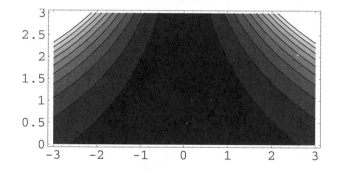

In[32]:= **ContourPlot[x²eʸ, {x, -3, 3}, {y, 0, 3}, AspectRatio→Automatic, PlotRange→All]**

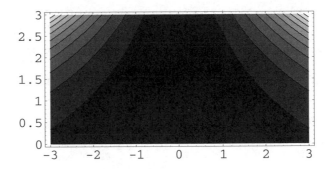

There are several other options that can be used exclusively with **ContourPlot** that will give you control over such things as shading and the number of contour lines. Set **ContourShading → False** to produce an unshaded plot. Set **Contours** to the number of contour lines you wish to have in your plot. Alternatively, set **Contours** to a *list* of of z values; the plot will have contour lines at the specified heights. This is useful for producing a single level curve. For example, the plot below shows the level curve at height 1 for the function $e^{\sin(xy)}$. It is essentially a plot of the curve defined by the implicit equation $e^{\sin(xy)} = 1$:

In[33]:= **ContourPlot[e$^{\text{Sin[xy]}}$, {x, -2π, 2π}, {y, -π, π},**
        AspectRatio → Automatic, PlotPoints → 100,
        ContourShading → False, Contours → {1}]

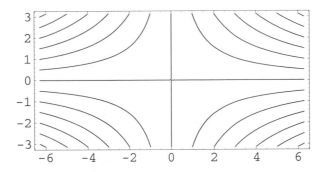

The setting **ContourLines → False** will produce a plot with no contour lines (only use this option when **ContourShading** has not been set to **False** or you'll end up with a blank white box). Adding **ContourStyle → Hue[1]** will produce a plot with red contour lines. You can also use **ContourStyle** to give each individual contour line a different style, although this is tedious if you have many contour lines. The plot below shows the level curves for the function $\sin(x)\cos(y)$ at height -0.5 in gray and at height 0.5 in black. Replace **GrayLevel** with **Hue** to get a full color plot:

```
In[34]:= ContourPlot[Sin[x] Cos[y], {x, -2π, 2π}, {y, -π, π},
            AspectRatio → Automatic, PlotPoints → 100,
            ContourShading → False, Contours → {-0.5, 0.5},
            ContourStyle → {{GrayLevel[0.5]}, {GrayLevel[0]}}]
```

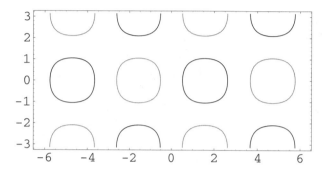

In general, the major disadvantage inherent in a contour plot is that the plot itself provides the viewer no means for determining the values assumed by the function. This is a consequence of squashing three dimensions into two. But with a little work this situation can be rectified – by placing a legend next to the plot that shows the range of values assumed by the function. The package **Graphics`Legend`** provides the command **ShowLegend** for this purpose:

```
In[35]:= Needs["Graphics`Legend`"]
```

```
In[36]:= c = ContourPlot[Cos[x] Sin[y], {x, 0, π}, {y, 0, π},
            PlotPoints → 20, DisplayFunction → Identity];
```

```
In[37]:= ShowLegend[c,
            {GrayLevel[1 - #]&, 11, "1", "-1",
            LegendPosition → {1.1, -0.5}, LegendSize → 1.2}]
```

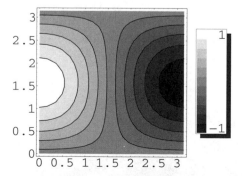

The first argument to **ShowLegend** is the plot. The second argument is a list containing four items and options; it controls the legend. Just copy the setting above, replacing 11 with the number of contour regions in your plot (11 is the default; it's always one more than the number of contour lines), and replacing 1 and −1 with the maximum and minimum values obtained by your function in the specified domain. Of course, you need to know what these values are, and it can be a bit of work to find out – try first making a contour plot to identify the approximate coordinates of the high and low points, then plugging those points into the function to determine the high and low values. The settings for the **LegendPosition** option are discussed in Section 3.8, on page 73. **LegendSize** is set to a scaling factor for the entire legend. It may need to be adjusted to get a good printout. Further details can be had in the Help Browser – push the **Master Index** radio button, then type **ShowLegend** in the text field and follow the link.

⚠ The strange-looking command **GrayLevel[1 - #]&** appearing in the **ShowLegend** command is an example of something called a *pure function*. Pure functions are discussed in the next chapter; see page 234 in Section 7.1.

Options for 3D Plots

The information in this section applies to any plotting command that generates a three-dimensional graphic. Such commands include **Plot3D**, **ContourPlot3D**, **ParametricPlot3D**, **CylindricalPlot3D**, and **SphericalPlot3D**.

Among the options that are the same as the familiar options for **Plot** (as described in Chapter 3, Section 3.5, see page 55) are such common settings as **AxesLabel**, **PlotLabel**, **PlotPoints**, and **PlotRange**. Set **AxesLabel** to a list of three axis names, each appearing in quotation marks; a typical setting is **AxesLabel → {"x","y","z"}**. **PlotLabel** works exactly as before; set it to a name enclosed in quotation marks. **PlotPoints** is set to 15 by default, meaning that the plot will be a patchwork surface composed of $14 \times 14 = 196$ little rectangles. **PlotPoints** often needs to be bumped up to a higher value to produce a satisfactory plot. However, doing so can make significant demands on system resources and can take a bit of time to render. Setting **PlotPoints** to 100 means each of the x and y domains are subdivided into 100 parts, and the resulting $100 \times 100 = 10{,}000$ points are individually plotted. It's usually a good idea to tinker with **PlotPoints** only after you've determined that the default setting is too low, and to increase it gradually. A setting of 40 is usually sufficient to produce an excellent plot:

```
In[38]:= Plot3D[e^Sin[xy], {x, -π, π}, {y, -π, π},
            AxesLabel → {"x ","y ","z "},
            PlotLabel → {"My Favorite Function"},
            PlotPoints → 40]
```

My Favorite Function

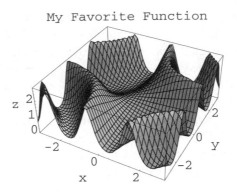

Use the setting **PlotRange → All** when you suspect that *Mathematica* is chopping off the top or bottom of your plot:

$$In[39]:= \textbf{Plot3D}\left[\frac{-x^5\,y^2+x^4\,y}{100}+e^{-(x^2+y^2)}, \{x, -3, 3\}, \{y, -3, 3\},\right.$$
$$\left.\textbf{PlotPoints} \to 30\right]$$

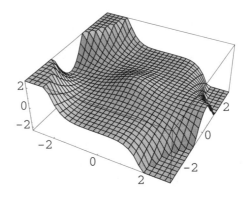

Note the change in scale on the z axis when **PlotRange → All** is added, and the loss of detail near the center of the plot:

$$In[40]:= \textbf{Plot3D}\left[\frac{-x^5\,y^2+x^4\,y}{100}+e^{-(x^2+y^2)}, \{x, -3, 3\}, \{y, -3, 3\},\right.$$
$$\left.\textbf{PlotPoints} \to 30, \textbf{PlotRange} \to \textbf{All}\right]$$

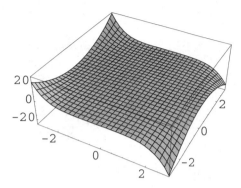

You can resize a plot exactly as before. Click once on the graphic and then use your mouse to drag on one of the corners until the graphic is the desired size.

The option **BoxRatios** determines the relative dimensions of the bounding box; it is analogous to the option **AspectRatio** used in two-dimensional plots. Set **BoxRatios** to a list of three numbers indicating the relative lengths of the x, y, and z dimensions of the graphic's bounding box:

In[41]:= **Plot3D[e$^{\text{Sin[xy]}}$, {x, -2π, 2π}, {y, -π, π},**
    BoxRatios → {1, 1, 0.2}, PlotPoints → 60]

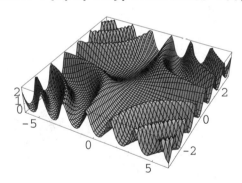

Setting the option **Axes → False** will remove the numbers and tick marks from the three labeled axes, but leave the frame box. Setting the option **Boxed → False** will remove the frame box but leave the three labeled axes. Add both of these settings to remove both box and axes:

In[42]:= **Plot3D$\left[\dfrac{\text{-x}^5\text{ y}^2\text{ +x}^4\text{ y}}{100}\text{ +e}^{-(x^2+y^2)}\text{, {x, -2, 2}, {y, -2, 2},}\right.$**
    PlotPoints → 30, PlotRange → All,
    Axes → False, Boxed → False$\Big]$

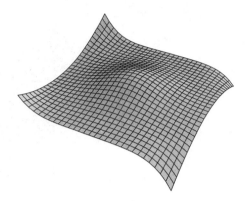

If you add the option **Lighting → False**, the plot will be shaded so that the low regions appear dark and the high regions appear light (this option works only with **Plot3D**, not with other 3D plotting commands such as **ParametricPlot3D**):

$$In[43] := \mathbf{Plot3D}\Big[\frac{-\mathbf{x}^5\,\mathbf{y}^2 + \mathbf{x}^4\,\mathbf{y}}{\mathbf{100}} + \mathbf{e}^{-(\mathbf{x}^2 + \mathbf{y}^2)}, \{\mathbf{x}, -2, 2\}, \{\mathbf{y}, -2, 2\},$$
$$\mathbf{PlotPoints \to 30, PlotRange \to All, Axes \to False,}$$
$$\mathbf{Boxed \to False, Lighting \to False}\Big]$$

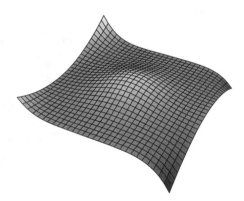

The setting **Mesh → False** will display the graphic sans black mesh lines (again, this works only with **Plot3D**, not with other 3D plotting commands such as **ParametricPlot3D**). It's a good idea to have **PlotPoints** set above its default value of 15 to get a nice smooth image:

$$In[44] := \mathbf{Plot3D}\Big[\frac{-\mathbf{x}^5\,\mathbf{y}^2 + \mathbf{x}^4\,\mathbf{y}}{\mathbf{100}} + \mathbf{e}^{-(\mathbf{x}^2 + \mathbf{y}^2)}, \{\mathbf{x}, -2, 2\}, \{\mathbf{y}, -2, 2\},$$
$$\mathbf{PlotPoints \to 30, PlotRange \to All, Axes \to False,}$$
$$\mathbf{Boxed \to False, Mesh \to False}\Big]$$

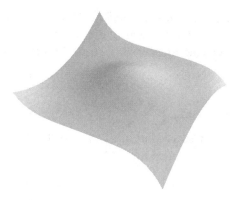

There are a host of other options for the 3D plotting commands. The next section describes how to change the viewpoint. Type and enter **??Plot3D** to see a listing of all of the options (and their default settings) for **Plot3D**. You can then highlight the name of any option, go to the **Help** menu and choose **Find in Help...** (version 3 of *Mathematica*), or **Find Selected Function...** (version 4 of *Mathematica*).

Another Point of View

Another useful option for three-dimensional plotting commands is **ViewPoint**. Set it to a list of three numbers: the coordinates of a point in space from which the graph is to be viewed. In this coordinate system, the origin is at the center of the plot. For instance, if you want to look back at a plot from the positive z direction, add the option **ViewPoint → {0,0,1}**, regardless of the domain of the function:

$$In[45]:= \textbf{Plot3D}\Big[\frac{-x^5\,y^2+x^4\,y}{100}+\mathbb{e}^{-(x^2+y^2)}, \{x,-2,2\}, \{y,-2,2\},$$
$$\textbf{PlotPoints → 30, PlotRange → All,}$$
$$\textbf{ViewPoint → \{0, 0, 1\}}\Big]$$

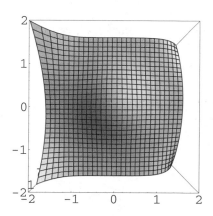

If you choose a point farther out along the same ray from the center of the plot, you will get the same viewing direction, but the perspective will be less severe. This will have the effect of flattening features that protrude in that direction:

$$In[46]:= \texttt{Plot3D}\left[\frac{-x^5\,y^2+x^4\,y}{100}+e^{-(x^2+y^2)}, \{x, -2, 2\}, \{y, -2, 2\},\right.$$
$$\left.\texttt{PlotPoints}\rightarrow 30, \texttt{PlotRange}\rightarrow \texttt{All},\right.$$
$$\left.\texttt{ViewPoint}\rightarrow \{0, 0, 3\}\right]$$

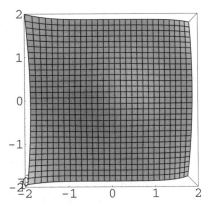

Unfortunately, it is not (yet) possible in *Mathematica* to click and drag on a plot to rotate it in real time. But there is a feature called the **3D ViewPoint Selector** that is almost as good. Using it is somewhat less than intuitive at first, but once you get the hang of it you will use it all the time. You have to try this to appreciate it, so get yourself seated in front of a computer running *Mathematica* and generate your favorite 3D plot.

Now if you have not added a **ViewPoint** option to your plot, click on the input cell and position the cursor exactly where it would have to be to add this option. Type a comma so that the next text you would need to type would be a **ViewPoint** setting. If you already have a **ViewPoint** setting in your input cell, highlight it with your mouse. Now go to the **Input** menu and select **3D ViewPoint Selector...**. A dialog box appears.

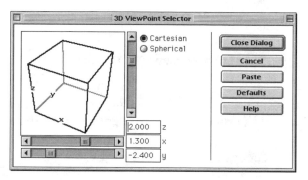

The 3D ViewPoint Selector

Use your mouse to drag on the cube and rotate it to the desired position (or use the sliders, or type numerical values directly in the three text fields). When you are done, push the **Paste** button. The dialog box will vanish, and the appropriate **ViewPoint** setting will be pasted in your input cell at the position of the cursor. You can now enter the cell. If you want to change the **ViewPoint** setting again, first highlight the current **ViewPoint** setting in the input cell, then bring up the **3D ViewPoint Selector** and proceed as above. Repeat as often as you please.

The important thing to remember about the **3D ViewPoint Selector** is that it simply provides a mechanism for pasting a setting for the **ViewPoint** option in an input cell. You *must* position the cursor at the appropriate place in that cell before going to the **3D ViewPoint Selector** and pushing the **Paste** button.

There is a standard package that can generate an animation of a given 3D graphic, making it spin around so you can view it from all sides. It works by generating several plots of the object, each with a different setting for the **ViewPoint** option, then animating the result. Information can be found in the Help Browser by pushing the **Master Index** radio button, typing **SpinShow** in the text field, and following the link that is displayed. An example of the input needed to produce such a sequence of plots is provided below. See Section 3.9 on page 77 for information on playing the movie:

$$In[47]:= \mathbf{myplot = Plot3D}\left[\frac{\mathbf{x * y}}{\mathbf{x^2 + y^2}} + \mathbf{e}^{-(x^2+y^2)}, \{\mathbf{x, -2, 2}\}, \{\mathbf{y, -2, 2}\},$$
$$\mathbf{Boxed \rightarrow False, Axes \rightarrow False}\big]$$

```
In[48]:= Needs["Graphics`Animation`"]
```

```
In[49]:= SpinShow[myplot, Frames → 20]
```

The output will be the frames for a short animation. We display them below –
read across the rows from left to right to follow the animation sequence.

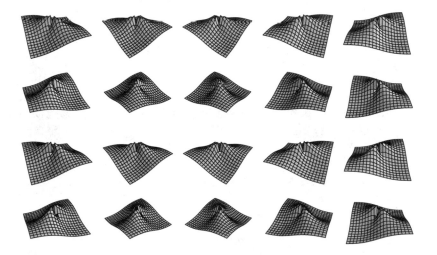

Plotting Level Surfaces and Implicitly Defined Functions

Just as it is possible to render a two-dimensional contour plot of a function of two
variables, it is possible to render a three-dimensional contour plot of a function of
three variables. Instead of level curves, there will be *level surfaces* – surfaces in
space upon which the value of the function is constant. The command **Contour-
Plot3D** is used for constructing a three-dimensional contour plot. To use it, you
must first load the package **Graphics`ContourPlot3D`**:

```
In[50]:= Needs["Graphics`ContourPlot3D`"]
```

By default, **ContourPlot3D** will plot the level surface $f(x, y, z) = 0$ when given
$f(x, y, z)$ as its first argument. The first argument is followed by three iterators
specifying the values to be assumed by x, y, and z, respectively. Here is an example.
We plot the surface described by the equation $xy^2 + yz^2 - zx^2 = 0$:

```
In[51]:= ContourPlot3D[x y² + y z² - z x²,
          {x, -3, 3}, {y, -3, 3}, {z, -3, 3}]
```

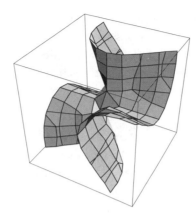

The command **ContourPlot3D** works by subdividing the given region in space into little cubes, then checking to see if a portion of the level surface resides within each of the little cubes. Cubes containing a portion of the surface are then subdivided into still smaller cubes and the process is repeated – the algorithm is *recursive*. You can control this subdividing process with the **PlotPoints** option. By default it is set to the value **{3,5}**, which means that initially three points are sampled in each of the three coordinate directions (so that the region in space is initially subdivided into $(3-1)^3 = 8$ little cubes), and in the next recursive pass, five points are sampled from each little cube that contains a portion of the surface (so each such little cube is divided into $(5-1)^3 = 64$ smaller cubes). To get a better rendering of the surface, try a setting of **PlotPoints → {4,6}** or **PlotPoints → {5,7}**. But beware that these higher settings may require significant amounts of time and memory – don't bump up the **PlotPoints** setting until you've determined that the default setting is too low:

```
In[52]:= ContourPlot3D[x y² + y z² - z x²,
         {x, -3, 3}, {y, -3, 3}, {z, -3, 3},
         PlotPoints → {4, 6}]
```

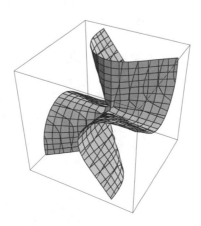

If you want to see the level surface $f(x, y, z) = 3$, add the option **Contours** → **{3}**. If you want to see several level surfaces at once, such as $f(x, y, z) = 1$, $f(x, y, z) = 2$, and $f(x, y, z) = 3$, add the option **Contours→{1,2,3}**. Here are three concentric ellipsoids; each is a level surface of the function $f(x, y, z) = 2x^2 + y^2 + z^2$:

In[53]:= **ContourPlot3D[2x² + y² + z²,**
    {x, -3, 3}, {y, -1, 1}, {z, -1, 1},
    Contours → {1, 2, 3}, PlotPoints → {5, 7}]

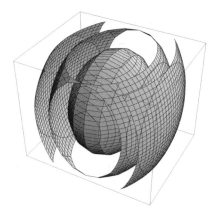

An *implicitly defined* function of two variables is an equation in the variables x, y, and z, for which an explicit algebraic solution of the form $z = f(x, y)$ may not exist. There is no built-in command **ImplicitPlot3D** that plots such functions. However, it is a simple matter to plot implicitly defined functions using **ContourPlot3D**. Given an implicit equation of the form $f(x, y, z) = g(x, y, z)$, you can create a graph by using the expression $f(x, y, z) - g(x, y, z)$ as the first argument to **ContourPlot3D**. This works because the level surface $f(x, y, z) - g(x, y, z) = 0$ is the same as the surface defined by the equation $f(x, y, z) = g(x, y, z)$.

Here is a plot of the surface defined by the equation $x^2 + y^2 = 2 + \sin z$:

In[54]:= **ContourPlot3D[x² + y² - (2 + Sin[z]),**
    {x, -3, 3}, {y, -3, 3}, {z, 0, 2π}]

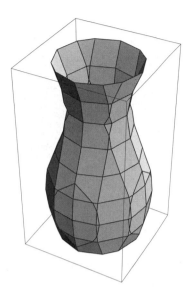

It is a simple matter to automate this process by defining a custom command for plotting implicitly defined functions. Here's how:

```
In[55]:= implicitPlot3D[f_ == g_, args__]:=
             ContourPlot3D[f - g, args]
```

To use **implicitPlot3D**, type the equation for an implicitly defined function as the first argument, followed by iterators for x, y, and z, and by any optional arguments accepted by **ContourPlot3D**. Put *two* underscores after **args** on the left side of the definition; this indicates that **args** stands for a sequence of one *or more* arguments. In this example, **args** represents the three iterators and any optional arguments.

⚠ To find out more about one versus two underscores, go to the Help Browser and type **Blank** (for information on one underscore), or **Blank-Sequence** (for information on two underscores).

Here is a plot of the surface defined by the equation $\cos^2 x + \sin^2 y = 1 + \sin z$:

```
In[56]:= implicitPlot3D[Cos[x]^2 + Sin[y]^2 == 1 + Sin[z],
            {x, 0, 2π}, {y, π/2, 5π/2}, {z, 0, 2π}, PlotPoints → {5, 7}]
```

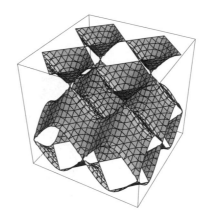

Differentiation of Functions of Two or More Variables

Calculating Partial Derivatives

You can calculate the partial derivatives of a function of two or more variables with the **D** command. This works just as in Chapter 5:

```
In[57]:= Clear[f, x, y];
         f[x_, y_] := Sin[x² - y²]
```

```
In[58]:= D[f[x, y], x]
Out[58]= 2 x Cos[x² - y²]
```

```
In[59]:= D[f[x, y], y]
Out[59]= -2 y Cos[x² - y²]
```

Use replacement rules to evaluate a derivative at a particular point:

$$In[60]:= \%/.\left\{x \to 0, y \to \sqrt{\pi}\right\}$$

$$Out[60]= 2\sqrt{\pi}$$

Alternatively, you can calculate partial derivatives with the palette version of the **D** command by using the $\boxed{\partial_\square \blacksquare}$ button on the **BasicInput** palette. The subscript indicates the variable with respect to which the derivative should be taken. Move from one placeholder to the next with the TAB key:

```
In[61]:= ∂ₓ f[x, y]
Out[61]= 2 x Cos[x² - y²]
```

The best way to use the palette button is first to type and highlight the expression whose partial derivative you desire, and then to push the palette button. If you deviate from this convention by pushing the palette button *first*, then using the TAB key to move to the placeholder where the function is to be entered, be sure to put grouping parentheses around the function so that you don't end up only differentiating the first summand appearing in the function:

```
In[62]:= ∂ₓ x² + x y
Out[62]= 2 x + x y
```

```
In[63]:= ∂ₓ (x² + x y)
Out[63]= 2 x + y
```

To find the second partial $\frac{\partial^2 f}{\partial x^2}$, you can use the **D** command exactly as in Chapter 5:

```
In[64]:= D[f[x, y], {x, 2}]
Out[64]= 2 Cos[x² - y²] - 4 x² Sin[x² - y²]
```

To find the mixed partial $\frac{\partial^2 f}{\partial y \partial x}$, simply do this:

```
In[65]:= D[f[x, y], y, x]
Out[65]= 4 x y Sin[x² - y²]
```

Alternatively, you may use the $\boxed{\partial_{\Box,\,\Box}\blacksquare}$ key on the **BasicInput** palette:

```
In[66]:= ∂ₓ, ₓ f[x, y]
Out[66]= 2 Cos[x² - y²] - 4 x² Sin[x² - y²]
```

```
In[67]:= ∂ᵧ, ₓ f[x, y]
Out[67]= 4 x y Sin[x² - y²]
```

Derivatives higher than the second partials require the **D** command:

```
In[68]:= D[f[x, y], {x, 3}, {y, 4}]
Out[68]= 96 x³ Cos[x² - y²] - 576 x y² Cos[x² - y²] -
         128 x³ y⁴ Cos[x² - y²] + 144 x Sin[x² - y²] +
         384 x³ y² Sin[x² - y²] - 192 x y⁴ Sin[x² - y²]
```

The Gradient

The *gradient* of a function of two or more variables is the vector whose components are the partial derivatives of the function. For instance, in the case of a function

$f(x, y)$ of two variables, the gradient is

$$\nabla f(x, y) = \partial_x f(x, y)\vec{\imath} + \partial_y f(x, y)\vec{\jmath}.$$

There is no built-in command for producing gradients, but if you need to make extensive use of them it is not hard to create your own gradient-generating command:

```
In[69]:= grad[f_,vars_List]:=
            Table[D[f,vars[[i]]],{i,Length[vars]}]
```

This command takes two arguments. The first is the function whose gradient you wish to compute. The second is the list of variables used in defining the function:

```
In[70]:= grad[x^2y^3,{x,y}]
```
$Out[70]= \{2 \, x \, y^3, \ 3 \, x^2 \, y^2\}$

$In[71]:= \text{grad}\left[\dfrac{x_1{}^2 x_2{}^3 x_4{}^4}{x_3{}^5}, \{x_1, x_2, x_3, x_4\}\right]$

$Out[71]= \left\{ \dfrac{2 \, x_1 \, x_2^3 \, x_4^4}{x_3^5}, \ \dfrac{3 \, x_1^2 \, x_2^2 \, x_4^4}{x_3^5}, \ -\dfrac{5 \, x_1^2 \, x_2^3 \, x_4^4}{x_3^6}, \ \dfrac{4 \, x_1^2 \, x_2^3 \, x_4^3}{x_3^5} \right\}$

⚠ It's not too hard to see how the definition for the **grad** command works. The output is a list whose ith member is the partial derivative of f with respect to the ith variable. The **Table** command is used to generate this list, with i assuming values from 1 to however many variables are present.

You can evaluate the gradient at any point using replacement rules:

```
In[72]:= g=grad[x^2y^3,{x,y}]/.{x→2,y→3}
```
$Out[72]= \{108, 108\}$

Below we show the unit vector $\vec{u}$ with its tail at the point $(2, 3)$ that points in the direction of the gradient vector $\vec{g}$, superimposed on a contour plot of $f(x, y) = x^2y^3$ showing the contour at height $f(2, 3)$. This is accomplished using the **vector** command that is defined in the subsection "Rendering Vectors in the Plane" of Section 6.1 on page 173. As long as the axes are given the same scale (the option **AspectRatio→Automatic** guarantees this), the gradient vector will be perpendicular to the level curve. It is in this sense that the gradient points in the direction of steepest ascent:

$In[73]:=$ **u = $\dfrac{\text{g}}{\sqrt{\text{g} \cdot \text{g}}}$**

$Out[73]=$ $\left\{\dfrac{1}{\sqrt{2}}, \dfrac{1}{\sqrt{2}}\right\}$

$In[74]:=$ **v = vector[u, {2, 3}];**

$In[75]:=$ **c = ContourPlot[x²y³, {x, 0, 4}, {y, 1, 5},**
            Contours → {2²3³}, ContourShading → False,
            DisplayFunction → Identity];

$In[76]:=$ **Show[c, v, AspectRatio → Automatic,**
            DisplayFunction → $DisplayFunction]

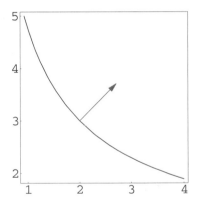

There is a simple means for simultaneously plotting a number of gradient vectors over a rectangular domain (as opposed to just plotting the one at $(2, 3)$ as we did above). See "Plotting a Two-Dimensional Vector Field" in Section 6.5, page 221 for a description of the command **PlotGradientField**.

You can take a *directional derivative* by taking the dot product of the gradient with the unit vector that points in the desired direction. Here is an expression representing the directional derivative of the function $f(x, y) = x^2 y^3$ in the direction of the vector $3\vec{\imath} - \vec{\jmath}$:

$In[77]:=$ **grad[x²y³, {x, y}] . $\dfrac{\{3, -1\}}{\sqrt{\{3, -1\} . \{3, -1\}}}$**

$Out[77]=$ $-\dfrac{3 \, x^2 \, y^2}{\sqrt{10}} + 3 \sqrt{\dfrac{2}{5}} \, x \, y^3$

To evaluate the directional derivative at a particular point, use replacement rules:

$In[78]:=$ **%/.{x→2,y→3}**

$Out[78]=$ $108\sqrt{\dfrac{2}{5}}$

Optimization

The *critical points* of a function are those points where the first partials are zero or do not exist. If the function is to assume a relative maximum or minimum value in the interior of its domain, it can only do so at a critical point.

For simple functions, such as polynomials of low degree, the **Solve** command can find those critical points where the first partials are zero:

$In[79]:=$ **f[x_, y_] := 12 y³ + 4x² - 10x y**

$In[80]:=$ **Solve[{∂ₓ f[x, y] == 0, ∂_y f[x, y] == 0}, {x, y}]**

$Out[80]=$ $\left\{ \{x \to 0, y \to 0\}, \left\{x \to \dfrac{125}{288}, y \to \dfrac{25}{72}\right\}\right\}$

Note that the **Solve** command works just as in Chapter 4, where it was used to solve systems of linear equations (see Section 4.8, page 126) – the first argument is a list of equations to be solved, and the second is a list of variables for which a solution is sought. The output is a list of replacement rules. Each rule gives a value for x and for y that simultaneously satisfies both equations. If you have already defined the gradient command **grad** (see page 196 above) you can also do this:

$In[81]:=$ **Solve[grad[f[x, y], {x, y}] == {0, 0}, {x, y}]**

$Out[81]=$ $\left\{ \{x \to 0, y \to 0\}, \left\{x \to \dfrac{125}{288}, y \to \dfrac{25}{72}\right\}\right\}$

You may be able to determine whether f has a relative maximum or minimum at either of these points in a completely algebraic fashion by examining the *discriminant* and the second partials when evaluated at the critical points. Recall that the discriminant of f is the expression

$$\Delta_f = (\partial_{x,x} f)(\partial_{y,y} f) - (\partial_{x,y} f)^2.$$

The standard test to determine the status of the critical point (x, y) is as follows:

- If $\Delta_f > 0$ and $\partial_{x,x} f > 0$, then (x, y) is a relative minimum.
- If $\Delta_f > 0$ and $\partial_{x,x} f < 0$, then (x, y) is a relative maximum.
- If $\Delta_f < 0$, then (x, y) is a saddle point.
- If $\Delta_f = 0$, then the test is inconclusive.

Let's carry out this test for the point $(x, y) = (\frac{125}{288}, \frac{25}{72})$. We first isolate the replacement rule that corresponds to this point:

```
In[82]:= pt = %[[2]]
```

$$Out[82]= \left\{x \to \frac{125}{288}, y \to \frac{25}{72}\right\}$$

Here is the discriminant, evaluated at this point by applying the replacement rule **pt**. We see that it is positive:

```
In[83]:= (∂x,xf[x, y]) * (∂y,yf[x, y]) - (∂x,yf[x, y])²/.pt
Out[83]= 100
```

Note that the second partial with respect to x is also positive at this critical point:

```
In[84]:= ∂x,xf[x, y]/.pt
Out[84]= 8
```

We conclude that f has a *minimum* at the point $(\frac{125}{288}, \frac{25}{72})$. We can confirm our work with a contour plot. The critical point appears dead center in the plot. Recall that in a contour plot, darker regions are low and lighter regions are high:

```
In[85]:= ContourPlot[f[x, y], {x, 120/288, 130/288}, {y, 24/72, 26/72}]
```

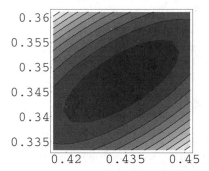

If you are not so lucky as to be working with a function that is a polynomial, the **Solve** command may not be able to find the critical points. The same issues that are discussed in Chapter 4 pertain here. Just as **Solve** can accept a list of equations to be solved simultaneously, so can **NSolve** and **FindRoot**. You may need to invoke these commands when the **Solve** command is unable to find a solution.

Integrating Functions of Two or More Variables

Iterated Integrals

Evaluating iterated integrals is easy. You can use the same old **Integrate** command (from Section 5.9, see page 150) by simply adding another iterator (for definite integrals) or another variable (for indefinite integrals):

$In[86]:=$ **Integrate[$x^2\ y^2$, {y, 1, 3}, {x, 0, 2}]**

$Out[86]=$ $\dfrac{208}{9}$

$In[87]:=$ **Integrate[$x^2\ y^2$, y, x]**

$Out[87]=$ $\dfrac{x^3\ y^3}{9}$

In the examples above, we integrated first with respect to x, then with respect to y; that is, the iterators are given in the same order that the integral *signs* are written in standard mathematical notation. The palette version of **Integrate** makes the order of integration more transparent. First type and highlight the function you wish to integrate, then push the appropriate integration button on the **BasicInput** palette and fill in the placeholders for the *inner* integral, using the TAB key to move from one placeholder to the next. Now highlight the entire expression and push the integration button a second time, fill in the placeholders, and enter:

$In[88]:=$ $\displaystyle\int_1^3 \left(\int_0^2 x^2\ y^2\ dx \right) dy$

$Out[88]=$ $\dfrac{208}{9}$

$In[89]:=$ $\displaystyle\int \left(\int x^2\ y^2\ dx \right) dy$

$Out[89]=$ $\dfrac{x^3\ y^3}{9}$

It is perfectly alright to use as bounds in an inner integral expressions involving variables appearing in an outer integral. For double integrals, this allows integration over nonrectangular regions in the plane. Here we integrate over the region bounded by the circle of radius 2 centered at the origin:

$In[90]:=$ $\displaystyle\int_{-2}^2 \left(\int_{-\sqrt{4-y^2}}^{\sqrt{4-y^2}} x^2\ y^2\ dx \right) dy$

$Out[90]=$ $\dfrac{8\ \pi}{3}$

Here we (attempt to) integrate over the region bounded by the sphere of radius 2 centered at the origin:

$$In[91]:= \int_{-2}^{2} \left(\int_{-\sqrt{4-z^2}}^{\sqrt{4-z^2}} \left(\int_{-\sqrt{4-y^2-z^2}}^{\sqrt{4-y^2-z^2}} x^2\, y^2 z^2\, dx \right) dy \right) dz$$

```
Integrate::gener : Unable to check convergence.
```

$$Out[91]= \frac{2048\,\pi}{945}$$

The warning here is disturbing. A better approach to such an integral, even when using a tool as powerful as *Mathematica*, is to use another coordinate system. See the subsection "Integrating in Other Coordinate Systems" in Section 6.4 on page 219 for details.

6.3   Parametric Curves and Surfaces

Parametric Curves in the Plane

A *parametric* representation of a curve is a *vector-valued* function of one variable; for each input t, the function returns a vector $(x(t), y(t))$ in the plane. You can define a parametric function in *Mathematica* as a list consisting of two real-valued functions. The first represents the x coordinate, and the second represents the y coordinate:

```
In[92]:= s[t_]:={Cos[t] +t, Sin[t]}
```

You can now find your position in the plane for any value of t:

$$In[93]:= s\left[\frac{\pi}{4}\right]$$

$$Out[93]= \left\{ \frac{1}{\sqrt{2}} + \frac{\pi}{4}, \frac{1}{\sqrt{2}} \right\}$$

To plot a parametric function, use the command **ParametricPlot**:

```
In[94]:= ParametricPlot[Evaluate[s[t]], {t, 0, 10π}]
```

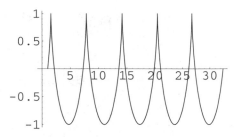

ParametricPlot takes two arguments. The first is the function you wish to plot. Note that if you have previously named this function (ours has the name **s[t]**), you need to wrap it in the **Evaluate** command (for an explanation, see Section 3.8, page 74). The second argument is an iterator for the independent variable (**t** in this example).

You need not restrict yourself to simple functions. You will find that **Parametric Plot** can effortlessly render some very interesting curves:

$$In[95]:= \ \texttt{c[t\_]} := \left\{ \int_0^t \texttt{Sin[u}^2\texttt{]du}, \int_0^t \texttt{Cos[u}^2\texttt{]du} \right\}$$

$$In[96]:= \ \texttt{ParametricPlot[Evaluate[c[t]], \{t, -10, 10\}]}$$

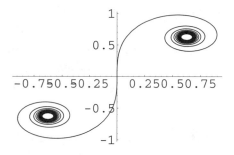

The *derivative* of the parametric function $(x(t), y(t))$ is $(x'(t), y'(t))$. You can differentiate a parametric function just as you did with real-valued functions:

```
In[97]:= D[s[t],t]
Out[97]= {1-Sin[t], Cos[t]}
```

```
In[98]:= s'[t]
Out[98]= {1-Sin[t], Cos[t]}
```

If $\bar{s}(t)$ represents *position* at time t, then the *velocity* vector is $\bar{s}'(t)$, and *speed* is the magnitude of this vector. To compute speed, say at time $t = 3$, you can do this:

```
In[99]:= √s'[3].s'[3]//N
Out[99]= 1.31063
```

If you have defined the **norm** command (as described on page 172), it is even easier:

```
In[100]:= norm[s'[3]]//N
Out[100]= 1.31063
```

You can even get a formula for speed as a function of t:

```
In[101]:= Clear[t];
          norm[s'[t]]// Simplify
Out[101]= √(2-2 Sin[t])
```

If you have the defined the **vector** command (as described in the subsection "Rendering Vectors in the Plane" of Section 6.1 on page 173), you can easily create an animation showing a parametric plot being traced out. This will enable you to see which values of t correspond to which points in the parametric plot – in particular, you will be able to determine the direction in which the curve is traced out as t increases. First create a parametric plot, and give it a name (such as **p**):

```
In[102]:= r[t_] := {t³ +2t - 1, t^(1/3) +1}
```

```
In[103]:= p = ParametricPlot[Evaluate[r[t]], {t, 0, 2}]
```

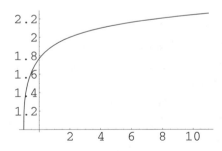

Now use the **Do** command to create the frames of a movie. **Do** works just like **Table** – the first argument is an expression (in this case the graphic-generating **Show** command), the second an iterator that controls how many times the expression is to be evaluated. Since the parametric plot **p** was created with t running from 0 to 2, we do the same here, incrementing t in units of $\frac{1}{2}$:

```
In[104]:= Do[Show[p, vector[r[t]]], {t, 0, 2, 0.5}]
```

Here are the individual frames, shown side by side. The actual output will be a sequence of graphics cells, stacked one on top of the other. To animate them, double click on their grouping bracket, and choose **Animate Selected Graphics** from the **Cell** menu.

Here is another plot of $\vec{r}(t)$ with $0 \le t \le 2$, together with the vector $\vec{r}(1)$ (shown with its tail at the origin) and with the vector $\vec{r}'(1)$ (shown with its tail at the point $\vec{r}(1)$). Note how $\vec{r}'(1)$ is tangent to the curve:

$In[105]:=$ **v = vector[r'[1], r[1]];**
$In[106]:=$ **w = vector[r[1]];**

$In[107]:=$ **Show[p, v, w]**

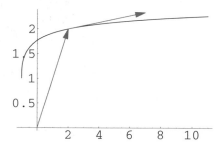

Parametric Curves in Space

Parametric curves in three-space are just like parametric curves in the plane, except that they are constructed as a list of *three* real-valued functions. The first function represents the x coordinate, the second represents the y coordinate, and the third represents the z coordinate:

$$In[108]:= \mathbf{s[t\_]:=\left\{\frac{t^2}{50}Sin[t], \frac{t^2}{50}Cos[t], t\right\}}$$

You can now find your position in three-space for any value of t:

$$In[109]:= \mathbf{s\left[\frac{\pi}{4}\right]}$$
$$Out[109]= \left\{\frac{\pi^2}{800\sqrt{2}}, \frac{\pi^2}{800\sqrt{2}}, \frac{\pi}{4}\right\}$$

To plot a parametric function in space, use the built-in command **Parametric-Plot3D**:

In[110]:= **ParametricPlot3D[Evaluate[s[t]], {t, 0, 8π},**
          AxesLabel → {"x", "y", "z"}]

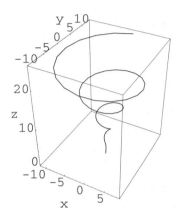

ParametricPlot3D takes two arguments. The first is the function you wish to plot. Note that if you have previously named this function (ours has the name **s[t]**), you need to wrap it in the **Evaluate** command. The second argument is an iterator for the independent variable (**t** in this example). We added the **AxesLabel** option to make it easy to determine which direction is which; note the axes labels on the plot. For more information regarding plot options for three-dimensional plots, see the section in this chapter called **Three-Dimensional Plotting Tips** on page 178.

You can differentiate as with real-valued functions. You have two choices:

In[111]:= **D[s[t], t]**
Out[111]= $\left\{\dfrac{1}{50}t^2\,\text{Cos}[t] + \dfrac{1}{25}t\,\text{Sin}[t], \dfrac{1}{25}t\,\text{Cos}[t] - \dfrac{1}{50}t^2\,\text{Sin}[t], 1\right\}$

In[112]:= **s'[t]**
Out[112]= $\left\{\dfrac{1}{50}t^2\,\text{Cos}[t] + \dfrac{1}{25}t\,\text{Sin}[t], \dfrac{1}{25}t\,\text{Cos}[t] - \dfrac{1}{50}t^2\,\text{Sin}[t], 1\right\}$

If $\vec{s}(t)$ represents *position* at time t, then the *velocity* vector is $\vec{s}'(t)$, and *speed* is the magnitude of this vector. To compute speed, say at time $t = 3$, you can do this:

In[113]:= **√s'[3].s'[3] // N**
Out[113]= 1.02313

If you have defined the **norm** command (as described on page 172), it is even easier:

```
In[114]:= norm[s'[3]]//N
Out[114]= 1.02313
```

You can get a general formula for speed at time t with ease:

```
In[115]:= Clear[t];
          norm[s'[t]]//Simplify
```

$$Out[115]= \frac{1}{50} \sqrt{2500 + 4\,t^2 + t^4}$$

Parametric Surfaces in Space

A surface in space can be parametrized much like a curve in space, but rather than using a single independent variable t, we use a pair of independent variables u and v. Whereas a parametrization of a curve in space is a continuous function from an *interval* of the real line to three-space, a parametrization of a surface is a continuous function from a *rectangle* in the plane to three-space. The image of each coordinate pair (u, v) is a point in space, a 3-tuple. The possibilities for such parametrizations are impressive. *Mathematica* is instrumental in helping to visualize the surfaces that result. The command needed is the same as the one used for visualizing curves in space, **ParametricPlot3D**. The only change is that a second iterator is added to accommodate the second variable. Here is an example:

```
In[116]:= Φ[u_, v_] := {u * v, u, v²}
```

```
In[117]:= ParametricPlot3D[
            Evaluate[Φ[u, v]], {u, -3, 3}, {v, -2, 2}]
```

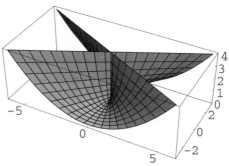

The rectangular region in the u–v plane with $-3 \leq u \leq 3$ and $-2 \leq v \leq 2$ is mapped continuously via Φ to the surface in $\mathbb{R}^3$ shown above.[2] Here's another example; we map a rectangle in the u–v plane to a torus:

```
In[118]:= Φ[u_, v_]:=
            {Cos[u](2+Cos[v]), Sin[u](2+Cos[v]), Sin[v]}
```

```
In[119]:= ParametricPlot3D[
            Evaluate[Φ[u, v]], {u, 0, 2π}, {v, 0, 2π}]
```

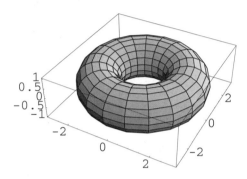

It's often informative to watch the surface render, for as it develops you can "see inside." Simply resize the graphic with your mouse (click once on the graphic, then drag a corner) to replay the construction sequence.

Differentiation works just as with parametrized curves. Here is the partial derivative with respect to v:

```
In[120]:= ∂_v Φ[u, v]
Out[120]= {-Cos[u] Sin[v], -Sin[u] Sin[v], Cos[v]}
```

It is easy to define a command that will generate a *surface of revolution*. If f is a real-valued function of one variable, such as $z = f(x) = \sin(x) - x$, you can produce the surface of revolution obtained by rotating the graph of f about the z axis as follows:

```
In[121]:= surface[f_, u_, v_]:= {v Cos[u], v Sin[u], f[v]}
```

---

[2] This surface is known as the Whitney umbrella. It is named after the American mathematician Hassler Whitney (1907–1989), who studied the connections between algebra and topology (a branch of geometry).

Here's an example with $f(x) = \sin x - x$:

```
In[122]:= f[x_]:= Sin[x] - x;
          ParametricPlot3D[
             Evaluate[surface[f, u, v]], {u, 0, 2π}, {v, 0, 4π}]
```

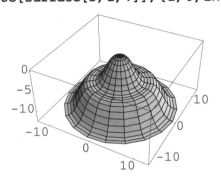

There is also a package that can generate surfaces of revolution, not only about the z axis, but around any axis imaginable. For more information, go to the Help Browser, push the **Master Index** radio button, and start typing **SurfaceOf-Revolution**, then follow the link that appears. The package can be loaded with the command **Needs["Graphics`SurfaceOfRevolution`"]**.

6.4 Other Coordinate Systems

Polar Coordinates

Conversion to and from Cartesian Coordinates

A point in polar coordinates is determined by its distance r from the origin and the angle θ from the positive x axis to the ray running from the origin to the point, measured counterclockwise, in radians.

To convert between polar and Cartesian coordinates you need to know the conversion formulas, and the geometry and trigonometry that goes into them. The formulas can be briefly summarized as follows:

Polar $\to$ Cartesian	Cartesian $\to$ Polar
$x = r \cos \theta$	$r = \sqrt{x^2 + y^2}$
$y = r \sin \theta$	$\theta = \begin{cases} \arctan(\frac{y}{x}) & x > 0 \\ \arctan(\frac{y}{x}) + \pi & x < 0,\ y \geq 0 \\ \arctan(\frac{y}{x}) - \pi & x < 0,\ y < 0 \\ \frac{\pi}{2} & x = 0,\ y > 0 \\ -\frac{\pi}{2} & x = 0,\ y < 0 \end{cases}$

In going from Cartesian to polar coordinates, finding θ is a bit messy – the formulae above will produce a value of θ with $-\pi < \theta \le \pi$. *Mathematica* makes things much easier with its **ArcTan** command. The **ArcTan** command usually takes a single number as its argument, and returns a value between $-\frac{\pi}{2}$ and $\frac{\pi}{2}$, the arc tangent of that number. But you can also feed it an *x–y* pair. **Arc-Tan[x,y]** will return the angle θ for the point (x, y), with $-\pi < \theta \le \pi$. So life is easy: in converting from Cartesian to polar coordinates, $\theta = $ **ArcTan[x,y]**. For instance:

In[123]:= **ArcTan[1, 1]**

Out[123]= $\dfrac{\pi}{4}$

In[124]:= **ArcTan[0, 1]**

Out[124]= $\dfrac{\pi}{2}$

In[125]:= **ArcTan[-1, 1]**

Out[125]= $\dfrac{3\pi}{4}$

In[126]:= **ArcTan[-1, -1]**

Out[126]= $-\dfrac{3\pi}{4}$

It is now a simple matter to automate the conversion process by creating the following commands:

In[127]:= **toPolar[x_, y_]:=** $\left\{ \sqrt{x^2 + y^2} \text{, ArcTan[x, y]} \right\}$**//Simplify**

In[128]:= **toCart[r_, θ_]:= {r * Cos[θ], r * Sin[θ]}//Simplify**

Here are some examples:

In[129]:= **toPolar** $\left[-1, \sqrt{3} \right]$

Out[129]= $\left\{ 2, \dfrac{2\pi}{3} \right\}$

In[130]:= **toCart** $\left[10, \dfrac{\pi}{12} \right]$

Out[130]= $\left\{ \dfrac{5(1+\sqrt{3})}{\sqrt{2}}, \dfrac{5(-1+\sqrt{3})}{\sqrt{2}} \right\}$

Plotting in Polar Coordinates

You have a couple of choices. You can load in the package:

>   *In[131]:=* **Needs["Graphics`Graphics`"]**

and then have access to the command **PolarPlot**, which takes as its first argument the radius r as a function of the angle θ, and as a second argument an iterator for θ. However, it is a simple matter to define a similar command on your own without loading any package. We prefer this approach for two reasons. First, it's high time you started doing this sort of thing – you will need to soon in any event – and this provides a simple example. Second, the **PolarPlot** command in the **Graphics** package produces by default a plot whose axes share the same scale; this can at times result in a graphic that is too short and fat or too tall and thin. Here's how to produce your own **polarPlot** command:

>   *In[132]:=* **polarPlot[r_, {θ_, θmin_, θmax_}, opts___] :=**
>   **ParametricPlot[{r * Cos[θ], r * Sin[θ]},**
>   **{θ, θmin, θmax}, opts]**

This command just tells *Mathematica* to set $x = r \cos\theta$ and $y = r \sin\theta$, and to generate a parametric plot. Be sure to put three underscores after **opts** on the left-hand side of the definition. This will enable you to add any options that can be accepted by **ParametricPlot**.

⚠ Three underscores indicate that the argument **opts** may or may not be present when the command is used, so that **opts** stands for a pattern consisting of zero or more items (separated by commas). For more information, go to the Help Browser and type **BlankNullSequence** in the text field, then follow the link to the *Mathematica* Book.

By default, the command **polarPlot** will produce plots with the same default aspect ratio used by **Plot** and **ParametricPlot**. Add the option **AspectRatio → Automatic** to give both axes the same scale:

>   *In[133]:=* **polarPlot$\left[\dfrac{1}{1 - Sin[θ]}, \left\{θ, \dfrac{-5\pi}{4}, \dfrac{\pi}{4} \right\} \right]$**

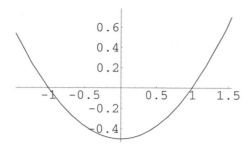

```
In[134]:= polarPlot[θ + Sin[θ²], {θ, 0, 10π},
            AspectRatio → Automatic,
            PlotPoints → 400, Axes → False]
```

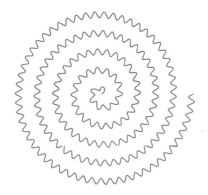

The command **polarPlot** is a simple construction, and as such it is unable to accept (as **Plot** and **ParametricPlot** can) a *list* of functions to be plotted simultaneously. If you need to view several functions at once, add this second definition that will instruct *Mathematica* what to do if you input a list of functions:

```
In[135]:= polarPlot[r_List, {θ_, θmin_, θmax_}, opts___] :=
            ParametricPlot[
                Transpose[{r * Cos[θ], r * Sin[θ]}] // Evaluate,
                {θ, θmin, θmax}, opts]
```

Here's an example. The two curves below meet at the origin:

```
In[136]:= polarPlot[{√θ, -√θ}, {θ, 0, 4π},
            AspectRatio → Automatic, Axes → False]
```

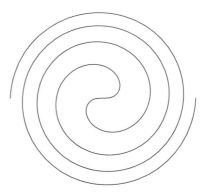

⚠ Note that we have defined *two* different commands, each with the name **polarPlot**. Because the second definition has one of its arguments restricted (to lists), it is the definition that *Mathematica* will attempt to use first. Only when the command is called and that argument is *not* a list will the first definition be used.

Parametric Plotting in Polar Coordinates

There is no built-in command for this, but it's easy to write the command yourself. If r and θ are each functions of the parameter t, then $x = r\cos\theta$ and $y = r\sin\theta$ are also functions of t, and can be plotted using **ParametricPlot**. Here's how we formalize this:

```
In[137]:= polarParametricPlot[{r_, θ_}, args__]:=
            ParametricPlot[{r*Cos[θ], r*Sin[θ]}, args]
```

Put two underscores after **args** on the left side of the definition (two underscores means that **args** represents one or more arguments separated by commas). In this case **args** stands for the required iterator for t *and* any options that might be added.

Here's an example:

```
In[138]:= Clear[r, θ, t];
            r[t_]:= t Sin[t];
            θ[t_]:= e^t
```

```
In[139]:= polarParametricPlot[{r[t], θ[t]}, {t, 0, π},
            AspectRatio→Automatic, Axes→False]
```

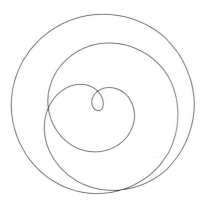

Cylindrical and Spherical Coordinates

Conversion to and from Cartesian Coordinates

When translating from one coordinate system to another it is imperative that you understand the geometry and trigonometry used to generate the conversion formulae. Otherwise you will be placing your faith entirely in the computer, never a good idea. However, it would be nice to be able to automate the process, or to be able to ask *Mathematica* for a conversion formula that you might have forgotten. To automate the translation process, you will need to load a package:

In[140]:= **Needs["Calculus`VectorAnalysis`"]**

Now you will have access to the commands **CoordinatesToCartesian** and **CoordinatesFromCartesian**. Each of these commands takes two arguments. The first is the point whose coordinates you want to translate, and the second is the name of the coordinate system to or from which the translation should occur:

In[141]:= **CoordinatesFromCartesian$\left[\left\{-\sqrt{2},\ \sqrt{2},\ 3\right\},$ Cylindrical$\right]$**

Out[141]= $\left\{2,\ \dfrac{3\,\pi}{4},\ 3\right\}$

In[142]:= **CoordinatesToCartesian$\left[\left\{2,\ \dfrac{3\pi}{4},\ 3\right\},$ Cylindrical$\right]$**

Out[142]= $\left\{-\sqrt{2},\ \sqrt{2},\ 3\right\}$

Working with spherical coordinates in this package demands that you pay careful attention to *Mathematica*'s conventions for this coordinate system. By default, points expressed in spherical coordinates are of the form **{ρ,φ,θ}**, where ρ is the distance of the point from the origin, ϕ is the angle from the vector determined by the point to the positive z axis, and θ is the angle used in polar and cylindrical coordinates. The second and third coordinate positions are transposed in many standard calculus texts, so beware!

In[143]:= **CoordinatesFromCartesian$\left[\left\{-2, 2, 2\sqrt{2}\,\right\}, \text{Spherical}\right]$**

Out[143]= $\left\{4, \dfrac{\pi}{4}, \dfrac{3\,\pi}{4}\right\}$

In[144]:= **CoordinatesToCartesian$\left[\left\{4, \dfrac{\pi}{4}, \dfrac{3\pi}{4}\right\}, \text{Spherical}\right]$**

Out[144]= $\left\{-2, 2, 2\,\sqrt{2}\right\}$

Best of all, you can also use these commands to help you remember the conversion formulas:

In[145]:= **Clear[ρ, ϕ, θ];**
         CoordinatesToCartesian[{ρ, ϕ, θ}, Spherical]

Out[145]= $\{\rho \, \text{Cos}[\theta] \, \text{Sin}[\phi], \rho \, \text{Sin}[\theta] \, \text{Sin}[\phi], \rho \, \text{Cos}[\phi]\}$

In[146]:= **Clear[x, y, z];**
         CoordinatesFromCartesian[{x, y, z}, Spherical]

Out[146]= $\left\{\sqrt{x^2 + y^2 + z^2}, \text{ArcCos}\left[\dfrac{z}{\sqrt{x^2 + y^2 + z^2}}\right], \text{ArcTan}[x, y]\right\}$

If you are not familiar with the **ArcTan[x,y]** notation, see the subsection "Polar Coordinates" at the beginning of this section on page 208.

⚠ It is worth noting that the package **Calculus`VectorAnalysis`** supports more than a dozen coordinate systems. Cartesian, cylindrical, and spherical are simply the most common. For more information, go to the Help Browser, push the **Master Index** radio button, and begin by typing **VectorAnalysis** in the text field. Hit **Go To** to find out more than you ever wanted to know about other coordinate systems.

Plotting a Function of Two Variables in Cylindrical Coordinates

If you wish to plot a function of two variables given in cylindrical coordinates – that is, z is given as a function of the radius r and angle θ – use the command **CylindricalPlot3D**. It works much like **Plot3D**: the first argument is an expression in r and θ, the second and third arguments are iterators for r and θ, respectively. To use this command, you must first load the package

Graphics`ParametricPlot3D`:

In[147]:= **Needs["Graphics`ParametricPlot3D`"]**

In[148]:= **CylindricalPlot3D[θ, {r, 0, 3}, {θ, 0, 2π}]**

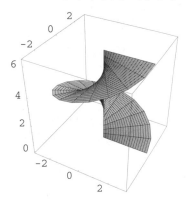

CylindricalPlot3D will produce a plot whose domain is circular (as opposed to the rectangular domains produced by **Plot3D**). This provides a method for plotting any function over a circular domain centered at the origin: translate the expression for the function to polar coordinates, then plot with **Cylindrical-Plot3D**. Here, for example, is the paraboloid given by $f(x, y) = x^2 + y^2$, shown over a circular domain of radius 2:

In[149]:= **CylindricalPlot3D[r², {r, 0, 2}, {θ, 0, 2π},**
    Boxed → False, Axes → False, PlotPoints → 40,
    BoxRatios → {1, 1, 2}]

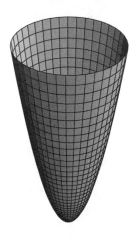

CylindricalPlot3D accepts most of the options that **Plot3D** does. A discussion of these options is in the subsection "Three-Dimensional Plotting Tips" of Section 6.2 on page 178.

Parametric Plotting in Cylindrical Coordinates

If r and θ and z are each parametrized by a variable such as t, you can plot the curve that results from the parametrization with relative ease. Although there is no built-in command for this, you can create the command **parametricCylindricalPlot** as follows:

In[150]:= **parametricCylindricalPlot[{r_, θ_, z_}, args__] :=**
    ParametricPlot3D[{r * Cos[θ], r * Sin[θ], z}, args]

This command simply invokes **ParametricPlot3D** after converting the arguments from cylindrical to Cartesian coordinates. Be sure to put two underscores after **args** on the left-hand side of the defining equation; two underscores mean that **args** stands for a sequence of one or more arguments. Here **args** represents the required iterator for *t and* any options you may add – this will allow you to use any of the options allowed by **ParametricPlot3D**. For more information regarding plot options for three-dimensional plots, see the subsection "Three-Dimensional Plotting Tips" of Section 6.2 on page 178.

Here is an example of a curve that resides along the cylinder whose equation in cylindrical coordinates is $r = 1$:

In[151]:= **parametricCylindricalPlot[**
    {1, t, Cos[20t]}, {t, 0, 2π},
    PlotPoints → 400, Boxed → False, Axes → False]

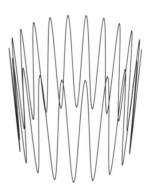

Plotting a Function of Two Variables in Spherical Coordinates

If, in spherical coordinates, ρ is a function of ϕ and θ, you can produce a plot of this function with the command **SphericalPlot3D**. This will enable you to plot some pretty wild surfaces, and to easily make pictures of spheres. You must first load the package **Graphics`ParametricPlot3D`**:

In[152]:= **Needs["Graphics`ParametricPlot3D`"]**

Using **SphericalPlot3D** is much like using **Plot3D** – the first argument is the expression for the radius ρ given in terms of ϕ and θ. The second and third arguments are iterators for ϕ and θ, respectively (note that ϕ, the angle from the positive z axis, comes *first*). Here are two hemispheres, each with the equation $\rho = 2$:

In[153]:= **SphericalPlot3D$\left[2, \left\{\phi, 0, \dfrac{\pi}{2}\right\}, \{\theta, 0, 2\pi\}\right]$**

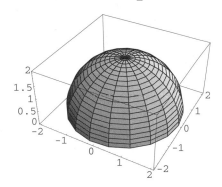

In[154]:= **SphericalPlot3D[2, {ϕ, 0, π}, {θ, 0, π}]**

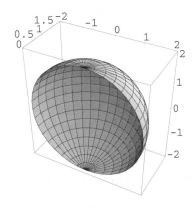

And here is a plot of the surface with the simple equation $\rho = \theta$:

$In[155]:=$ **SphericalPlot3D$\left[\theta, \{\phi, 0, \pi\}, \left\{\theta, 0, \dfrac{7\pi}{2}\right\}, \right.$**

   $\left.\text{Boxed} \rightarrow \text{False}, \text{Axes} \rightarrow \text{False}, \text{PlotPoints} \rightarrow 60\right]$

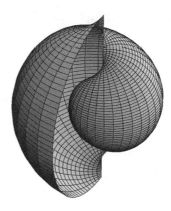

Most of the options that can be used with the command **Plot3D** will also work for **SphericalPlot3D**. A discussion of these options is in the subsection "Three-Dimensional Plotting Tips" of Section 6.2 on page 178.

Parametric Plotting in Spherical Coordinates

If ρ and ϕ and θ are each parametrized by a variable such as t, you can plot the curve that results from the parametrization with relative ease. Although there is no built-in command for this, you can create the command **parametricSphericalPlot** as follows:

$In[156]:=$ **parametricSphericalPlot[$\{\rho_-, \phi_-, \theta_-, \}$, args$_{--}$]$:=$**
   ParametricPlot3D[
      $\{\rho * \text{Sin}[\phi] * \text{Cos}[\theta], \rho * \text{Sin}[\phi] * \text{Sin}[\theta], \rho * \text{Cos}[\phi]\}$,
      args]

This command simply invokes **ParametricPlot3D** after converting the arguments from spherical to Cartesian coordinates. Be sure to put two underscores after **args** on the left-hand side of the defining equation; two underscores mean that **args** stands for a sequence of one or more arguments. Here **args** represents the required iterator for t *and* any options you may add – this will allow you to use any of the options allowed by **ParametricPlot3D**. For more information regarding plot options for three-dimensional plots, see the subsection "Three-Dimensional Plotting Tips" of Section 6.2 on page 178.

Here is an example of a curve that resides along the sphere whose equation in spherical coordinates is $\rho = 1$:

In[157]:= **parametricSphericalPlot[{1, t, 20t}, {t, 0, π},**
          PlotPoints → 400, Boxed → False, Axes → False]

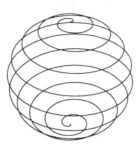

Integrating in Other Coordinate Systems

If you can set up an integral and it has a solution, chances are that *Mathematica* can evaluate it. You need no new *Mathematica* knowledge to switch to other coordinate systems. You do need to know how to convert from one coordinate system to the other, however.

For example, here is the integral of the function $f(x, y) = x^2 y^2$ evaluated over the circle of radius 2 centered at the origin (we evaluated this integral in Cartesian coordinates on page 200 at the end of Section 6.2). We first convert the integrand $x^2 y^2$ to polar coordinates:

In[158]:= **Clear[x, y, r, θ];**
          x^{2}y^2/.{x → r Cos[θ], y → r Sin[θ]}//Simplify
Out[158]= $r^4 Cos[\theta]^2 Sin[\theta]^2$

We can now integrate, replacing $dx\,dy$ with $r\,dr\,d\theta$. Since we are integrating over the circular region of radius 2 centered at the origin, we use $0 \leq r \leq 2$ and $0 \leq \theta \leq 2\pi$ as our bounds of integration:

In[159]:= $\int_0^{2\pi} \left(\int_0^2 \text{ \% r dr} \right) d\theta$

Out[159]= $\dfrac{8\pi}{3}$

And how about the triple integral of the function $x^2 y^2 z^2$ evaluated over the sphere of radius 2 centered at the origin? We attempted this integral in Cartesian coordinates in Section 6.2 on page 201 and got a disturbing warning message. Here we achieve success by converting to spherical coordinates. We first use the conversion formulas to express the integrand as a function of ρ, ϕ, and θ. Now what were those conversion formulas?

```
In[160]:= Needs["Calculus`VectorAnalysis`"]
```

```
In[161]:= Clear[ρ, φ, θ];
          CoordinatesToCartesian[{ρ, φ, θ}, Spherical]
Out[161]= {ρ Cos[θ] Sin[φ], ρ Sin[θ] Sin[φ], ρ Cos[φ]}
```

Here is the converted integrand:

```
In[162]:= x²y²z²/.{x → %[[1]], y → %[[2]], z → %[[3]]}
          //Simplify
Out[162]= ρ⁶ Cos[θ]² Cos[φ]² Sin[θ]² Sin[φ]⁴
```

And now we integrate, replacing $dx\,dy\,dz$ with $\rho^2\sin(\phi)\,d\rho\,d\phi\,d\theta$. Since we wish to integrate over the sphere of radius 2 centered at the origin, we choose as our bounds of integration $0 \le \rho \le 2$, $0 \le \phi \le \pi$, and $0 \le \theta \le 2\pi$. The result agrees with the one we obtained earlier:

```
In[163]:= ∫₀²π (∫₀π (∫₀² % ρ² Sin[φ] dρ) dφ) dθ
Out[163]= 2048π / 945
```

6.5 Vector Fields

Defining a Vector Field

Recall that a parametrized curve is a vector-valued function of one variable, that is, it's a function taking $\mathbb{R} \to \mathbb{R}^2$ or a function taking $\mathbb{R} \to \mathbb{R}^3$. A *vector field* is a vector-valued function of two or more variables. It is a function taking $\mathbb{R}^2 \to \mathbb{R}^2$ or $\mathbb{R}^3 \to \mathbb{R}^3$. You define a two-dimensional vector field exactly as you might expect:

```
In[164]:= Clear[f, x, y];
          f[x_, y_] := {x⁴ + y⁴ - 6x²y² - 1, 4x³y - 4xy³}
```

A three-dimensional vector field has one more variable and produces a vector in three-space:

```
In[165]:= Clear[g, x, y, z];
          g[x_, y_, z_] := {y - z, z - x, x - y}
```

Plotting a Two-Dimensional Vector Field

You will need to load the package **Graphics`PlotField`**:

In[166]:= **Needs["Graphics`PlotField`"]**

You now have access to the command **PlotVectorField**:

In[167]:= **Clear[f, x, y];**
f[x_, y_] := {x⁴ + y⁴ − 6x²y² − 1, 4x y³ − 4x³y}

In[168]:= **PlotVectorField[f[x, y], {x, 0, 3}, {y, 0, 3}]**

The first argument to **PlotVectorField** is the vector field to be plotted (you can type an explicit formula or the name of a previously named field, such as **f[x,y]** above). It is followed by two iterators, one for each of the two variables. Each side of the rectangular domain is subdivided into 15 equal pieces, and at each of the $15 \times 15 = 225$ points of the resulting grid the tail of a vector is placed, the value of the vector field at that point. The lengths of the vectors are scaled so that even the longest vectors will not overlap one another. You can change the number of subdivisions of each side of the rectangle from 15 to any other value using the **PlotPoints** option. Beware that higher settings of this option will slow things down considerably. For simple fields, however, a lower setting may be appropriate. A setting of 10 requires *Mathematica* to only compute $10 \times 10 = 100$ vectors, rather than 225, and so will execute in roughly half the time:

In[169]:= **PlotVectorField[{y, x}, {x, -1, 1}, {y, -1, 1},**
PlotPoints → 10]

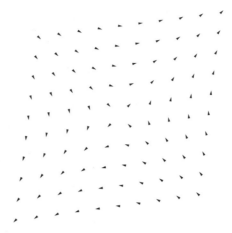

A very similar and sometimes useful command is **PlotGradientField**. It works like **PlotVectorField** except that you use a *real*-valued function of two variables as the first argument. The gradient of such a function is a two-dimensional vector field, the *gradient field* of the function. This gradient field is then plotted. Here is another way to generate the plot for the field f shown earlier, for that field happens to be a gradient field:

$In[170]:=$ **PlotGradientField** $\left[\frac{1}{5}x^5 + x\,y^4 - 2x^3y^2 - 1,\right.$

$\left.\{x, 0, 3\}, \{y, 0, 3\}, \text{PlotPoints} \rightarrow 10\right]$

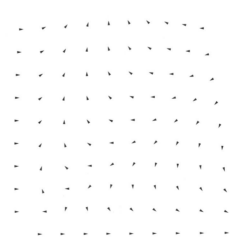

Plotting a Three-Dimensional Vector Field

You will need to load the package **Graphics`PlotField3D`**:

```
In[171]:= Needs["Graphics`PlotField3D`"]
```

You now have access to the command **PlotVectorField3D**. It works very much like **PlotVectorField**:

```
In[172]:= Clear[g, x, y, z];
          g[x_, y_, z_] := {-y, x, 0}
```

```
In[173]:= PlotVectorField3D[g[x, y, z],
            {x, 0, 1}, {y, 0, 1}, {z, 0, 1}]
```

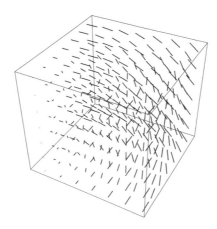

The option **PlotPoints** is set to 7 by default, yielding a total of $7^3 = 343$ vectors in the plot. The arrowheads are left off the vectors, for they tend to make a complicated graphic even more difficult to read. You can put the arrowheads back on by adding the option setting **VectorHeads → True**. Use the **3D ViewPoint Selector** to try several **ViewPoint** settings; this is useful for finding a perspective that clearly reveals a pattern:

```
In[174]:= PlotVectorField3D[g[x, y, z],
            {x, 0, 1}, {y, 0, 1}, {z, 0, 1},
            PlotPoints → 5, VectorHeads → True,
            ViewPoint → {0, 0, 5}]
```

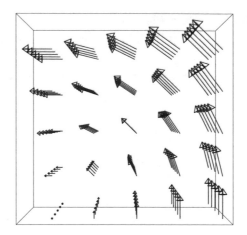

As in the two-dimensional case, there is also a command **PlotGradient-Field3D**. Use as the first argument a real-valued function of three variables to get a plot of that function's gradient field:

In[175]:= **h[x_, y_, z_] := x²y − z**

In[176]:= **field = PlotGradientField3D[h[x, y, z],
        {x, 0, 1}, {y, 0, 1}, {z, 0, 1}, PlotPoints → 4]**

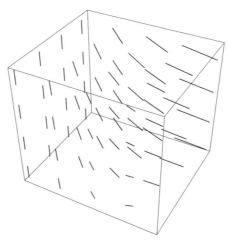

When working with gradient fields, there is a powerful visual aid available to help reconcile the spatial difficulties inherent in 3D vector field plots. You can superimpose a few level surfaces of the function $h(x, y, z)$, and use the fact that the gradient vectors are perpendicular to the level surfaces. It will often make the plot much clearer. Here is an example (see the sub-subsection "Plotting Level Surfaces and Implicitly Defined Functions" in Section 6.2 on page 190 for more information on plotting level surfaces):

```
In[177]:= Needs["Graphics`ContourPlot3D`"]
```

```
In[178]:= surface = ContourPlot3D[h[x, y, z],
            {x, 0, 1}, {y, 0, 1}, {z, 0, 1},
            Contours → {h[0.5, 0.5, 0.2], h[0.5, 0.5, 0.8]},
            PlotPoints → {3, 4}, DisplayFunction → Identity];
```

```
In[179]:= Show[field, surface]
```

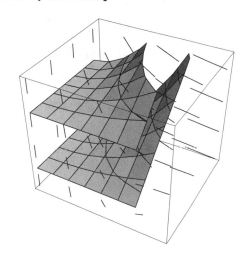

Divergence and Curl of a Three-Dimensional Vector Field

The *divergence* of a three-dimensional vector field $f(x, y, z) = f_1(x, y, z)\vec{\imath} + f_2(x, y, z)\vec{\jmath} + f_3(x, y, z)\vec{k}$ is the scalar function

$$\operatorname{div} f(x, y, z) = \partial_x f_1 + \partial_y f_2 + \partial_z f_3.$$

The *curl* of f is the three-dimensional vector field

$$\operatorname{curl} f(x, y, z) = (\partial_y f_3 - \partial_z f_2)\vec{\imath} + (\partial_z f_1 - \partial_x f_3)\vec{\jmath} + (\partial_x f_2 - \partial_y f_1)\vec{k}.$$

In order to compute divergence and curl with *Mathematica*, you need to load the package **Calculus`VectorAnalysis`**:

In[180]:= **Needs["Calculus`VectorAnalysis`"]**

You now have access to the commands **Div** and **Curl** to find the divergence and curl, respectively, of any three-dimensional vector field.

Div and **Curl** each take two arguments. The first is the vector field, and the second is the coordinate system in which you are working (and the names of the three variables for that system). Typical choices are **Cartesian[x,y,z]**, **Cylindrical[r, θ, z]**, or **Spherical[ρ, ϕ,θ]**:

In[181]:= **Clear[f, x, y, z];**
            f[x_ , y_ , z_] := {x^2 y, z, x y z}

In[182]:= **Div[f[x, y, z], Cartesian[x, y, z]]**
Out[182]= 3 x y

In[183]:= **Curl[f[x, y, z], Cartesian[x, y, z]]**
Out[183]= {-1 + x z, -y z, -x^2}

Here is an example in cylindrical coordinates:

In[184]:= **g[r_ , θ_ , z_] := {r^{2}z, -θ, z}**

In[185]:= **Div[g[r, θ, z], Cylindrical[r, θ, z]]**
Out[185]= $\dfrac{-1 + r + 3\ r^2\ z}{r}$

In[186]:= **Curl[g[r, θ, z], Cylindrical[r, θ, z]]**
Out[186]= $\left\{0,\ r^2,\ -\dfrac{\theta}{r}\right\}$

If you will be doing several computations all in one coordinate system, you can set that coordinate system as the default. This will enable you to use the commands **Div** and **Curl** without the second argument. The default coordinate system is specified with the command **SetCoordinates**:

In[187]:= **SetCoordinates[Cartesian[x, y, z]]**

```
In[188]:= Curl[f[x, y, z]]
```
$Out[188]= \{-1 + x\,z, \ -y\,z, \ -x^2\}$

6.6   Line Integrals and Surface Integrals

Line Integrals

Here is a parametrization of a curve $c(t)$ that joins the point $(-1, -1)$ to the point $(2, 2)$ as t runs from -1 to 2:

```
In[189]:= Clear[c, t, x, y];
          x[t_] := t;
          y[t_] := t³ - t² - t;
          c[t_] := {x[t], y[t]}
```

```
In[190]:= curve = ParametricPlot[Evaluate[c[t]], {t, -1, 2}]
```

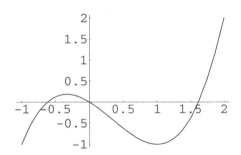

Here is a vector field in the plane:

```
In[191]:= Clear[f];
          f[x_, y_] := {x⁴ + y⁴ - 6x²y² - 1, 4x³y - 4x y³}
```

```
In[192]:= Needs["Graphics`PlotField`"]
```

```
In[193]:= field = PlotVectorField[f[x, y], {x, -1, 2}, {y, -1, 2}]
```

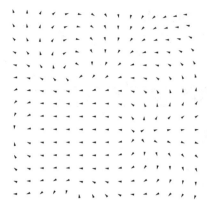

And here is a plot of the curve superimposed on the plot of vector field:

In[194]:= **Show[field, curve]**

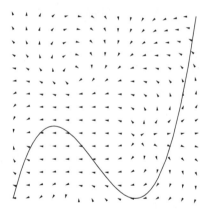

The line integral of the field f along the curve c can be evaluated with ease. Here is the integrand:

In[195]:= **f[x[t],y[t]].c'[t]**
Out[195]= $-1+t^4-6\,t^2\,(-t-t^2+t^3)^2+(-t-t^2+t^3)^4+$
$\qquad (-1-2\,t+3\,t^2)\,(4t^3\,(-t-t^2+t^3)-4t\,(-t-t^2+t^3)^3)$

In[196]:= **Simplify[%]**
Out[196]= $-1-4\,t^4-16\,t^5-12\,t^6+40\,t^7+41\,t^8-64\,t^9-18\,t^{10}+40\,t^{11}-11\,t^{12}$

And here is the line integral:

$$In[197]:= \int_{-1}^{2} \% \, dt$$

$$Out[197]= \frac{54102}{5005}$$

$$In[198]:= \mathbf{N[\%]}$$

$$Out[198]= 10.8096$$

Line integrals in three or more dimensions are just as easy to evaluate. Plots for three-dimensions will require use of the commands **ParametricPlot3D** (for the curve) and **PlotVectorField3D** (for the vector field).

Surface Integrals

Here is a surface:

```
In[199]:= Clear[Φ, u, v, x, y, z];
          x[u_, v_] := (1 - v^2) Sin[u];
          y[u_, v_] := (1 - v^2) Sin[2 u];
          z[u_, v_] := v;
          Φ[u_, v_] := {x[u, v], y[u, v], z[u, v]}

In[200]:= surface = ParametricPlot3D[Evaluate[Φ[u, v]],
          {u, 0, 2π}, {v, -1, 1},
          PlotPoints → 30, ViewPoint -> {0, -2, 2}]
```

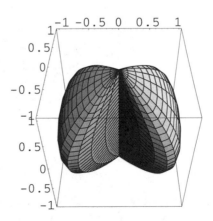

And here is a three-dimensional vector field:

$In[201]:=$ **f[x_, y_, z_] := $\left\{2x, 2y, \dfrac{1}{z}\right\}$**

$In[202]:=$ **Needs["Graphics`PlotField3D`"]**

$In[203]:=$ **field = PlotVectorField3D[f[x, y, z],**
        {x, -1, 1}, {y, -1, 1}, {z, -1, 1},
        PlotPoints → 4, VectorHeads → True]

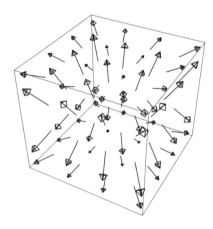

$In[204]:=$ **Show[field, surface]**

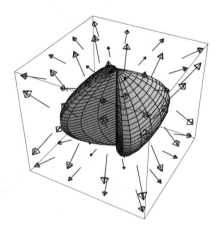

The surface integral can be evaluated with ease. Here is the integrand. Be sure to use the cross product × and not the (larger) multiplication operator × when pulling that symbol off the **BasicInput** palette:

$In[205]:=$ **f[x[u, v], y[u, v], z[u, v]].($\partial_u \Phi$[u, v] × $\partial_v \Phi$[u, v])**

$Out[205]=$ $2(1-v^2)(2\,\mathrm{Cos}[2\,u]-2\,v^2\mathrm{Cos}[2\,u])\,\mathrm{Sin}[u]\,+$
$\qquad 2(1-v^2)(-\mathrm{Cos}[u]+v^2\mathrm{Cos}[u])\,\mathrm{Sin}[2\,u]\,+$
$\qquad \dfrac{1}{v}(4\,v\,\mathrm{Cos}[2\,u]\,\mathrm{Sin}[u]-4v^3\mathrm{Cos}[2\,u]\,\mathrm{Sin}[u]\,-$
$\qquad 2v\,\mathrm{Cos}[u]\,\mathrm{Sin}[2\,u]+2v^3\mathrm{Cos}[u]\,\mathrm{Sin}[2\,u])$

$In[206]:=$ **Simplify[%]**

$Out[206]=$ $-4(2-3\,v^2+v^4)\,\mathrm{Sin}[u]^3$

Now we evaluate the integral:

$In[207]:=$ $\displaystyle \int_{-1}^{1}\left(\int_{0}^{2\pi} \% \, \mathbf{du}\right)\mathbf{dv}$

$Out[207]=$ 0

Chapter 7

Linear Algebra

7.1 Matrices

Entering Matrices

Traditionally, matrices are denoted by capital letters, but in *Mathematica* you will want to use lowercase letters, since capitals are reserved for built-in functions.[1] To enter a matrix in *Mathematica* first type the name of your matrix followed by an equal sign. Then select **Create Table/Matrix/Palette...** in the **Input** menu. A dialogue box will appear.

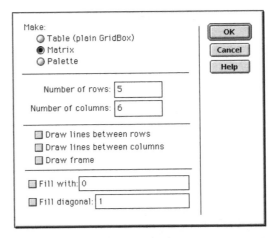

The Create Table/Matrix/Palette... dialogue box

---

[1] If you really can't live in a world where matrices are denoted by lowercase letters, you can use uppercase letters provided you do *not* use those letters that are the names of built-in commands or constants: C, D, E, I, K, N, and O.

Select **Matrix** and enter the correct number of rows and columns, then click **OK**. A matrix of the appropriate dimensions will appear in a fresh input cell with a placeholder for each entry. Click on the first placeholder and type a value, and then use the TAB key to move to the next. Enter the cell when you have finished:

$$
In[1]:= \textbf{mat1} = \begin{pmatrix} 2 & 3 & 4 & 5 & 6 & 7 \\ 1 & 1 & 1 & 1 & 1 & 1 \\ 4 & 5 & 4 & 5 & 4 & 5 \\ 11 & 2 & 2 & 2 & 2 & 2 \\ 0 & 0 & 0 & 0 & 0 & 1 \end{pmatrix}
$$

```
Out[1]= {{2,3,4,5,6,7},{1,1,1,1,1,1},{4,5,4,5,4,5},
          {11,2,2,2,2,2},{0,0,0,0,0,1}}
```

Look carefully at the output above. *Mathematica* thinks of a matrix as a list of lists. Each row is enclosed in curly brackets with entries separated by commas, the rows are separated by commas, and the entire matrix is enclosed in curly brackets. You can enter a matrix in this form also, but it can be a little messy:

```
In[2]:= mat2 = {{1,2,3 },{3,4,5},{5,6,7}}
Out[2]= {{1,2,3},{3,4,5},{5,6,7}}
```

The command **MatrixForm** is used to display matrices. It works much like **TableForm** – feed it a list of lists, and it will produce a nicely formatted rectangular array with brackets on the sides. It is best not to use the **MatrixForm** command when defining a matrix, as it would then be impossible to perform some operations. It is better to simply request that the output be in **MatrixForm** whenever you want a nice look at your matrix:

```
In[3]:= mat2 // MatrixForm
Out[3]//MatrixForm=
```

$$
\begin{pmatrix} 1 & 2 & 3 \\ 3 & 4 & 5 \\ 5 & 6 & 7 \end{pmatrix}
$$

You can request that *Mathematica* output every matrix in **MatrixForm** by typing the following command at the beginning of a session:

```
In[4]:= $Post := If [MatrixQ[#], MatrixForm[#],#]&
```

```
In[5]:= mat1
Out[5]//MatrixForm=
```

$$\begin{pmatrix} 1 & 2 & 3 \\ 3 & 4 & 5 \\ 5 & 6 & 7 \end{pmatrix}$$

In order to avoid confusion we will continue to affix **// MatrixForm** to all our inputs in this chapter.

⚠ **$Post** is a global variable whose value, if set, is a function that will be applied to every output generated in the current session. The simplest setting would be something like **$Post:=MatrixForm**, which would put *every* output cell into **MatrixForm**. This would work if every output were a matrix, but it would produce unwanted behavior if nonmatrix output were generated. Hence the rather intimidating setting above.

The command **If[MatrixQ[#], MatrixForm[#],#]&** is an example of something called a *pure function*. It looks rather fancy and cryptic, but the idea of a pure function is quite simple, and from the perspective of programming, is also quite elegant. In order to understand the working of a pure function, you need to understand the two symbols **#** and **&**. The symbol **#** represents the argument of the function, and the symbol **&** is used to separate the definition of the function from the argument. So, for instance, the input **#²&[3]** would produce the output 9. In essence, we have created a function whose name **#²&** reveals precisely what it does.

In the **If[MatrixQ[#], MatrixForm[#],#]&** example above, things are only a little more complicated. Understand first that the argument **#** will represent an output generated in the current session. The effect of the function will be to put matrix output into **MatrixForm**, but to leave nonmatrix output alone. This is accomplished with the **If** command, which takes three arguments. The first is a condition. The second is what is returned if the condition is true. The third is what is returned if the condition is false. The condition is checked with the **MatrixQ** command. **MatrixQ[x]** returns True if x is a matrix and False otherwise.

See the *Mathematica* Book for more details about pure functions (in the Help Browser, click on the **Master Index** radio button, and type **pure functions**).

Mathematica is happy to report the dimensions of your matrix. When fed a matrix as input, the **Dimensions** command returns a list containing the number of rows and columns in the matrix, respectively:

```
In[6]:= Dimensions[mat1]
Out[6]= {5,6}
```

There are several commands that produce matrices quickly. The familiar **Table** command is perhaps the most common. To enter a general 3×4 matrix whose i, jth entry (the entry in row i and column j) is $a[i, j]$, type:

```
In[7]:= Clear[a];
        Table[a[i,j],{i,3},{j,4}] // MatrixForm
Out[7] //MatrixForm=
```

$$\begin{pmatrix} a[1,1] & a[1,2] & a[1,3] & a[1,4] \\ a[2,1] & a[2,2] & a[2,3] & a[2,4] \\ a[3,1] & a[3,2] & a[3,3] & a[3,4] \end{pmatrix}$$

The first iterator gives the number of rows, and the second gives the number of columns.

To get a 3×5 matrix with random integer entries between 0 and 50, type:

```
In[8]:= Table[Random[Integer,{0,50}],{3},{5}]
        // MatrixForm
Out[8] //MatrixForm=
```

$$\begin{pmatrix} 31 & 9 & 24 & 41 & 38 \\ 4 & 31 & 30 & 14 & 21 \\ 20 & 46 & 44 & 19 & 26 \end{pmatrix}$$

The next command gives a 5×5 matrix whose i, jth entry is $i + 2j$:

```
In[9]:= Table[i + 2j,{i,5},{j,5}]// MatrixForm
Out[9] //MatrixForm=
```

$$\begin{pmatrix} 3 & 5 & 7 & 9 & 11 \\ 4 & 6 & 8 & 10 & 12 \\ 5 & 7 & 9 & 11 & 13 \\ 6 & 8 & 10 & 12 & 14 \\ 7 & 9 & 11 & 13 & 15 \end{pmatrix}$$

The iterators can be set to start at values other than 1:

In[10]:= **Table[i + 2j, {i,-2,3}, {j,0,2}] // MatrixForm**

Out[10] // MatrixForm =

$$\begin{pmatrix} -2 & 0 & 2 \\ -1 & 1 & 3 \\ 0 & 2 & 4 \\ 1 & 3 & 5 \\ 2 & 4 & 6 \\ 3 & 5 & 7 \end{pmatrix}$$

To get a 3×4 zero matrix you can type this:

In[11]:= **Table[0, {3}, {4}] // MatrixForm**

Out[11] // MatrixForm =

$$\begin{pmatrix} 0 & 0 & 0 & 0 \\ 0 & 0 & 0 & 0 \\ 0 & 0 & 0 & 0 \end{pmatrix}$$

You can also produce a zero matrix by using the **Create Table/Matrix/Palette...** dialog box in the **Input** menu. Just check the **Fill with 0** box.

We can produce a 4×4 lower triangular matrix with entries on and below the diagonal equal to $i + 2j$, and above the diagonal equal to 0, by typing:

In[12]:= **Table[If[i ≥ j, i + 2j ,0], {i,4}, {j,4}]**
             // MatrixForm

Out[12] // MatrixForm =

$$\begin{pmatrix} 3 & 0 & 0 & 0 \\ 4 & 6 & 0 & 0 \\ 5 & 7 & 9 & 0 \\ 6 & 8 & 10 & 12 \end{pmatrix}$$

The **If** command takes three arguments. The first is a condition. The second is what is returned if the condition is true. The third is what is returned if the condition is false.

The **Array** command works much like the **Table** command but uses a function (either built-in or user-defined) rather than an expression to compute the entries. For a function f that takes two arguments, the command

$$\text{\textbf{Array}}[f, \{m,n\}]$$

will give the $m \times n$ matrix whose i, jth entry is $f(i, j)$. For example, using the built-in function **Min** for f produces a matrix where each entry is the minimum of the row number and column number of that entry's position:

```
In[13]:= Array[Min,{4,5}]// MatrixForm
Out[13]//MatrixForm=
```

$$\begin{pmatrix} 1 & 1 & 1 & 1 & 1 \\ 1 & 2 & 2 & 2 & 2 \\ 1 & 2 & 3 & 3 & 3 \\ 1 & 2 & 3 & 4 & 4 \end{pmatrix}$$

Here is a second example, this time with a user-defined function:

```
In[14]:= Clear[f];
         f[i_,j_]:= i^3 + j^2;
         Array[f,{2,3}]// MatrixForm
Out[14]//MatrixForm=
```

$$\begin{pmatrix} 2 & 5 & 10 \\ 9 & 12 & 17 \end{pmatrix}$$

The most efficient way to produce the general matrix with entries $a[i, j]$ is with the **Array** command:

```
In[15]:= Clear[a];
         Array[a,{2,4}]// MatrixForm
Out[15]//MatrixForm=
```

$$\begin{pmatrix} a[1,1] & a[1,2] & a[1,3] & a[1,4] \\ a[2,1] & a[2,2] & a[2,3] & a[2,4] \end{pmatrix}$$

The command below gives the identity matrix of the desired size:

```
In[16]:= IdentityMatrix[4]// MatrixForm
Out[16]//MatrixForm=
```

$$\begin{pmatrix} 1 & 0 & 0 & 0 \\ 0 & 1 & 0 & 0 \\ 0 & 0 & 1 & 0 \\ 0 & 0 & 0 & 1 \end{pmatrix}$$

This can also be accomplished with the **Create Table/Matrix/Palette...** dialogue box in the **Input** menu by checking the **Fill with 0** and **Fill Diagonal with 1** boxes.

The following command gives a diagonal matrix with the enclosed list on the diagonal:

In[17]:= **DiagonalMatrix[{a,b,c,d}]// MatrixForm**
Out[17]//MatrixForm=
$$\begin{pmatrix} a & 0 & 0 & 0 \\ 0 & b & 0 & 0 \\ 0 & 0 & c & 0 \\ 0 & 0 & 0 & d \end{pmatrix}$$

Editing Matrices

It is a simple matter to add another row or column to an existing matrix. Start with either a matrix generated by the **Create Table/Matrix/Palette...** dialogue box, or any **MatrixForm** output. To add a row, click on the matrix just above where you want a new row to appear and press the CONTROL and RETURN keys at the same time. A row of placeholders will appear. To add a new column, click on the matrix where you want the new column to appear. Press the CONTROL and COMMA keys at the same time, and a column of placeholders will appear. If the original matrix appeared in a **MatrixForm** output cell, the modified matrix will appear in a new input cell. You can also use the **Edit** menu for these tasks: look in the **Expression Input** submenu for **Add Row** and **Add Column**:

$$\mathtt{mat1} = \begin{pmatrix} 2 & 3 & 4 & 5 & \square & 6 & 7 \\ 1 & 1 & 1 & 1 & \square & 1 & 1 \\ \square & \square & \square & \square & \square & \square & \square \\ 4 & 5 & 4 & 5 & \square & 4 & 5 \\ 11 & 2 & 2 & 2 & \square & 2 & 2 \\ 0 & 0 & 0 & 0 & \square & 0 & 1 \end{pmatrix}$$

There are several useful commands for composing and separating matrices found in the **LinearAlgebra`MatrixManipulation`** package. Before you can use these commands you need to load the package:

In[18]:= **Needs["LinearAlgebra`MatrixManipulation`"]**

You will then have access to the commands **AppendRows**, **AppendColumns**, **BlockMatrix**, **TakeRows**, **TakeColumns**, **TakeMatrix**, and **SubMatrix**. Here are some examples.

The command **AppendRows** will join the rows in several matrices to form a larger matrix:

```
In[19]:= Clear[mat1, mat2,a,b,c,d,e,f,x,y,z,w,p,q];
         mat1 = ( a  b  c ) ;   mat2 = ( x  y  z ) ;
                ( d  e  f )            ( w  p  q )
         AppendRows[mat1,mat2]// MatrixForm
Out[19]//MatrixForm=
         ( a  b  c  x  y  z )
         ( d  e  f  w  p  q )
```

And the command **AppendColumns** will join the columns of several matrices:

```
In[20]:= AppendColumns[mat1,mat2] // MatrixForm
Out[20]//MatrixForm=
         ( a  b  c )
         ( d  e  f )
         ( x  y  z )
         ( w  p  q )
```

The command **BlockMatrix** will form a matrix by joining submatrices. Each submatrix acts like a single entry in the new matrix:

```
In[21]:= BlockMatrix[{{mat1,mat2},{mat2,Table[0,{2},{3}]}}]
         // MatrixForm
Out[21]//MatrixForm=
         ( a  b  c  x  y  z )
         ( d  e  f  w  p  q )
         ( x  y  z  0  0  0 )
         ( w  p  q  0  0  0 )
```

There are several commands for extracting submatrices. We'll use a general 5×5 matrix to get a good look at what is happening:

```
In[22]:= Clear[a,mat];
         mat =Array[a, {5,5}]; mat// MatrixForm
Out[22]//MatrixForm=
         ( a[1,1]  a[1,2]  a[1,3]  a[1,4]  a[1,5] )
         ( a[2,1]  a[2,2]  a[2,3]  a[2,4]  a[2,5] )
         ( a[3,1]  a[3,2]  a[3,3]  a[3,4]  a[3,5] )
         ( a[4,1]  a[4,2]  a[4,3]  a[4,4]  a[4,5] )
         ( a[5,1]  a[5,2]  a[5,3]  a[5,4]  a[5,5] )
```

The following command will return the first three rows of the matrix **mat**:

In[23]:= **TakeRows[mat,3]//MatrixForm**

Out[23] //MatrixForm=

$$\begin{pmatrix} a[1,1] & a[1,2] & a[1,3] & a[1,4] & a[1,5] \\ a[2,1] & a[2,2] & a[2,3] & a[2,4] & a[2,5] \\ a[3,1] & a[3,2] & a[3,3] & a[3,4] & a[3,5] \end{pmatrix}$$

To get the last two rows, type:

In[24]:= **TakeRows[mat,-2]//MatrixForm**

Out[24] //MatrixForm=

$$\begin{pmatrix} a[4,1] & a[4,2] & a[4,3] & a[4,4] & a[4,5] \\ a[5,1] & a[5,2] & a[5,3] & a[5,4] & a[5,5] \end{pmatrix}$$

And to get rows 2 through 4, type:

In[25]:= **TakeRows[mat,{2,4}]//MatrixForm**

Out[25] //MatrixForm=

$$\begin{pmatrix} a[2,1] & a[2,2] & a[2,3] & a[2,4] & a[2,5] \\ a[3,1] & a[3,2] & a[3,3] & a[3,4] & a[3,5] \\ a[4,1] & a[4,2] & a[4,3] & a[4,4] & a[4,5] \end{pmatrix}$$

There are similar commands for extracting columns:

In[26]:= **TakeColumns[mat,2]//MatrixForm**

Out[26] //MatrixForm=

$$\begin{pmatrix} a[1,1] & a[1,2] \\ a[2,1] & a[2,2] \\ a[3,1] & a[3,2] \\ a[4,1] & a[4,2] \\ a[5,1] & a[5,2] \end{pmatrix}$$

In[27]:= **TakeColumns[mat,-4]//MatrixForm**

Out[27] //MatrixForm=

$$\begin{pmatrix} a[1,2] & a[1,3] & a[1,4] & a[1,5] \\ a[2,2] & a[2,3] & a[2,4] & a[2,5] \\ a[3,2] & a[3,3] & a[3,4] & a[3,5] \\ a[4,2] & a[4,3] & a[4,4] & a[4,5] \\ a[5,2] & a[5,3] & a[5,4] & a[5,5] \end{pmatrix}$$

```
In[28]:= TakeColumns[mat,{3,5}]//MatrixForm
Out[28]//MatrixForm=
```

$$\begin{pmatrix} a[1,3] & a[1,4] & a[1,5] \\ a[2,3] & a[2,4] & a[2,5] \\ a[3,3] & a[3,4] & a[3,5] \\ a[4,3] & a[4,4] & a[4,5] \\ a[5,3] & a[5,4] & a[5,5] \end{pmatrix}$$

The command **TakeMatrix** will return a submatrix. This command takes three arguments: the name of the matrix, the indices of the upper left corner of the desired submatrix, and the indices of the lower right corner of the submatrix:

```
In[29]:= TakeMatrix[mat,{2,3},{4,4}]//MatrixForm
Out[29]//MatrixForm=
```

$$\begin{pmatrix} a[2,3] & a[2,4] \\ a[3,3] & a[3,4] \\ a[4,3] & a[4,4] \end{pmatrix}$$

The command **SubMatrix** also takes three arguments: the name of the matrix, the indices of the upper left corner of the desired submatrix, and the dimensions of the submatrix:

```
In[30]:= SubMatrix[mat,{2,3},{3,2}]//MatrixForm
Out[30]//MatrixForm=
```

$$\begin{pmatrix} a[2,3] & a[2,4] \\ a[3,3] & a[3,4] \\ a[4,3] & a[4,4] \end{pmatrix}$$

7.2 Performing Gaussian Elimination

Referring to Parts of Matrices

Always remember that internally, *Mathematica* thinks of a matrix as a list of lists. So to refer to a part of a matrix we use the same notation discussed in Section 3.11. on page 82. The basic rule is that you use double square brackets to refer to individual items in a list:

```
In[31]:= mat1
Out[31]= {{2,3,4,5,6,7},{1,1,1,1,1,1},{4,5,4,5,4,5},
            {11,2,2,2,2,2},{0,0,0,0,0,1}}
```

To get the second row, type:

```
In[32]:= mat1[[2]]
Out[32]= {1,1,1,1,1,1}
```

Or use the ▪**〚□〛** button found on the **BasicInput** palette. We'll do this for the remainder of the chapter, since it looks a bit nicer:

```
In[33]:= mat1〚2〛
Out[33]= {1,1,1,1,1,1}
```

To retrieve the entry in row 3, column 4, type:

```
In[34]:= mat1〚3, 4〛
Out[34]= 5
```

The most efficient method for extracting a column is different for versions 3 and 4 of *Mathematica*. If you are using version 4, you can extract the third column by typing:

```
In[35]:= mat1〚All,3〛
Out[35]= {4,1,4,2,0}
```

To extract a column in version 3 you should first use the **Transpose** command to interchange the rows and columns of the matrix. Then pick out the desired column (now a row). You can format the output to look like a column with the **ColumnForm** command. For example, to get the third column, type:

```
In[36]:= Transpose[mat1]〚3〛 // ColumnForm
            4
            1
Out[36]=    4
            2
            0
```

Gaussian Elimination

A matrix is in *reduced row echelon form* if the first nonzero entry in each row is a 1 with only zeros above and beneath it. Furthermore, the rows must be arranged so that if one row begins with more zeros than another, then that row appears beneath the other. Any matrix can be put into reduced row echelon form by performing successive elementary row operations: multiplying a row by a nonzero constant, replacing a row by its sum with a multiple of another row, or interchanging two rows.

You can ask *Mathematica* to find the reduced row echelon form of a matrix by using the command **RowReduce**:

$$In[37]:= \textbf{mat} = \begin{pmatrix} 1 & 1 & 4 & 25 \\ 2 & 1 & 0 & 7 \\ -3 & 0 & 1 & -1 \end{pmatrix};$$

RowReduce[mat]//MatrixForm

Out[37]//MatrixForm=

$$\begin{pmatrix} 1 & 0 & 0 & 2 \\ 0 & 1 & 0 & 3 \\ 0 & 0 & 1 & 5 \end{pmatrix}$$

You can also perform "manual" row reduction. Use **mat[[*i*]]** to refer to the *i*th row of the matrix **mat**. To replace the second row with the sum of the second row and -2 times the first row, type:

$$In[38]:= \textbf{mat[[2]] = mat[[2]] - 2mat[[1]]};$$

mat//MatrixForm

Out[38]//MatrixForm=

$$\begin{pmatrix} 1 & 1 & 4 & 25 \\ 0 & -1 & -8 & -43 \\ -3 & 0 & 1 & -1 \end{pmatrix}$$

The first line performed the operation, and the semicolon suppressed the output; the second line asked *Mathematica* to display the revised matrix in **MatrixForm**. Next we can add 3 times the first row to the third row, and the second row to the first row:

$$In[39]:= \textbf{mat[[3]] = mat[[3]] + 3mat[[1]]};$$

mat[[1]] = mat[[1]] + mat[[2]];

mat//MatrixForm

Out[39]//MatrixForm=

$$\begin{pmatrix} 1 & 0 & -4 & -18 \\ 0 & -1 & -8 & -43 \\ 0 & 3 & 13 & 74 \end{pmatrix}$$

Now add 3 times the second row to the third row:

In[40]:= **mat [[3]] = mat [[3]] + 3 mat [[2]];**
            mat // MatrixForm

Out[40] // MatrixForm=
$$\begin{pmatrix} 1 & 0 & -4 & -18 \\ 0 & -1 & -8 & -43 \\ 0 & 0 & -11 & -55 \end{pmatrix}$$

Finally, we can multiply the third row by $-\frac{1}{11}$, multiply the second row by -1, add -8 times the third row to the second row, and add 4 times the third row to the first row:

In[41]:= **mat [[3]] = mat [[3]] $\left(-\dfrac{1}{11}\right)$;**
            mat [[2]] = -1 mat [[2]] ;
            mat [[2]] = mat [[2]] - 8 mat [[3]] ;
            mat [[1]] = mat [[1]] + 4 mat [[3]] ;
            mat // MatrixForm

Out[41] // MatrixForm=
$$\begin{pmatrix} 1 & 0 & 0 & 2 \\ 0 & 1 & 0 & 3 \\ 0 & 0 & 1 & 5 \end{pmatrix}$$

7.3   Matrix Operations

If two matrices have the same dimensions, we can compute their sum by adding the corresponding entries of the two matrices. In *Mathematica*, as in ordinary mathematical notation, we use the + operator for matrix sums:

In[42]:= **mat3 = $\begin{pmatrix} 1 & 0 & 0 \\ 2 & 3 & 4 \\ -1 & 5 & -1 \end{pmatrix}$; mat4 = $\begin{pmatrix} 2 & 2 & 3 \\ 0 & 0 & 1 \\ 5 & 5 & 5 \end{pmatrix}$;**
            mat3 + mat4 // MatrixForm

Out[42] // MatrixForm=
$$\begin{pmatrix} 3 & 2 & 3 \\ 2 & 3 & 5 \\ 4 & 10 & 4 \end{pmatrix}$$

We can also find their difference:

In[43]:= **mat3 - mat4 // MatrixForm**

Out[43] // MatrixForm=
$$\begin{pmatrix} -1 & -2 & -3 \\ 2 & 3 & 3 \\ -6 & 0 & -6 \end{pmatrix}$$

We can perform scalar multiplication:

In[44]:= **7 * mat3 // MatrixForm**

$$Out[44]= \begin{pmatrix} 7 & 0 & 0 \\ 14 & 21 & 28 \\ -7 & 35 & -7 \end{pmatrix}$$

And we can multiply matrices. The i, jth entry of the *product* of the matrix **a** with the matrix **b** is the dot product of the ith row of **a** with the jth column of **b**. Multiplication is only possible if the number of columns of **a** is equal to the number of rows of **b**.

In *Mathematica*, use the dot (i.e., the period) as the multiplication operator for matrices:

In[45]:= **mat3.mat4 // MatrixForm**

Out[45] // MatrixForm =

$$\begin{pmatrix} 2 & 2 & 3 \\ 24 & 24 & 29 \\ -7 & -7 & -3 \end{pmatrix}$$

Be careful to use the dot to perform matrix multiplication. The symbol * will simply multiply corresponding entries in the two matrices (not a standard matrix operation):

In[46]:= **mat3 * mat4 // MatrixForm**

Out[46] // MatrixForm =

$$\begin{pmatrix} 2 & 0 & 0 \\ 0 & 0 & 4 \\ -5 & 25 & -5 \end{pmatrix}$$

The **Transpose** command will produce the transpose of a matrix – the matrix obtained by switching the rows and columns of that matrix:

In[47]:= **Transpose[mat3] // MatrixForm**

Out[47] // MatrixForm =

$$\begin{pmatrix} 1 & 2 & -1 \\ 0 & 3 & 5 \\ 0 & 4 & -1 \end{pmatrix}$$

To find a power of a matrix use the command **MatrixPower**. The first argument is the matrix, and the second argument is the desired power:

$In[48]:=$ **MatrixPower[mat3,10] // MatrixForm**
$Out[48]//MatrixForm=$

$$\begin{pmatrix} 1 & 0 & 0 \\ 10249364 & 36166989 & 20498728 \\ 7834130 & 25623410 & 15668261 \end{pmatrix}$$

The *inverse* of a square matrix, if it exists, is the matrix whose product with the original matrix is the identity matrix. A matrix that has an inverse is said to be *nonsingular*. You can find the inverse of a nonsingular matrix with the **Inverse** command:

$In[49]:=$ **Inverse[mat3] // MatrixForm**
$Out[49]//MatrixForm=$

$$\begin{pmatrix} 1 & 0 & 0 \\ \dfrac{2}{23} & \dfrac{1}{23} & \dfrac{4}{23} \\ -\dfrac{13}{23} & \dfrac{5}{23} & -\dfrac{3}{23} \end{pmatrix}$$

It is a simple matter to check that the product of a matrix with its inverse is the identity:

$In[50]:=$ **%.mat3 // MatrixForm**
$Out[50]//MatrixForm=$

$$\begin{pmatrix} 1 & 0 & 0 \\ 0 & 1 & 0 \\ 0 & 0 & 1 \end{pmatrix}$$

⚠ Note that the **%** in the last input represents the inverse of **mat3** rather than the **MatrixForm** of that inverse. This is the reason for the cell tag $Out[48] // MatrixForm =$. If you refer to any such output cell (with **%** or **%%**, for instance), *Mathematica* will use the output generated before **MatrixForm** was applied. This makes it easy to incorporate **MatrixForm** output into new input.

The *determinant* of a square matrix is a number that is nonzero if and only if the matrix is nonsingular. Determinants are notoriously painful to compute by hand, but are a snap with *Mathematica*'s **Det** command:

$In[51]:=$ **Det[mat3]**
$Out[51]= -23$

Any matrix operation can be performed either on a matrix whose entries are numeric, or on a matrix whose entries are purely symbolic. For example, you can find the formula for the determinant of a general 3×3 matrix:

```
In[52]:= Clear[a]; mat5 = Array[a,{3,3}]; mat5//MatrixForm
Out[52]//MatrixForm=
```
$$\begin{pmatrix} a[1,1] & a[1,2] & a[1,3] \\ a[2,1] & a[2,2] & a[2,3] \\ a[3,1] & a[3,2] & a[3,3] \end{pmatrix}$$

```
In[53]:= Det[mat5]
Out[53]= -a[1,3] a[2,2] a[3,1] + a[1,2] a[2,3] a[3,1] +
         a[1,3] a[2,1] a[3,2]-a[1,1] a[2,3] a[3,2]-
         a[1,2] a[2,1] a[3,3] + a[1,1] a[2,2] a[3,3]
```

Notice how the determinant arises naturally in the inverse of a matrix. Here is the entry in the first row and first column of the inverse of **mat5**:

```
In[54]:= Inverse[mat5][[1, 1]]
Out[54]= (-a[2,3] a[3,2] + a[2,2] a[3,3])/
         (-a[1,3] a[2,2] a[3,1] + a[1,2] a[2,3] a[3,1] +
         a[1,3] a[2,1] a[3,2]-a[1,1] a[2,3] a[3,2]-
         a[1,2] a[2,1] a[3,3] + a[1,1] a[2,2] a[3,3])
```

Here is the same entry with the determinant replaced by the symbol **det**:

```
In[55]:= Inverse[mat5][[1, 1]]/. Det[mat5] → det
```
$$Out[55]= \frac{-a[2,3]\ a[3,2] + a[2,2]\ a[3,3]}{det}$$

The *trace* of a matrix is the sum of the entries along the main diagonal. In version 4 of *Mathematica*, the trace of a matrix may be calculated with the command **Tr**:

```
In[56]:= Tr[mat5]
Out[56]= a[1,1] + a[2,2] + a[3,3]
```

Getting version 3 of *Mathematica* to compute the trace of a matrix involves a little bit of work, simply because there is no built-in command (there is a command whose name is **Trace**, but it has nothing to do with linear algebra; don't use it to compute the trace of a matrix). You can define your own trace command by entering the following cell. Since the new command name **trace** looks a lot like the built-in command **Trace**, you may get a warning message when you enter this cell. You can ignore it, but remember that your command begins with a lower-case t.

```
In[57]:= trace[m_List] := Sum[m[[i, i]] , {i, Length[m]}]
         General::spell1 : Possible spelling error : new symbol
           name "trace" is similar to existing  symbol "Trace".
```

Here's an example:

```
In[58]:= trace[mat5]
Out[58]= a[1,1] + a[2,2] + a[3,3]
```

7.4 Solving Systems of Linear Equations

Nonhomogeneous Systems of Linear Equations

Suppose we want to solve a system of linear equations in the form $\mathbf{mx} = \mathbf{b}$, where $\mathbf{m}$ is the coefficient matrix, $\mathbf{x}$ is a column vector of variables, and $\mathbf{b}$ is a column vector. Such a system is called *nonhomogeneous* when $\mathbf{b}$ is a vector with at least one nonzero entry. *Mathematica* offers several options for solving such a system, and we will explore each in turn. In this first example $\mathbf{m}$ is a nonsingular matrix and the system has a unique solution. Enter the equation $\mathbf{mx} = \mathbf{b}$ by typing $\mathbf{m.x} == \mathbf{b}$. Note how *Mathematica* interprets this equation:

```
In[59]:= Clear[m, x, x1, x2, x3, x4, b];
         ⎛ 1   5  -4  1 ⎞        ⎛ x1 ⎞        ⎛ 1 ⎞
         ⎜ 3   4  -1  2 ⎟        ⎜ x2 ⎟        ⎜ 2 ⎟
     m = ⎜ 3   2   1  5 ⎟ ; x =  ⎜ x3 ⎟ ; b =  ⎜ 3 ⎟ ;
         ⎝ 0  -6   7  1 ⎠        ⎝ x4 ⎠        ⎝ 4 ⎠
     m . x == b
Out[59]= {{x1 + 5 x2 - 4 x3 + x4}, {3 x1 + 4 x2 - x3 + 2 x4},
          {3 x1 + 2 x2 + x3 + 5 x4}, {-6 x2 + 7 x3 + x4}} ==
          {{1}, {2}, {3}, {4}}
```

We can interpret this as a list of four linear equations, each in four variables.

We now use the command **AppendRows** to form the augmented matrix, and the command **RowReduce** to find the reduced row echelon form of the matrix. The command **AppendRows** is found in the **LinearAlgebra`MatrixManipulation`** package. Before you can use this command you need to load the package:

```
In[60]:= Needs["LinearAlgebra`MatrixManipulation`"]
```

```
In[61]:= AppendRows[m, b] // MatrixForm
Out[61] //MatrixForm=
         ⎛ 1   5  -4  1  1 ⎞
         ⎜ 3   4  -1  2  2 ⎟
         ⎜ 3   2   1  5  3 ⎟
         ⎝ 0  -6   7  1  4 ⎠
```

In[62]:= **RowReduce[%] // MatrixForm**

Out[62] // MatrixForm =

$$\begin{pmatrix} 1 & 0 & 0 & 0 & -\dfrac{127}{35} \\ 0 & 1 & 0 & 0 & \dfrac{141}{35} \\ 0 & 0 & 1 & 0 & \dfrac{139}{35} \\ 0 & 0 & 0 & 1 & \dfrac{13}{35} \end{pmatrix}$$

We conclude that $x_1 = -\frac{127}{35}$, $x_2 = \frac{141}{35}$, $x_3 = \frac{139}{35}$, and $x_4 = \frac{13}{35}$.

The command **LinearSolve** provides a quick means for solving systems that have a single solution:

In[63]:= **LinearSolve[m,b]**

$$Out[63] = \left\{\left\{-\frac{127}{35}\right\}, \left\{\frac{141}{35}\right\}, \left\{\frac{139}{35}\right\}, \left\{\frac{13}{35}\right\}\right\}$$

Yet another means of solving the system goes like this. We can solve the system $\mathbf{m}\,\mathbf{x} = \mathbf{b}$ for $\mathbf{x}$ by multiplying both sides on the left by $\mathbf{m}^{-1}$, to get $\mathbf{x} = \mathbf{m}^{-1}\mathbf{b}$:

In[64]:= **Inverse[m].b**

$$Out[64] = \left\{\left\{-\frac{127}{35}\right\}, \left\{\frac{141}{35}\right\}, \left\{\frac{139}{35}\right\}, \left\{\frac{13}{35}\right\}\right\}$$

We can also use the command **Solve** to solve this system, just as in Section 4.8 (see page 126). But we have to be careful using **Solve**. When we use the **Create Table/Matrix/Palette...** dialogue box to create **m,x**, and **b**, we find that both **m x** and **b** are lists of lists. The **Solve** command takes a list of equations as its first argument and a list of variables as its second argument – it unfortunately cannot accept lists of lists. There is a simple solution: We will have to re-enter **x** and **b** without using the **Create Table/Matrix/Palette....** dialogue box, expressing each as a single list. If we do this, the equation **m.x == b** is acceptable as input to the **Solve** command. Note how *Mathematica* interprets the equation **m.x == b** as a single list of equations when **x** and **b** are entered this way:

In[65]:= **Clear[x, b]; x={x1, x2, x3, x4}; b={1, 2, 3, 4};**
            m.x == b

Out[65]= {x1 + 5 x2 - 4 x3 + x4 == 1, 3 x1 + 4 x2 - x3 + 2 x4 == 2,
            3 x1 + 2 x2 + x3 + 5 x4 == 3, -6 x2 + 7 x3 + x4 == 4}

In[66]:= **Solve[m.x == b, x]**

$$Out[66] = \left\{\left\{x1 \to -\frac{127}{35}, x2 \to \frac{141}{35}, x3 \to \frac{139}{35}, x4 \to \frac{13}{35}\right\}\right\}$$

An *inconsistent* system of equations has no solutions. If we use the **Solve** command on such a system, the output will be an empty set of curly brackets:

```
In[67]:= Clear[m, x, b];

        ⎛ 1   1   1 ⎞
   m =  ⎜ 1   1   1 ⎟  ; x = {x1, x2, x3}; b = {1,  2,  -1};
        ⎝ 1  -1  -1 ⎠

        Solve[m.x == b, x]
Out[67]= {}
```

However, if we row-reduce, we can see the inconsistency in the system:

```
                          ⎛  1 ⎞
In[68]:= Clear[b]; b =    ⎜  2 ⎟   ; AppendRows[m , b]
                          ⎝ -1 ⎠
Out[68]= {{1,1,1,1},{1,1,1,2},{1,-1,-1,-1}}
```

```
In[69]:= RowReduce[%] // MatrixForm
Out[69]//MatrixForm=
        ⎛ 1  0  0  0 ⎞
        ⎜ 0  1  1  0 ⎟
        ⎝ 0  0  0  1 ⎠
```

The last row represents the impossible equation $0 = 1$.

If you use the **LinearSolve** command with an inconsistent system you will be told off:

```
In[70]:= LinearSolve[m , b]
          LinearSolve :: nosol : Linear equation encountered
             which has no solution.
Out[70]= LinearSolve[{{1,1,1},{1,1,1},{1,-1,-1}},
             {{1},{2},{-1}}]
```

And if you try to find the inverse of **m** you will be told off again:

```
In[71]:= Inverse[m] .b
          Inverse :: sing : Matrix {{1,1,1},{1,1,1},{1,-1,-1}}
             is singular.
Out[71]= Inverse[{{1,1,1},{1,1,1},{1,-1,-1}}]
             .{{1},{2},{-1}}
```

The remaining possibility for a system of equations is that there are an infinite number of solutions. The **Solve** command nicely displays the solution set in this situation:

```
In[72]:= Clear[m, x, b];
```

$$m = \begin{pmatrix} 2 & 3 & -4 \\ 4 & 6 & -8 \\ 1 & -1 & -1 \end{pmatrix}; \; x = \{x1, x2, x3\}; \; b = \{8, 16, 1\};$$

```
Solve[m.x == b, x]
```

Solve :: svars : Equations may not give solutions for all
  "solve" variables.

$$Out[72]= \left\{\left\{x1 \rightarrow \frac{11}{5} + \frac{7\,x3}{5}, x2 \rightarrow \frac{6}{5} + \frac{2\,x3}{5}\right\}\right\}$$

Be very careful when using the **LinearSolve** command. In a system having an infinite number of solutions it will return only one of them, giving no warning that there are others. In this example it returns only the solution where $x_3 = 0$:

```
In[73]:= LinearSolve[m,b]
```

$$Out[73]= \left\{\frac{11}{5}, \frac{6}{5}, 0\right\}$$

Row reduction gives the solution with little possibility for confusion:

$$In[74]:= \textbf{Clear[b]; } \; b = \begin{pmatrix} 8 \\ 16 \\ 1 \end{pmatrix};$$

```
RowReduce[AppendRows[m,b]] // MatrixForm
```

Out[74] //MatrixForm =

$$\begin{pmatrix} 1 & 0 & -\dfrac{7}{5} & \dfrac{11}{5} \\ 0 & 1 & -\dfrac{2}{5} & \dfrac{6}{5} \\ 0 & 0 & 0 & 0 \end{pmatrix}$$

Thus, for each real value assumed by x_3, there is a solution with $x_1 = \frac{11}{5} + \frac{7}{5}x_3$, and $x_2 = \frac{6}{5} + \frac{2}{5}x_3$.

The moral is that you should be very careful using the command **LinearSolve** unless you know you have a nonsingular matrix and hence a single solution. To check this, you can use the **Det** command, keeping in mind that a singular matrix has determinant zero. When in doubt it is best to use row reduction and your knowledge of linear algebra to find the solution vectors.

Homogeneous Systems of Equations

A system of equations of the form $\mathbf{mx} = \mathbf{0}$, where $\mathbf{m}$ is the coefficient matrix, $\mathbf{x}$ is a column vector of variables, and $\mathbf{0}$ is the zero vector, is called *homogeneous*. Note that $\mathbf{x} = \mathbf{0}$ is a solution to any homogeneous system. Now suppose $\mathbf{m}$ is a square matrix. Recall that such a system of linear equations has a unique solution if and only if $\mathbf{m}$ is nonsingular. Hence, we see that if $\mathbf{m}$ is nonsingular, a homogeneous system will have only the *trivial* solution $\mathbf{x} = \mathbf{0}$, while if $\mathbf{m}$ is singular the system will have an infinite number of solutions. The set of all solutions to a homogeneous system is called the *null space* of $\mathbf{m}$:

```
In[75]:= Clear[m];
```
$$m = \begin{pmatrix} 0 & 2 & 2 & 4 \\ 1 & 0 & -1 & -3 \\ 2 & 3 & 1 & 1 \\ -2 & 1 & 3 & -2 \end{pmatrix}; \; x = \begin{pmatrix} x1 \\ x2 \\ x3 \\ x4 \end{pmatrix}; \; b = \begin{pmatrix} 0 \\ 0 \\ 0 \\ 0 \end{pmatrix}; \; \texttt{Det[m]}$$
```
Out[75]= 0
```

```
In[76]:= RowReduce[AppendRows[m,b]] // MatrixForm
Out[76] //MatrixForm=
```
$$\begin{pmatrix} 1 & 0 & -1 & 0 & 0 \\ 0 & 1 & 1 & 0 & 0 \\ 0 & 0 & 0 & 1 & 0 \\ 0 & 0 & 0 & 0 & 0 \end{pmatrix}$$

This reduced form of the augmented matrix tells us that $x_1 = x_3$, $x_2 = -x_3$, and $x_4 = 0$. That is, any vector of the form $(t, -t, t, 0)$, where t is a real number, is a solution, and the vector $(1, -1, 1, 0)$ forms a *basis* for the solution space.[2]

The command **NullSpace** gives a set of basis vectors for the solution space of the homogeneous equation $\mathbf{mx} = \mathbf{0}$:

```
In[77]:= NullSpace[m]
Out[77]= {{1,-1,1,0}}
```

Using LinearSolve and NullSpace to Solve Nonhomogeneous Systems

We have seen that the **LinearSolve** command will only return one solution when a matrix equation $\mathbf{mx} = \mathbf{b}$ has an infinite number of solutions. This can be confusing at first, but you should understand that there is a reason for its behavior. If you were to take a the sum of the solution vector provided by **LinearSolve** with

---

[2] Bases are discussed in the next section of this chapter. See page 254.

any vector in the null space of **m**, you would get another solution vector. Moreover, every solution vector is of this form. Here's an example:

```
In[78]:= Clear[m,b];
        m = ( 0  2   2   4 )   ; b = ( 2 ) ;
            ( 1  0  -1  -3 )         ( 0 )
            ( 2  3   1   1 )         ( 0 )
```

```
In[79]:= LinearSolve[m,b]
Out[79]= {{-9},{7},{0},{-3}}
```

```
In[80]:= NullSpace[m]
Out[80]= {{1,-1,1,0}}
```

This tells us that there are an infinite number of solutions. For each real number t, there is a solution $(-9, 7, 0, -3) + t(1, -1, 1, 0)$. In other words, $x_1 = -9 + t$, $x_2 = 7 - t$, $x_3 = t$, and $x_4 = -3$. This is exactly what row reduction tells us, in slightly different language:

```
In[81]:= RowReduce[AppendRows[m,b]] // MatrixForm
Out[81]//MatrixForm=
        ( 1  0  -1  0  -9 )
        ( 0  1   1  0   7 )
        ( 0  0   0  1  -3 )
```

7.5   Vector Spaces

Span and Linear Independence

Suppose we are given a set $\{v_1, v_2, v_3, \ldots, v_n\}$ of vectors. Any vector that can be expressed in the form $a_1v_1 + a_2v_2 + a_3v_3 + \cdots + a_nv_n$ is said to be in the *span* of the vectors $v_1, v_2, v_3, \ldots, v_n$, where the coefficients a_i are scalars.[3] We can determine whether a given vector **b** is in the span of the vectors $v_1, v_2, v_3, \ldots,$ v_n by letting **m** be the matrix whose columns are $v_1, v_2, v_3, \ldots, v_n$, and then determining whether the equation $\mathbf{mx} = \mathbf{b}$ has a solution. A solution **x**, if it exists, provides values for the scalars a_i.

---

[3] The coefficients $a_1, a_2, \ldots, a_n$ are in general required to be members of the scalar field over which the vector space is defined. This is often the field of real numbers, but may also be the field of complex numbers or some other field.

For example, in real three-space, is the vector $\mathbf{b} = (1,2,3)$ in the span of the vectors $\mathbf{v}_1 = (10,4,5)$, $\mathbf{v}_2 = (4,4,7)$, and $\mathbf{v}_3 = (8,1,0)$?

```
In[82]:= Clear[v1, v2, v3, b, m, c];
         v1 = {10, 4, 5};
         v2 = {4, 4, 7};
         v3 = {8, 1, 0};
         b = {1, 2, 3};
         m = Transpose[{v1, v2, v3}];
         c = LinearSolve[m, b]
```
$$Out[82]= \left\{ \frac{3}{2}, -\frac{9}{14}, -\frac{10}{7} \right\}$$

We can now check that $\frac{3}{2}\mathbf{v}_1 - \frac{9}{14}\mathbf{v}_2 - \frac{10}{7}\mathbf{v}_3 = \mathbf{b}$.

```
In[83]:= c[[1]] v1 + c[[2]] v2 + c[[3]] v3
Out[83]= {1,2,3}
```

A set of vectors $\{\mathbf{v}_1, \mathbf{v}_2, \mathbf{v}_3, \ldots, \mathbf{v}_n\}$ is said to be *linearly independent* if every vector in their span can be expressed in a unique way as a linear combination $a_1\mathbf{v}_1 + a_2\mathbf{v}_2 + a_3\mathbf{v}_3 + \cdots + a_n\mathbf{v}_n$. Put another way, this means that the only way to express the zero vector as such a linear combination is to have each coefficient $a_i = 0$. If it is possible to write $a_1\mathbf{v}_1 + a_2\mathbf{v}_2 + \cdots + a_n\mathbf{v}_n = \mathbf{0}$ with at least one of the $a_i \neq 0$, then the set of vectors $\{\mathbf{v}_1, \mathbf{v}_2, \mathbf{v}_3, \ldots, \mathbf{v}_n\}$ is linearly *dependent*.

To check whether a set of vectors $\{\mathbf{v}_1, \mathbf{v}_2, \mathbf{v}_3, \ldots, \mathbf{v}_n\}$ is linearly independent, let $\mathbf{m}$ be the matrix whose columns are $\mathbf{v}_1, \mathbf{v}_2, \mathbf{v}_3, \ldots, \mathbf{v}_n$, and check that the equation $\mathbf{mx} = \mathbf{0}$ has only the trival solution:

```
In[84]:= NullSpace[m]
Out[84]= {}
```

Yes, these are independent vectors. Alternatively, we could check that the matrix whose rows (or columns) are $\mathbf{v}_1, \mathbf{v}_2, \mathbf{v}_3, \ldots, \mathbf{v}_n$, is nonsingular:

```
In[85]:= Det[{v1, v2, v3}]
Out[85]= 14
```

Bases

A *basis* for a vector space is a set of linearly independent vectors whose span includes every vector in the vector space. Given a spanning set of vectors $\{\mathbf{v}_1, \mathbf{v}_2, \mathbf{v}_3, \ldots, \mathbf{v}_n\}$ for a vector space we can easily obtain a basis for that space. Form a matrix whose rows are the vectors $\mathbf{v}_1, \mathbf{v}_2, \mathbf{v}_3, \ldots, \mathbf{v}_n$, and row-reduce:

```
In[86]:= Clear[v1, v2, v3, v4, m, a];
         v1 = {2, 1, 15, 10, 6};
         v2 = {2, -5 , -3, -2, 6};
         v3 = {0, 5, 15, 10, 0};
         v4 = {2, 6, 18, 8, 6};
         m = {v1, v2, v3, v4};
         RowReduce[m] // MatrixForm
```

Out[86] // MatrixForm =

$$\begin{pmatrix} 1 & 0 & 0 & -2 & 3 \\ 0 & 1 & 0 & -1 & 0 \\ 0 & 0 & 1 & 1 & 0 \\ 0 & 0 & 0 & 0 & 0 \end{pmatrix}$$

The nonzero rows of this matrix form a basis for the space spanned by the set $\{\mathbf{v}_1, \mathbf{v}_2, \mathbf{v}_3, \mathbf{v}_4\}$. This space is also called the *row space* of the matrix $\mathbf{m}$.

We can also find a basis consisting of a subset of the original vectors. If we row-reduce the matrix whose columns are the vectors $\mathbf{v}_1, \mathbf{v}_2, \mathbf{v}_3, \ldots, \mathbf{v}_n$, then the columns containing the *leading 1's* will form a basis for the column space, and the corresponding columns from the original matrix will also form a basis for the column space. (An entry in a row-reduced matrix is called a leading 1 if the entry is a 1 and it has only zeros to its left.)

```
In[87]:= Clear[v1, v2, v3, v4, m, a];
         v1 = {2,1,15,10,6};
         v2 = {2,-5, -3,-2,6};
         v3 = {0,5,15,10,0};
         v4 = {2,6,18,8,6};
         m = Transpose[{v1,v2,v3,v4}];
         RowReduce[m] // MatrixForm
```

Out[87] // MatrixForm =

$$\begin{pmatrix} 1 & 0 & \dfrac{5}{6} & 0 \\ 0 & 1 & -\dfrac{5}{6} & 0 \\ 0 & 0 & 0 & 1 \\ 0 & 0 & 0 & 0 \\ 0 & 0 & 0 & 0 \end{pmatrix}$$

The vectors $(1, 0, 0, 0, 0)$, $(0, 1, 0, 0, 0)$, and $(0, 0, 1, 0, 0)$ form a basis for the column space of **m**. The vectors from the same columns in **m** will also form a basis for the column space. Hence $\mathbf{v}_1$, $\mathbf{v}_2$, and $\mathbf{v}_4$ will form a basis for the space spanned by the set $\{\mathbf{v}_1, \mathbf{v}_2, \mathbf{v}_3, \mathbf{v}_4\}$. We can confirm that $\{\mathbf{v}_1, \mathbf{v}_2, \mathbf{v}_4\}$ is a linearly independent set:

```
In[88]:= NullSpace[Transpose[{v1, v2, v4}]]
Out[88]= {}
```

We see here an example of a general truth: a vector space may have many distinct bases. The number of vectors in any basis for that vector space, however, will always be the same. This number is called the *dimension* of the vector space.

Rank and Nullity

The dimension of the null space of a matrix is called the *nullity* of the matrix. We can find the nullity by using the **Length** command to count the vectors in a basis for the null space:

```
In[89]:= Length[NullSpace[m]]
Out[89]= 1
```

The *rank* of a matrix is the common dimension of the row space and the column space. The rank plus the nullity must equal the number of columns in a matrix. We can use this fact to compute the rank of **m**. The following command automates the process:

```
In[90]:= rank[m_List] :=
            Length[Transpose[m]] - Length[NullSpace[m]]
```

Let's try it:

```
In[91]:= rank[m]
Out[91]= 3
```

Orthonormal Bases and the Gram–Schmidt Process

A collection of vectors is *orthogonal* if the vectors are mutually perpendicular, i.e. if the dot product of every pair is 0. The set is *orthonormal* if, in addition to being orthogonal, each vector has length one. Given a basis for a vector space, we can use the Gram–Schmidt process to find an orthonormal basis for the same vector space. Computing the orthonormal basis by hand is not difficult, but it is tedious and lends itself to the commission of errors. We can automate the process by using the command **GramSchmidt**, which is found in the **LinearAlgebra** **`Orthogonalization`** package. To use it, you first must load this package:

In[92]:= **Needs["LinearAlgebra`Orthogonalization`"]**

The argument for the command **GramSchmidt** is a list of linearly independent vectors. The output is a list of mutually orthogonal unit vectors with the same span:

In[93]:= **Clear[v1, v2, v3, w1, w2, w3];**
     v1 = {2, 3, -4, 1, 0};
     v2 = {1, 5, -6, 10, -3};
     v3 = { 7, -2, 1, 1, 1};
     {w1, w2, w3} = GramSchmidt[{v1, v2, v3}]

Out[93]= $\left\{\left\{ \sqrt{\frac{2}{15}},\ \sqrt{\frac{3}{10}}, -2\ \sqrt{\frac{2}{15}}, \frac{1}{\sqrt{30}}, 0\right\},\right.$

$\left\{-4\ \sqrt{\frac{6}{1405}}, -\frac{1}{\sqrt{8430}}, 4\ \sqrt{\frac{2}{4215}}, \frac{83}{\sqrt{8430}}, -\sqrt{\frac{30}{281}}\right\}, \left\{\frac{5368}{\sqrt{38274729}},\right.$

$\left.\left.-706\ \sqrt{\frac{3}{12758243}}, \frac{1489}{\sqrt{38274729}}, \frac{1574}{\sqrt{38274729}}, 176\sqrt{\frac{3}{12758243}}\right\}\right\}$

It can be helpful to display such messy output as a table. This will obliterate the commas separating the various coordinate positions in each vector, but it is still easier to read:

In[94]:= **TableForm[%,**
       TableHeadings → {{"w1 = ", "w2 = ", "w3 = "}, None}]

Out[94] // TableForm =

w1 =	$\sqrt{\frac{2}{15}}$	$\sqrt{\frac{3}{10}}$	$-2\sqrt{\frac{2}{15}}$	$\frac{1}{\sqrt{30}}$	0
w2 =	$-4\ \sqrt{\frac{6}{1405}}$	$-\frac{1}{\sqrt{8430}}$	$4\ \sqrt{\frac{2}{4215}}$	$\frac{83}{\sqrt{8430}}$	$-\sqrt{\frac{30}{281}}$
w3 =	$\frac{5368}{\sqrt{38274729}}$	$-706\ \sqrt{\frac{3}{12758243}}$	$\frac{1489}{\sqrt{38274729}}$	$\frac{1574}{\sqrt{38274729}}$	$176\ \sqrt{\frac{3}{12758243}}$

It is easy to check that any pair of these vectors is orthogonal. Just enter a list whose items are dot products of every possible pair of distinct vectors. The output will be a list of zeros if the vectors in each pair are orthogonal:

In[95]:= **{w1.w2, w2.w3, w3.w1}**
Out[95]= **{0, 0, 0}**

And here we check that they are all unit vectors:

In[96]:= **norm[v_List] := $\sqrt{\text{v.v}}$;**
        {norm[w1], norm[w2], norm[w3]}

Out[96]= {1,1,1}

You can also produce an orthogonal basis that is not normalized. Just add the option **Normalized → False** to **GramSchmidt**:

In[97]:= **{w1, w2, w3} = GramSchmidt[{v1, v2, v3},**
         Normalized → False]

Out[97]= $\left\{\{2,3,-4,1,0\}, \left\{-\dfrac{12}{5}, -\dfrac{1}{10}, \dfrac{4}{5}, \dfrac{83}{10}, -3\right\}, \right.$
          $\left.\left\{\dfrac{5368}{843}, -\dfrac{706}{281}, \dfrac{1489}{843}, \dfrac{1574}{843}, \dfrac{176}{281}\right\}\right\}$

These vectors are still pairwise orthogonal:

In[98]:= **{w1.w2, w2.w3, w3.w1}**
Out[98]= {0,0,0}

But they are not unit vectors:

In[99]:= **{norm[w1], norm[w2], norm[w3]}**
Out[99]= $\left\{\sqrt{30}, \sqrt{\dfrac{843}{10}}, \sqrt{\dfrac{45403}{843}}\right\}$

The familiar concepts of vector length and the angle between pairs of vectors in Euclidean vector spaces can be generalized to other vector spaces that admit an *inner product* – a generalization of the dot product. As with the dot product, two vectors whose inner product is zero are said to be orthogonal. And a vector whose inner product with itself is 1 is said to be a unit vector.

The Gram–Schmidt process can be applied in any inner-product space. For example, consider the vector space P_2 of polynomials in the variable x of degree at most two with real coefficients. An inner product for this space is defined below:

In[100]:= **innerprod[p1_, p2_] := $\displaystyle\int_{-1}^{1}$ p1 $*$ p2 dx**

For instance, here is the inner product of a pair of vectors (polynomials) in this space:

In[101]:= **innerprod[1 + 2x + 3x^2, 2 + 4x]**
Out[101]= $\dfrac{40}{3}$

The set $\{1, x, x^2\}$ is a basis for P_2. We can use the command **GramSchmidt** to find an orthonormal basis for P_2 with respect to the inner product above. In order to do this, we have to specify this inner product with the **InnerProduct** option:

In[102]:= **{p1, p2, p3} = GramSchmidt[{1, x, x²},**
InnerProduct → innerprod] // Simplify

Out[102]= $\left\{ \dfrac{1}{\sqrt{2}}, \sqrt{\dfrac{3}{2}}\, x, \dfrac{1}{2}\sqrt{\dfrac{5}{2}}\left(-1 + 3\,x^2\right) \right\}$

Here we check that every pair of vectors in the new basis is orthogonal:

In[103]:= **{innerprod[p1, p2], innerprod[p2, p3],**
innerprod[p1, p3]}

Out[103]= {0,0,0}

And here we define the norm under this inner product and check that each of the vectors in the new basis is a unit vector:

In[104]:= **Clear[norm];**
norm[p_] := $\sqrt{\text{innerprod[p, p]}}$;
{norm[p1], norm[p2], norm[p3]}

Out[104]= {1,1,1}

7.6   Eigenvalues and Eigenvectors

Given an $n \times n$ matrix **m**, the nonzero vectors $\mathbf{v}_i$ such that $\mathbf{m}\mathbf{v}_i = \lambda_i\mathbf{v}_i$ are the *eigenvectors* of **m**, and the scalars λ_i are the *eigenvalues* of **m**. There are at most n eigenvalues. First we will use the commands **Eigenvalues**, **Eigenvectors**, and **Eigensystem** to find eigenvalues and eigenvectors. Then we will walk through the process "manually."

Finding Eigenvalues and Eigenvectors Automatically

Here is a simple matrix:

In[105]:= **Clear[m];**
m = Array[Min, {2, 2}]; m // MatrixForm

Out[105]//MatrixForm=

$\begin{pmatrix} 1 & 1 \\ 1 & 2 \end{pmatrix}$

To get the eigenvalues, type the following command (look for λ in the **BasicInput** palette):

$In[106]:=$ **{λ1, λ2} = Eigenvalues[m]**

$Out[106]=$ $\left\{\frac{1}{2}\left(3-\sqrt{5}\right),\frac{1}{2}\left(3+\sqrt{5}\right)\right\}$

For the eigenvectors, type:

$In[107]:=$ **{v1, v2} = Eigenvectors[m]**

$Out[107]=$ $\left\{\left\{\frac{1}{2}\left(-1-\sqrt{5}\right),1\right\},\left\{\frac{1}{2}\left(-1+\sqrt{5}\right),1\right\}\right\}$

We find two eigenvalues and two eigenvectors. Let's check that $\mathbf{mv}_1 = \lambda_1\mathbf{v}_1$:

$In[108]:=$ **m.v1 // Simplify**

$Out[108]=$ $\left\{\frac{1}{2}\left(1-\sqrt{5}\right),\frac{1}{2}\left(3-\sqrt{5}\right)\right\}$

$In[109]:=$ **λ1*v1// Simplify**

$Out[109]=$ $\left\{\frac{1}{2}\left(1-\sqrt{5}\right),\frac{1}{2}\left(3-\sqrt{5}\right)\right\}$

You can easily check that $\mathbf{mv}_2 = \lambda_2\mathbf{v}_2$ as well.

The command **Eigensystem** gives both the eigenvalues and the eigenvectors. The output is a list whose first item is a list of eigenvalues and whose second item is a list of corresponding eigenvectors:

$In[110]:=$ **Eigensystem[m]**

$Out[110]=$ $\left\{\left\{\frac{1}{2}\left(3-\sqrt{5}\right),\frac{1}{2}\left(3+\sqrt{5}\right)\right\},\right.$

$\left.\left\{\left\{\frac{1}{2}\left(-1-\sqrt{5}\right),1\right\},\left\{\frac{1}{2}\left(-1+\sqrt{5}\right),1\right\}\right\}\right\}$

We can ask that the output of any of these commands be numerical approximations by replacing **m** with **N[m]**:

$In[111]:=$ **Eigensystem[N[m]]**

$Out[111]=$ {{2.61803,0.381966},
        {{-0.525731,-0.850651},{-0.850651,0.525731}}}

Even with a simple matrix the eigenvalues can be quite complicated and involve complex numbers:

```
In[112]:= Clear[m];
          m = Array[Min, {3, 3}]; m // MatrixForm
Out[112] //MatrixForm=
```

$$\begin{pmatrix} 1 & 1 & 1 \\ 1 & 2 & 2 \\ 1 & 2 & 3 \end{pmatrix}$$

```
In[113]:= Eigenvalues[m]
```

$$Out[113]= \left\{2 + \frac{7^{2/3}}{\left(\frac{3}{2}\left(9 + I\sqrt{3}\right)\right)^{1/3}} + \frac{\left(\frac{7}{2}\left(9 + I\sqrt{3}\right)\right)^{1/3}}{3^{2/3}}, \right.$$

$$2 - \frac{\left(\frac{7}{2}\right)^{2/3}\left(1 + I\sqrt{3}\right)}{\left(3\left(9 + I\sqrt{3}\right)\right)^{1/3}} - \frac{\left(1 - I\sqrt{3}\right)\left(\frac{7}{2}\left(9 + I\sqrt{3}\right)\right)^{1/3}}{2 \cdot 3^{2/3}},$$

$$\left. 2 - \frac{\left(\frac{7}{2}\right)^{2/3}\left(1 - I\sqrt{3}\right)}{\left(3\left(9 + I\sqrt{3}\right)\right)^{1/3}} - \frac{\left(1 + I\sqrt{3}\right)\left(\frac{7}{2}\left(9 + I\sqrt{3}\right)\right)^{1/3}}{2 \cdot 3^{2/3}}\right\}$$

Here it appears that the eigenvalues are complex numbers. That can happen, but in this case we are just seeing real numbers expressed in a manner that makes use of the imaginary number I (the square root of -1, also commonly written as i), much as we might write i^2 for the real number -1. The simplest way to deal with complex output such as this is to ask for a numerical approximation. Edit the last input cell, replacing **m** by **N[m]**. To get *exact* real eigenvalues, you can apply the command **ComplexExpand** to the output above:

```
In[114]:= ComplexExpand[%]
Out[114]=
```

$$\left\{2 + 2\sqrt{\frac{7}{3}}\operatorname{Cos}\left[\frac{1}{3}\operatorname{ArcTan}\left[\frac{1}{3\sqrt{3}}\right]\right],\right.$$

$$2 - \sqrt{\frac{7}{3}}\operatorname{Cos}\left[\frac{1}{3}\operatorname{ArcTan}\left[\frac{1}{3\sqrt{3}}\right]\right] - \sqrt{7}\operatorname{Sin}\left[\frac{1}{3}\operatorname{ArcTan}\left[\frac{1}{3\sqrt{3}}\right]\right],$$

$$\left. 2 - \sqrt{\frac{7}{3}}\operatorname{Cos}\left[\frac{1}{3}\operatorname{ArcTan}\left[\frac{1}{3\sqrt{3}}\right]\right] + \sqrt{7}\operatorname{Sin}\left[\frac{1}{3}\operatorname{ArcTan}\left[\frac{1}{3\sqrt{3}}\right]\right]\right\}$$

```
In[115]:= N[%]
Out[115]= {5.04892, 0.307979, 0.643104}
```

The faster alternative is:

```
In[116]:= Eigenvalues[N[m]]
Out[116]= {5.04892,0.643104,0.307979}
```

For an $n \times n$ matrix *Mathematica* will always return n eigenvalues even if they are not all distinct. The eigenvalues will occur in the same frequency as the roots of the characteristic polynomial (as explained in the next section). *Mathematica* will also output n eigenvectors. If there are fewer than n linearly independent eigenvectors, the output may contain one or more zero vectors. These zero vectors are there for bookkeeping only; actual eigenvectors are nonzero by definition:

```
In[117]:= Clear[m];
          m = ( 2  1  0
                0  2  0  );
                0  0  0
          Eigensystem[m]
Out[117]= {{0,2,2},{{0,0,1},{1,0,0},{0,0,0}}}
```

Finding Eigenvalues and Eigenvectors Manually

Even though *Mathematica* can produce eigenvalues and eigenvectors very quickly, it is still sometimes enlightening to go through the process "manually." To find the eigenvalues we first form the *characteristic polynomial*, which is the determinant of the matrix $\lambda \mathbf{I} - \mathbf{m}$, where $\mathbf{m}$ is a square matrix, λ is an indeterminate, and $\mathbf{I}$ is the identity matrix of the same dimensions as $\mathbf{m}$:

```
In[118]:= Clear[m];
          m = ( 2  -1  0
               -1   2  0  );
                0   0  3
          c=Det[λ IdentityMatrix[3] - m]
Out[118]= -9 + 15 λ-7 λ² + λ³
```

Next, we find the roots of the characteristic polynomial:

```
In[119]:= Solve[c == 0,λ]
Out[119]= {{λ → 1},{λ → 3},{λ → 3}}
```

There are two eigenvalues $\lambda = 1$ and $\lambda = 3$. The eigenvalue 3 is reported twice because it occurs twice as a root of the characteristic polynomial c. We can see this clearly by factoring c:

```
In[120]:= Factor[c]
Out[120]= (-3 + λ)² (-1 + λ)
```

Of course, most characteristic polynomials will not factor so nicely. To find the eigenspace of each eigenvalue λ_i we will find the null space of the matrix $\lambda_i \mathbf{I} - \mathbf{m}$:

```
In[121]:= NullSpace[1 * IdentityMatrix[3] - m]
Out[121]= {{1,1,0}}
```

```
In[122]:= NullSpace[3 * IdentityMatrix[3] - m]
Out[122]= {{0,0,1},{-1,1,0}}
```

The eigenspace for the eigenvalue $\lambda = 1$ has one basis vector: $(1, 1, 0)$. The eigenspace for the eigenvalue $\lambda = 3$ has two basis vectors: $(0, 0, 1)$ and $(-1, 1, 0)$.

Let's have *Mathematica* check our work:

```
In[123]:= Eigensystem[m]
Out[123]= {{1,3,3},{{1,1,0},{0,0,1},{-1,1,0}}}
```

Diagonalization

A square matrix $\mathbf{m}$ is called *diagonalizable* if there exists a diagonal matrix $\mathbf{d}$ and an invertible matrix $\mathbf{p}$ such that $\mathbf{m} = \mathbf{pdp}^{-1}$. An $n \times n$ matrix is diagonalizable if and only if it has n linearly independent eigenvectors. In this case the matrix $\mathbf{p}$ will be the matrix whose columns are the eigenvectors of $\mathbf{m}$ and the matrix $\mathbf{d}$ will have the eigenvalues of $\mathbf{m}$ along the diagonal:

```
In[124]:= Clear[m, p];
          m = ⎛  2  -1  0 ⎞
              ⎜ -1   2  0 ⎟ ;
              ⎝  0   0  3 ⎠
          Eigensystem[m]
Out[124]= {{1,3,3},{{1,1,0},{0,0,1},{-1,1,0}}}
```

```
In[125]:= p = Transpose[%[[2]]]; p // MatrixForm
Out[125] // MatrixForm=
          ⎛ 1  0  -1 ⎞
          ⎜ 1  0   1 ⎟
          ⎝ 0  1   0 ⎠
```

In[126]:= **d = DiagonalMatrix[%%⟦1⟧]; d // MatrixForm**

Out[126]//MatrixForm=

$$\begin{pmatrix} 1 & 0 & 0 \\ 0 & 3 & 0 \\ 0 & 0 & 3 \end{pmatrix}$$

Let's check that $\mathbf{m} = \mathbf{p}\mathbf{d}\mathbf{p}^{-1}$:

In[127]:= **p.d.Inverse[p] // MatrixForm**

Out[127]//MatrixForm=

$$\begin{pmatrix} 2 & -1 & 0 \\ -1 & 2 & 0 \\ 0 & 0 & 3 \end{pmatrix}$$

In[128]:= **% == m**

Out[128]= True

7.7 Visualizing Linear Transformations

A *linear transformation F* is a function from one vector space to another such that for all vectors **u** and **v** in the domain, $F(\mathbf{u} + \mathbf{v}) = F(\mathbf{u}) + F(\mathbf{v})$, and such that for all scalars k, $F(k\,\mathbf{v}) = k\,F(\mathbf{v})$. Once bases have been specified for each vector space, a linear transformation F can be represented as multiplication by a matrix **m**, so that $F(\mathbf{v}) = \mathbf{m}\mathbf{v}$ for all vectors **v** in the domain of F.

We can better understand a linear transformation by studying the effect it has on geometric figures in its domain. *Mathematica* can be used to visualize the effect of a linear transformation from $\mathbb{R}^2$ to $\mathbb{R}^2$ on a geometric object in the plane. We first produce a simple polygonal shape by specifying the coordinates of its vertices. We can then apply a linear transformation to each of these points and see where they land. Examining the geometric changes tells us how the linear transformation behaves.

First we will produce a square. We start with a list of points – the vertices of the square. The command **Polygon** will produce a shaded polygon whose vertices are the points in a list, and the command **Graphics** will store the polygon as a graphics object. We can adjust the shading or color of the graphic by adding graphics options such as **GrayLevel** or **RGBColor**. To render the square we use the command **Show**. We can add plot options to the **Show** command to add axes and to adjust their scaling. For more information on the possible settings for these options see Section 3.5.

```
In[129]:= square =
            Graphics[{GrayLevel[0.5],
              Polygon[{{0, 0}, {0, 1}, {1, 1}, {1, 0}}]
            }];
```

```
In[130]:= Show[square, Axes → True, AspectRatio → Automatic]
```

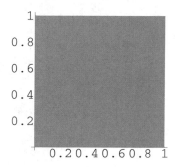

We can use the command **Line** instead of **Polygon** to produce only the edges of the polygon. A line segment is drawn between each successive pair of points in the vertex list:

```
In[131]:= emptysquare =
            Graphics[
              Line[{{0, 0}, {0, 1}, {1, 1}, {1, 0}, {0, 0}}]
            ];
```

```
In[132]:= Show[emptysquare, AspectRatio → Automatic]
```

To produce a regular polygon with more than three or four sides, use the **Table** command to help create the list of points for the vertices. Here, for instance, we produce a pentagon:

```
In[133]:= pentagon =
            Graphics[{GrayLevel[0.5],
              Polygon[
                Table[{Cos[2π/5k], Sin[2π/5k]}, {k, 0, 5}]
              ]
            }];
```

```
In[134]:= Show[pentagon, AspectRatio → Automatic]
```

To view the effects of a linear transformation on any of these polygonal shapes, we simply apply the transformation to each vertex. Since the transformation is *linear*, the line segment joining each pair of vertices will be transformed to the line segment joining the images of the vertices under the transformation. This means that the image of the original polygon will still be a polygon – the polygon whose vertices are the images of the vertices of the original polygon.

For example, let's examine the effects of various linear transformations on the square. In each case, the area of the original square is increased by a factor whose value is the determinant of the transformation matrix. A linear transformation of the form $F(\mathbf{v}) = k\,\mathbf{v}$ is a *dilation* if $k > 1$ and is a *contraction* if $0 < k < 1$. The matrix of a dilation or a contraction will be the identity matrix multiplied by the scalar k. The effect of such a transformation will be to radially expand or contract the plane about the origin. The area of any transformed polygon will change by a factor of k^2, which is the value of the determinant of the transformation matrix.

For example, the darker square below is the original figure, and the lighter region is the dilated square (with $k = 3$). Be sure to list the smaller region as the second argument in the **Show** command so it will be rendered after (and hence on top of) the larger region. If they are listed in the opposite order, the larger region will block the smaller region from view:

```
In[135]:= m = ( 3 0
              0 3 );
         square2 =
           Graphics[{GrayLevel[0.7],
             Polygon[{m.{0, 0}, m.{1, 0}, m.{1, 1}, m.{0, 1}}]
           }];
```

```
In[136]:= Show[square2, square,
            Axes → True, AspectRatio → Automatic]
```

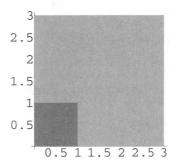

A *reflection* is a linear transformation that maps a vector to its mirror image about some line through the origin. In the example below we reflect the square about the *y* axis. Again, the original square is dark, and the image is light:

```
In[137]:= Clear[m];
         m = ( -1 0
               0 1 );
         square3 =
           Graphics[{GrayLevel[0.7],
             Polygon[{m.{0, 0}, m.{1, 0}, m.{1, 1}, m.{0, 1}}]
           }];
```

```
In[138]:= Show[square3, square,
            Axes → True, AspectRatio → Automatic]
```

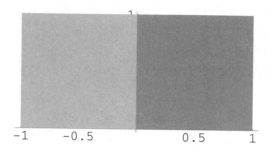

A *rotation* through the angle θ is a linear transformation that will rotate each vector about the origin through the angle θ. The matrix of a counterclockwise rotation through the angle θ with respect to the standard basis is given in the next input cell. Here's a rotation of the square counterclockwise through an angle of $\frac{\pi}{3}$ radians:

```
In[139]:= Clear[m];
          θ = π/3;
          m = ( Cos[θ]   -Sin[θ]
                Sin[θ]    Cos[θ] );
          square4 =
            Graphics[{GrayLevel[0.7],
              Polygon[{m.{0, 0}, m.{1, 0}, m.{1, 1}, m.{0, 1}}]
            }];

In[140]:= Show[square, square4,
              Axes → True, AspectRatio → Automatic]
```

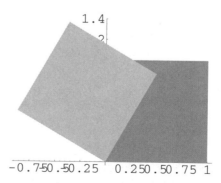

We can also examine the effects of a matrix whose entries are randomly chosen. Here each entry of the matrix we produce is a real number randomly selected between −2 and 2:

```
In[141]:= Clear[m];
          m = Table[Random[Real, {-2, 2}], {i, 2}, {j, 2}];
          m // MatrixForm
```

$$Out[141]= \begin{pmatrix} 1.17637 & 1.0904 \\ 0.951413 & -1.59858 \end{pmatrix}$$

```
In[142]:= square5 =
            Graphics[{GrayLevel[0.7],
              Polygon[{m.{0, 0}, m.{1, 0}, m.{1, 1}, m.{0, 1}}]
            }];
```

```
In[143]:= Show[square5, square,
            Axes → True, AspectRatio → Automatic]
```

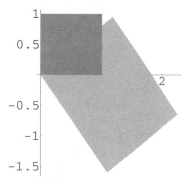

It's difficult to determine just what **m** is doing on the basis of its effect on the square. However, it is clear that this transformation is more than merely the composition of dilations, rotations, and reflections, for none of these transformations will elongate a figure, and the image square has been elongated.

We can create a somewhat more interesting figure to transform by hand-drawing a picture. To do this, first click once on an existing graphic so that a border appears around it. Now hold down the COMMAND key (Mac OS – on a Mac the COMMAND key has the ⌘ symbol on it) or the CONTROL key (Windows), and click on some points with your mouse. Do it in such a way that they trace the outline of an interesting shape. When you are done, copy your points by going to the **Edit** menu and selecting **Copy**. Now click once below the graphic to start a new input cell, and choose **Paste** from the **Edit** menu. A list containing your points will be pasted in the cell. After pasting, edit the cell by giving the list a name (we call ours **v**) and adding a semicolon at the end so you won't have to look at it again. Now enter the cell:

```
In[144]:= v = {{0.288711, 0.181614}, {0.234659, 0.227944},
        {0.219216, 0.30516}, {0.265546, 0.390098},
        {0.234659, 0.428706}, {0.234659, 0.467314},
        {0.265546, 0.4982}, {0.265546, 0.482757},
        {0.273268, 0.529087}, {0.296432, 0.505922},
        {0.304154, 0.490479}, {0.350484, 0.490479},
        {0.365927, 0.513644}, {0.38137, 0.536808},
        {0.404535, 0.505922}, {0.419978, 0.490479},
        {0.404535, 0.444149}, {0.396813, 0.413263},
        {0.373648, 0.390098}, {0.404535, 0.382376},
        {0.435421, 0.366933}, {0.443143, 0.328325},
        {0.435421, 0.25883}, {0.481751, 0.281995},
        {0.504916, 0.328325}, {0.489473, 0.359211},
        {0.481751, 0.390098}, {0.520359, 0.359211},
        {0.528081, 0.320603}, {0.535802, 0.274274},
        {0.497194, 0.235666}, {0.443143, 0.204779},
        {0.412257, 0.189336}, {0.358205, 0.15845}};
```

Let's get a look at this beast:

```
In[145]:= cat = Graphics[{GrayLevel[0.5], Polygon[v]}];
```

```
In[146]:= Show[%, Axes → True, AspectRatio → Automatic]
```

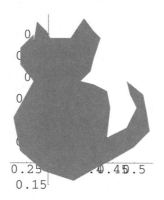

Here is what Mr. Cat looks like after the linear transformation **m** is applied:

```
In[147]:= cat2 =
        Graphics[{GrayLevel[0.7],
          Polygon[Table[m.v[[i]], {i, Length[v]}]]
        }];
```

```
In[148]:= Show[cat, cat2,
            Axes → True, AspectRatio → Automatic]
```

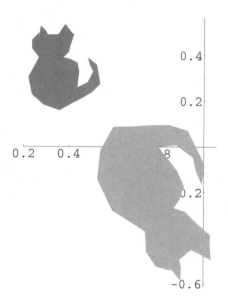

Notice that by studying the effects of a linear transformation on a figure such as this one (a figure with less symmetry than a square), properties of the transformation can be garnered. In this case, we note that in addition to stretching and rotating Mr. Cat, this transformation effected a reflection as well (which accounts for the backwards orientation of the tail in the transformed cat).

We can also produce *three-dimensional* polyhedra and see the effect on them when applying a linear transformation from $\mathbb{R}^3$ to $\mathbb{R}^3$. Below we produce a tetrahedron by listing all the points that we want connected. There will be a line segment between each successive pair of points in the list. The points are stored as a 3D graphics object by applying the command **Graphics3D**. They are rendered, as before, with the **Show** command:

$$In[149]:= v = \left\{ \{0, 0, 0\}, \{1, 0, 0\}, \right.$$
$$\left\{ \cos\left[\frac{\pi}{3}\right], \sin\left[\frac{\pi}{3}\right], 0 \right\}, \{0, 0, 0\},$$
$$\left\{ 0.5, \ 0.5 * \sin\left[\frac{\pi}{3}\right], \ \sin\left[\frac{\pi}{3}\right] \right\}, \left\{ \cos\left[\frac{\pi}{3}\right], \sin\left[\frac{\pi}{3}\right], 0 \right\},$$
$$\left. \left\{ 0.5, \ 0.5 * \sin\left[\frac{\pi}{3}\right], \ \sin\left[\frac{\pi}{3}\right] \right\}, \{1, 0, 0\} \right\};$$

In[150]:= **tetrahedron = Graphics3D[Line[v]];**
  Show[tetrahedron, Boxed → False]

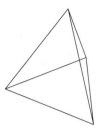

Now let's rotate this tetrahedron counterclockwise about the z axis through an angle of $-\frac{2\pi}{3}$ radians. We specify that the rotated tetrahedron should have lines three times as thick as the original with the graphics option **Absolute-Thickness[3]**:

In[151]:= **Clear[m];**
  $\theta = -\dfrac{2\pi}{3};$
  $m = \begin{pmatrix} \textbf{Cos[}\theta\textbf{]} & \textbf{-Sin[}\theta\textbf{]} & \textbf{0} \\ \textbf{Sin[}\theta\textbf{]} & \textbf{Cos[}\theta\textbf{]} & \textbf{0} \\ \textbf{0} & \textbf{0} & \textbf{1} \end{pmatrix};$
  tetrahedron2 =
   Graphics3D[{AbsoluteThickness[3],
    Line[Table[m.v⟦i⟧, {i, Length[v]}]]
    }];

In[152]:= **Show[tetrahedron, tetrahedron2, Boxed → False]**

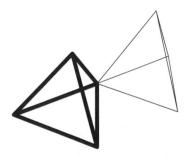

Another approach is to look at transformations of the unit cube. To construct the cube, we start with six lists, one for the vertices of each face of the cube:

```
In[153]:= f1 = {{0, 0, 0}, {1, 0, 0}, {1, 1, 0}, {0, 1, 0}};
          f2 = {{0, 0, 1}, {1, 0, 1}, {1, 1, 1}, {0, 1, 1}};
          f3 = {{0, 0, 0}, {0, 0, 1}, {1, 0, 1}, {1, 0, 0}};
          f4 = {{0, 0, 0}, {0, 0, 1}, {0, 1, 1}, {0, 1, 0}};
          f5 = {{1, 1, 1}, {1, 1, 0}, {1, 0, 0}, {1, 0, 1}};
          f6 = {{1, 1, 1}, {1, 1, 0}, {0, 1, 0}, {0, 1, 1}};
```

The easiest way to graph the cube is by using a *pure function*. It is an elegant way of defining a function without naming it, although it ends up looking rather cryptic to the uninitiated (see the discussion in the subsection "Entering Matrices" of Section 7.1 for more information on the workings of pure functions; the **Map** command is discussed in Section 5.5 on page 140. The input below instructs *Mathematica* to produce a list of polygons; each of **f1** through **f6** is placed in the position marked **#**:

```
In[154]:= cube =
          Map[
             Graphics3D[{Polygon[#]}]&, { f1, f2, f3, f4, f5, f6}
          ];
```

```
In[155]:= Show[cube, Boxed → False]
```

We now form the matrix of a linear transformation from $\mathbb{R}^3$ to $\mathbb{R}^3$. This one has entries that are randomly selected real numbers, each between -2 and 2:

```
In[156]:= Clear[m];
          m = Table[Random[Real, { -2, 2}], {i, 3}, { j, 3}];
          m // MatrixForm
```

$$Out[156]= \begin{pmatrix} 1.2853 & 0.571593 & -1.06052 \\ -1.23804 & 0.146722 & -0.0718004 \\ -1.88748 & 0.799463 & -0.215795 \end{pmatrix}$$

The quickest way to construct a graphic of the transformed cube is given below – again using pure functions. Use the **Show** command to display both. Note that the volume of the transformed cube is equal to the determinant of **m**:

```
In[157]:= cube1 =
          Map[
            Graphics3D[{Polygon[#]}]&,
            Map[Table[m.#[[i]], {i, 4}]&, {f1, f2, f3, f4, f5, f6}]
          ];
```

```
In[158]:= Show[cube1, cube, Axes → True]
```

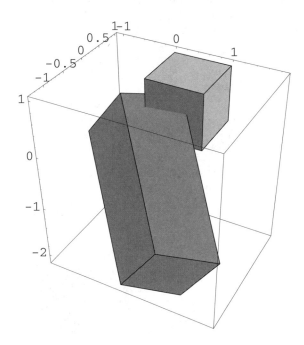

Index